T0147101

THE YEAR OF LIVING *virtuously*

(WEEKENDS OFF)

THE YEAR OF LIVING
virtuously

(WEEKENDS OFF)

TERESA JORDAN

COUNTERPOINT
CALIFORNIA

Library of Congress Cataloging-in-Publication Data

Jordan, Teresa.
The year of living virtuously : weekends off / Teresa Jordan.
pages cm
ISBN 978-1-61902-588-2
1. Jordan, Teresa. 2. Conduct of life—Biography. 3. Virtues—Miscellanea.
4. Life—Miscellanea. I. Title.
BJ1547.5.J67A3 2014
179'.9—dc23
2014014420

Cover design by Natalya Balnova
Interior Design by Neuwirth & Associates

COUNTERPOINT
Los Angeles and San Francisco, CA
www.counterpointpress.com

Printed in the United States of America

I need more to be alert than wise.
—KIM STAFFORD, *The Muses Among Us*

The first step is introspection—exclusive contemplation of the self. But whoever stops there goes only halfway. The second step must be genuine observation outward—spontaneous, sober observation of the external world.
—NOVALIS, *Pollen and Fragments*

FOR HAL

*The patron saint of banjos
and other more highly strung instruments*

CONTENTS

INTRODUCTION

I n the 1880s, a young Marcel Proust answered a series of questions in a friend's "confession album." The confession album was a British tradition, a friendship book that set out a series of questions meant to probe values, interests, and personality. The form intrigued Proust, and he answered the questions twice, at ages thirteen and twenty, and remained engaged enough by his own responses that he published them in a literary review many years later. Other luminaries enjoyed the form as well, including Queen Victoria's second son, Alfred, and Claude Debussy. The confession album was a parlor game shared among friends, a sort of Facebook of its day. What we now call the Proust Questionnaire comes down to us as a staple of the celebrity interview, a popular and long-standing feature of publications such as *The New York Times Magazine* and *Vanity Fair*.

A few months ago, my husband, folklorist and public radio producer Hal Cannon, and I were asked to respond to a version of the Proust Questionnaire for an online magazine called *12 Questions*. The publication focuses on folks who largely fly under the radar but are nonetheless, in the editors' view, "interesting people doing cool stuff." Flattered to be seen in such a light, we agreed.

Among other things, the questionnaire asked us to define virtue and sin. Hal's definition of sin was simple but clear: making the world go backward through human action. I liked his response and adapted it for my own definition of virtue: making the world go *forward* through human action. I went on to explain that righteousness scares me to death and seems to underlie most of the really horrifying atrocities throughout history. I wrote that I appreciated my mother's take on things: she was a good-enough housekeeper, a good-enough mom, a good-enough friend, a good-enough wife and business partner in the Wyoming cattle ranch that made up our family enterprise. She had a strong sense of right and wrong, took responsibility for her transgressions, and had a generous and forgiving nature. Her husband and friends adored her, and so did I. I'd like to follow in her footsteps, I wrote, but I get dogmatic at times.

The query had come by email, and like I do with so many things that stack up in the in-box, I dispatched my response with haste. Only later did I question my decision, when asked to condense my thoughts about virtue to a sentence or two, to invoke my mother. I admired her. We were close, and when she died during my junior year of college, it felt like the sun had fallen out of the sky. All these years later, her memory is a beneficent presence, a solid base of warmth and common sense that continues to inform me.

But at the time I responded to the questionnaire, I had nearly finished an experiment I called *The Year of Living Virtuously (Weekends Off)*, an online journal inspired by Benjamin Franklin's list of thirteen virtues and the seven deadly sins. For months, I had been counterpoising stories about how virtue and vice play out in ordinary life with the views of theologians, philosophers, ethicists, evolutionary biologists, and a whole range of scholars and scientists within the emerging field of consciousness studies. And with all these experts and ethicists to choose from, I singled out my mom?

It retrospect it is not so surprising that I offered a fragment of my mother's story to address a deep philosophical issue. Whether we embrace the family mores or react vigorously against them, for many of us, perhaps even for most, our basic ethical grounding begins at home. Her example gave me a shorthand entry into philosophical territory. In the way a picture is worth a thousand words, a story can take the place of a lengthy dissertation. The desire to enter into a discussion of virtue and vice through story was, after all, what led me to Benjamin Franklin's list of virtues and provided the impetus for *The Year of Living Virtuously (Weekends Off)* in the first place.

———◄○►———

Benjamin Franklin was in his early twenties when he embarked on what he called his "bold and arduous project of arriving at moral perfection." He set out a list of twelve virtues he hoped to master, and then added a thirteenth—humility—after a friend pointed out his prideful nature, a comment prompted, perhaps, by the sheer audacity of the undertaking. So much virtue all at once daunted even young Franklin, and he determined to concentrate on each merit in turn, a week at a time, charting his progress in a notebook by marking each transgression with a dot. Thirteen virtues divided the year tidily into four courses, and he expected that, "by a number of courses, I should be happy in viewing a clean book."

Alas, Franklin never achieved a "clean book," and from the vantage of his seventy-ninth year, he looked back on his youthful endeavor with bemusement, noting that "I was surpris'd to find myself so much fuller of faults than I had imagined." By that time, he had made peace with at least some of them, "for something, that pretended to be reason, was every now and then suggesting to me that such extream niccty as I exacted of myself might be a kind of foppery in morals, which, if it were known, would make me ridiculous. . . ."

An adage about the Founding Fathers suggests that "George Washington was first in war, first in peace, and first in the hearts of his countrymen, but Benjamin Franklin was first in everything else." A prodigious writer, inventor, scientist, statesman, diplomat, and revolutionary thinker, he introduced himself throughout his life as "Benjamin Franklin, Printer," and he stood, above all, as America's first great communicator. If he'd had the technology, I'm sure he would have been our first blogger as well. His virtue project, with its weekly attentions, is tailor-made for the form, and he would have enjoyed both the discipline and the public nature of the practice. Even near the end of his life, long after he had ceased keeping track, he used tales of his youthful earnestness to flirt with the ladies of Paris, and he sometimes regaled them with the ivory slates that had replaced his original charts on paper.

Benjamin Franklin is my favorite Founding Father. A visionary genius in virtually every field he set his hand to, he comes down to us nonetheless at an amazingly human scale, and he embodies the traits I most appreciated in the isolated Wyoming ranch community where I grew up. He believed himself master of his own destiny and that he could make himself into anything he had the guts to imagine. Driven by honesty, integrity, curiosity, and hard work, he had a hearty sense of humor and an almost childlike appetite for play. He had an earnest desire not only to do good but also to *be* good, coupled with a bemused acceptance of human frailty, his own and that of others. These are values I grew up believing were quintessentially American, values I miss as the country I love grows more divided each day.

In the fall of 2010, I decided to adapt Franklin's project as a blog, using his virtues as a starting point and peppering them with a second list that had long intrigued me, the seven deadly sins. As a practical matter, I hungered to start writing seriously again after concentrating for some years on visual art. I wanted to set up a practice to hone my literary muscles after so much disuse, and it struck me that the virtues and vices would provide provocative triggers, and the blog, with its public commitment, would shame me into a modicum of discipline which, when it comes to writing, has never been my strong suit.

But my interest in adopting Franklin's project ran deeper than a desire for structural convenience. In the din of the ever-more-bombastic culture wars, I wondered if his perhaps antiquated notions of virtue might offer guidance to a nation increasingly divided by angry righteousness.

I didn't think I had much to add to the national shouting match over the hot-button issues of the day such as abortion, gay marriage, global warming, gun rights, corporate greed, or political intransigence. Nor did I seek moral perfection, something that seems not only hopelessly out of reach but also, as Franklin blithely suggested (and as terrorism affirms in more radical terms), more dangerous than desirable. Rather, it was the mindfulness implicit in young Franklin's cause that intrigued me. How virtue and vice play out in everyday life invites the big questions: What do we mean when we call someone a good person? What does it take to live wholeheartedly? How do we learn to live authentically? How can we repair our transgressions?

I began with Franklin's list:

TEMPERANCE: Eat not to dullness; drink not to elevation.

SILENCE: Speak not but what may benefit others or yourself; avoid trifling conversation.

ORDER: Let all your things have their places; let each part of your business have its time.

RESOLUTION: Resolve to perform what you ought; perform without fail what you resolve.

FRUGALITY: Make no expense but to do good to others or yourself; i.e., waste nothing.

INDUSTRY: Lose no time; be always employ'd in something useful; cut off all unnecessary actions.

SINCERITY: Use no hurtful deceit; think innocently and justly, and, if you speak, speak accordingly.

JUSTICE: Wrong none by doing injuries, or omitting the benefits that are your duty.

MODERATION: Avoid extremes; forbear resenting injuries so much as you think they deserve.

CLEANLINESS: Tolerate no uncleanliness in body, cloaths, or habitation.

TRANQUILITY: Be not disturbed at trifles, or at accidents common or unavoidable.

CHASTITY: Rarely use venery but for health or offspring, never to dullness, weakness, or the injury of your own or another's peace or reputation.

HUMILITY: Imitate Jesus and Socrates.

For the most part, Franklin focused on practical rather than spiritual values, and several of his definitions seem surprisingly generous for the Puritan age, a reminder that liberality is not solely the invention of recent decades. In addition, there are a panoply of attributes he left out of his charts—though not out of his life—that intrigue me, such as faith, gratitude, generosity, courage, and forgiveness, and during the course of the year, I ranged freely among them.

As for the vices, I considered more than those specifically mentioned among the seven deadly sins. That list, codified by Pope Gregory I in 590 AD, comes down to us in contemporary language as lust, gluttony, greed, sloth, anger, envy, and pride. The Catholic Church considers these the Cardinal Sins, the vices that give birth to all others. Here, too, I roamed far afield, curious about such topics as defensiveness, fear, and stubbornness, sins subordinate to the Big Seven, but worthy of consideration in their own right.

Ordinary strengths and weaknesses shape the quality of our relationships and determine whether, on balance, we contribute to our communities—help the world go forward through human action—or incur a great cost. I think of Shakespeare's King Lear, whose tragic flaws were no greater than the foibles we recognize in ourselves and our families and friends. Lear was not a murderer or a pedophile or even a thief. He was simply needy, demanding proof of his daughters' love, and susceptible to flattery. Blind to both his youngest daughter's authentic devotion and to the counsel of his closest friend, he turned against them both in his quickness to wrath. From these most human of failings, all hell broke loose.

I suspect that most of us recognize some version of the King Lear story in our own lives, a series of events set in motion by a simple misstep or misunderstanding that festers and separates us from someone we love. These don't have to be events worthy of Elizabethan drama to nonetheless wreak havoc on the kingdom of the heart.

For me, this came in my early twenties, shortly after my mother's death. I had been close to both of my parents, but in ways I only understood much later, my mother had provided the emotional intelligence that held my family together. Without her to mediate between us, my father and I grew apart. In the summer after I graduated from college, we had a misunderstanding from which we never recovered. We remained devoted to each other—I suppose *dutiful* would be the more accurate term—but we never really trusted each other again. Nearly thirty years later, shortly before my father died, my brother told me a story that made me realize that I had never understood the source of the breach in the first place.

This is a small story, and no kingdoms were at stake. But our inarticulateness and mutual recalcitrance nonetheless robbed us of each other and affected our other relationships, something I explore around the theme of stubbornness in the chapter "Holding On for Dear Life." I know my personal story is not unusual, and my curiosity about how these sorts of everyday events, both good and ill, profoundly affect our interactions motivates this project.

I am equally intrigued with our internal lives, in what one of my favorite writers, E. B. White, so accurately deemed "man's fantastic battle with himself." Most of us have a sense of how we would like to interact with the world, but we often fall short. We know we should wrap up the notes for tomorrow's meeting, but we click on another episode of *30 Rock* instead; we believe in organic broccoli, but we wolf down a Big Mac; we emerge from a meditation on inner peace to find ourselves suddenly enraged by the telemarketer on the phone. Though self-improvement is one of America's favorite pastimes, we don't seem to be advancing at a pace that puts the self-help industry at risk.

So as I looked to the lives and events around me for insight, I found myself exploring as well the breakthroughs in neuro- and cognitive science that lend insight into human behavior. The debate between nature and nurture is an old one and will probably never completely be resolved, which is why *The Year of Living Virtuously (Weekends Off)* is a weave of story and science.

As I took each topic in turn, I often found a starting point in a memory from my childhood on the ranch, something that reminded me how much moral training we absorb, for better or worse, as children. Other times, I found inspiration in literature, biography, scientific research, and current events, newly aware of how much the models that surround us provide a boundless training ground. Benjamin Franklin was the inspiration for this project but not its focus; still, I found myself returning to him often as a touchstone as I searched out contemporary examples of the creativity, originality, open-mindedness, tolerance, and good humor that made him so effective in times even more challenging than our own.

Poets who work in traditional verse often talk about the heuristic quality of form, the unexpected leaps of imagination that happen when trying to fit an idea into the structure of, say, a sonnet or a villanelle. Using the virtues and vices as triggers offered me similar heuristic surprises.

Sometimes, a small personal event sent me searching for the right topic with which to explore it. One week, after I had lashed out at an offhand remark of my husband's with unreasonable defensiveness, I found myself thinking about those who stand at the first line of defense and remain calm. A meditation on courage and mindfulness, "Choosing Your Battles" weaves together the stories of a military leader in Iraq, a policewoman in Wisconsin, and a group of Trappist monks killed by Islamic extremists in Algeria. Other times, a topic inspired me to see something out of my own life in a new light. When I considered empathy, I found myself deep within a childhood memory of a fire and watched, as if viewing a film, as a young girl's awareness extended for the first time beyond her own concerns.

Other posts, while inspired by personal concerns, focused almost entirely outward. I am often anxious about the smallest things; in a quest to understand tranquility, I turned to stories of two men who found grace in conditions that evoke my greatest fears. "The Long Road" tells the stories of Terry Waite, the hostage negotiator who himself was held hostage in Lebanon for five years, and Brooke Hopkins, a retired professor from the University of Utah whose bicycle accident left him quadriplegic.

If the project often led me into more serious contemplation than what I initially expected, many of the posts have their measure of whimsy. In that fantastic battle with the self, the angel on one shoulder and the devil on the other bicker in ways that seem more suited to sitcom than drama. In my particular dance with ineptitude, I find that sloth, grumpiness, and procrastination often figure as the biggest clowns.

The composer Philip Glass once told an interviewer that, for him, composing music was a form
of concentrated listening. He didn't compose
music so much as attune himself to something that
was already there but very far away. He likened it
to the sound of an underground river. "You don't
know where it comes from," he said, "and you
don't know where it is going. The only difference is
whether you are listening to it or not."

RESOLUTION

On the Eve of a New Year

Be always at war with your vices, at peace with your neighbors, and let each new year find you a better man.
—Benjamin Franklin

A New Year's resolution is something that goes in one year and out the other.
—Anonymous

The last three mornings, I have awakened with a stiff neck. A few years back, I herniated a couple of disks, so the slightest crick makes me nervous, but this current discomfort has yielded easily to a low dose of ibuprofen and a little stretching. Still, aches and pains are the body's way of saying, "time's a-wasting." It's New Year's Eve, and I really should get on with those resolutions for a healthier life.

Every time I get a tweak in my neck, I think of a passage from "Coon Tree" by E. B. White. *Stuart Little* and *Charlotte's Web* enchanted me as a child (and still do), but it's White's essays that I return to time and again. "To essay" means to weigh or test, and it also means to venture out. White was a grand perambulator, and in the course of walking around a topic, he drew in pretty much everything that caught his eye.

In this manner, he worked his own stiff neck into "Coon Tree," a meditation on the unstoppable march of technology and the attractions of simplicity. As in much of his writing, White started with close observation of what was immediately at hand

and then moved outward into the big questions of the world. In 1956, when he wrote "Coon Tree," he suffered physical pain:

> My doctor has ordered me to put my head in traction for ten minutes twice a day. (Nobody can figure out what to do with my head, so now they are going to give it a good pull, like an exasperated mechanic who hauls off and gives his problem a smart jolt with the hammer.) I have rigged a delightful traction center in the barn, using a canvas halter, a length of clothesline, two galvanized pulleys, a twelve-pound boat anchor, a milking stool, and a barn swallow. I set everything up so I could work the swallow into the deal, because I knew he would enjoy it, and he does. While his bride sits on the eggs and I sit on the milking stool, he sits on a harness peg a few feet away, giggling at me throughout the ten-minute period and giving his mate a play-by-play account of man's fantastic battle with himself, which in my case must look like suicide by hanging.

We enter the season where many of us review our shortcomings and resolve to do better. I can never resist the New Year and its promise of a fresh start. Surely, if only I articulate my intentions clearly enough, I will finally transform into the organized, productive, fit, unflappable, and unfailingly generous soul I aspire to be. But I've danced the resolution tango a few dozen times by now, and some part of me can't help sitting off to the side, like E. B. White's swallow, and wondering if this isn't just one more example of woman's fantastic battle with herself. It's enough to give me a stiff neck.

In 1942, a few years after White moved from Manhattan to a farm in Maine with his wife and son, he wrote "Memorandum," a list of some two hundred things he should do to prepare the farm for winter. "Today I should carry the pumpkins and squash from the back porch to the attic," he begins. "The nights are too frosty to leave them outdoors any longer." He details what is necessary to prepare the mooring, the chicken coop, the pigsty, the sheep shed, the barn; to clean up the last of the corn and the windfall apples; to split and stack the wood. He even mentions the birthday gift he should buy for his wife, which is overdue, and the fact that he needs a haircut. He uses the phrase "I ought to" forty-five times, and the pleasure of the piece is that he knows exactly what he should do and how to do it, and he isn't going to do any of it right now. A good portion of the list will not be accomplished in the near future, and some of it never will be. Farm work, like writing and self-improvement, never yields to the perfection we hold for it. But there is power in lining out the possible. If we do it with sincerity, some portion of intention will pull us along.

"There are two faces to discipline," White said in an interview for the *Paris Review.* "If a man (who writes) feels like going to a zoo, he should by all means go to a zoo. He might even be lucky, as I once was when I paid a call at the Bronx Zoo and found myself attending the birth of twin fawns. It was a fine sight, and I lost no time writing a piece about it. The other face of discipline is that, zoo or no zoo, diversion or no diversion, in the end a man must sit down and get the words on paper, and against great odds." The same holds true for the farm. No matter how much pleasure we enjoy watching the family of raccoons in the tree outside the bedroom window, at some point we must guard the corn against their predations.

"If the world were merely seductive," White told another interviewer, "that would be easy. If it were merely challenging, that would be no problem. But I arise in the morning torn between a desire to improve (or save) the world and a desire to enjoy (or savor) the world. That makes it hard to plan the day." But plan we do—because we can, and because, by our nature, we must. It is part of how we both savor and save our own lives.

TEMPERANCE

Please Pass the Peppermints

Eat not to dullness; drink not to elevation.
—Benjamin Franklin

Everything in moderation, including moderation.
—Julia Child

I had the pleasure recently of reading a work-in-progress from a talented young memoirist, Melenie Freedom Flynn, in which she recounted a scene from a childhood road trip across the Oregon desert. Seven or eight years old, tired and bored, she lay in the backseat gazing up at the car ceiling, sucking on one peppermint Life Saver after another until she had run through an entire pack and the top of her mouth was burned raw.

The scene has stayed with me, familiar in the way it captured that sort of private, absentminded eating that is paradoxically attentive, more involved with sensation than appetite. I, too, have heard that inner voice: "One more, just one more . . ." until the last morsel has disappeared, and I rest heavy with remorse and also strangely relieved to be released from a spell.

I love food. I love its textures and flavors and colors and smells. I love the way it imbeds itself in memory. At the mere mention of peppermint Life Savers, I have one pressed to the roof of my mouth, my tongue circling between the hole in the center and the Braille on its surface that spells out its name. The burn of sugar, the cold splash of peppermint, the way the sinuses expand and the throat grows thick and numb: one more, just one more.

The single most magnificent food I ever ate, however, stands as a monument to a moment of rare restraint. I encountered it in February 2002, during the Winter Olympics, when my husband and I attended a dinner put on by the James Beard Foundation at Abravanel Hall, home of Utah's Salt Lake Symphony.

A quiet bevy of tuxedo-clad waiters served appetizers in the foyer as we circulated around a collection of famous Steinways, including Vladimir Horowitz's gleaming ebony piano that had followed him around the world, even shipping in a bulletproof case to Moscow; "Rhapsody in Blue," a piano the color of lapis lazuli that commemorated George Gershwin's hundredth birthday; and Steinway's newest commission, a chartreuse piano with a flaming glass top created by artist Dale Chihuly, whose "Olympic Tower"—a four-story-high tornado of red glass ten-drils—soared above us.

But this swirl of music and color and light receded into the background when I dipped a tiny spoon into a porcelain demitasse cup to taste what the waiter introduced as a foie gras cappuccino, a mousse of pâté topped with a cloud of truffle-infused mashed potatoes and a crust of rock salt. "Dig deep," he told me. "You need to experience all three tastes at once."

Oh my. . . . The buttery sensation of pâté and the comforting warmth of potato; the musky, nutty infusion of truffle, rising like smoke from the back of the throat to be more inhaled than tasted; the sweet, granular shock of salt. I know this sounds like a cliché—and I can only say that nothing like this has happened to me before or since—but everything else came to a standstill. I don't know how long I took to eat that perfect little portion, no more than an ounce, one tiny, deep spoonful at a time. I woke as if from a trance to find the waiter standing in front of me with a bemused look on his face and a newly filled tray, asking if I wanted another. I'll never know what wisdom graced me to decline. A second serving would have ruined everything.

I don't often say no to more of a good thing. As I summon my favorite food memories, most of them revolve around excess, and I'm surprised to notice that it's not actually the food I remember so much as the occasion. My favorite of all Thanksgivings took place during my final year of college when many of my friends and I stayed on campus to finish our senior theses. The day dawned sunny and warm, and we played touch football in the quad before we gathered to cook turkey and ham and the pheasants that some of our group had bagged earlier that fall. We tripped over each other in the kitchen, lubricating our culinary efforts with margaritas and red wine, stepping outside from time to time to have a smoke or throw a Frisbee to the dogs.

Finally everything was ready, but I don't remember the meal as well as I remember how we all ended up on the floor under the table after we had finished it, groaning and laughing and telling stories and dozing off until somehow, quite late in the afternoon, we rallied and headed outside to let the dogs pull us, Iditarod-style, on skateboards around the neighborhood.

Except for the smokes and the dogs and the Frisbees and the skateboards, it was an experience not entirely different from that Olympic dinner in 2002. For after my extraordinary temperance during the appetizer course, I gave in with abandon to what followed. We moved upstairs to a banquet room set with white linen and crystal, and we embarked on a voyage through several more courses that included scallops and filet mignon and frizzled leeks and uncountable glasses of very good wine.

This all took place over a decade ago, and many of the details are hazy. I don't remember the names of anyone who shared our table, or even what we talked about. How can I forget such things about people with whom I had such a good time? I'll blame it on the wine pairings, and maybe especially on the final snifters of brandy that we took with us into the Salt Lake City Art Center next door for an after-hours tour of the Chihuly glass exhibit.

The lights were turned down low, and each piece of backlit glass seemed enchanted. We felt like kids who had broken into a toy store on Christmas Eve. We giggled in whispers as we passed through a forest of glass vases, an underwater garden of glass anemones, and a corridor of neon-bright drawings on Plexiglas to arrive in a room called the Persian Pergola, where we looked up through a glass ceiling that supported hundreds, maybe even thousands, of colorful glass orbs. Somehow we understood that we would enjoy this more if we lay down—did the director suggest this?—and so we found ourselves tucked in close to each other on the floor, holding hands and laughing effervescently as we gazed into what heaven must look like if God turns out to be a glassblower.

Temperance has its place, I know. I had felt its grace only hours before. But just then, on the floor of the Persian Pergola— and now, in the glow of memory—there must also be a place for childlike abandon.

CLEANLINESS

Cleanliness and Its Caveats

Don't bleed on the carpet.
—ANONYMOUS MOTHER

Quiet now cobwebs; dust go to sleep. I'm rocking my baby,
and babies don't keep.
—NURSERY RHYME

My mother always said that she did not want to be known for her housekeeping. She was not a slob, but neither was she overly fastidious, a poise that left her time for reading, play, and genuine connection. She has been gone now for close to forty years, and I still miss her. If I leave behind a reputation anything close to hers for good sense, good humor, and a loving nature, I will have succeeded in my time on this earth.

The challenge of good-enough housekeeping on the ranch was considerable. We inhabited an unpaved world, and two kids, two dogs, two cats, a husband, and a never-ending parade of neighbors and hired hands brought a considerable amount of the great outdoors inside. My mother must have felt a kinship with the Illinois farm woman who copied "The Housewife's Lament" into her diary in the 1800s: "I spend my whole life in a battle with dirt."

When I was an infant, we had a brindle Great Dane named Cerberus the size of a Shetland pony. I suffered from colic, prone to fits of noisy anxiety, but according to the family story, I calmed right down if I could curl up next to Cerberus. I was particularly happy when he licked my face or sucked on the back of my head. Practical in this as in all things, my mother decided that if I insisted on sticking my head in the dog's mouth, she could dispense with sterilizing my bottles. I grew up with a healthy immune system and a love of dogs, and I thank her for both.

Cleanliness is and always has been a function of culture and personal disposition. When Benjamin Franklin listed it as one of his virtues, he enjoined himself to "tolerate no uncleanliness in body, cloaths, or habitation." Bodily cleanliness meant something different to Franklin than what we assume today. For a number of his years in Philadelphia, it was against the law to bathe more than once a month, a caution inherited from across the pond. Ever since the Black Death, Europeans held a dim view of bathing, which was said to invite disease by opening the pores. When the English cleric John Wesley preached in 1778 that "cleanliness is next to godliness," he referred to clothes rather than the body. Linen was believed to wick dirt, and a well-turned-out man changed his linen often.

At least during his years as an American envoy in London, Franklin enjoyed "air baths," sitting for an hour a day undressed in front of an open window. By that time, he was generous of belly, and there is something hearty and delightful about the image of him seated in a Windsor chair, wearing nothing but his spectacles as he read and caught the breezes, a sight that more than one neighbor must have remarked upon for it to have come down to us through history.

Franklin died in 1790, about the time that bathing started to increase in popularity. Pennsylvania Hospital installed shower baths in 1799, and Philadelphia built its first public bathhouse in 1801, but bathing came into its own as a hygienic practice only after the germ theory gained acceptance in the mid-1800s.

A culture's bathing practices, though, depend on more than medical concerns. Early Christianity, alone among the major religions, discouraged personal hygiene, partly in reaction against the decadent indulgence of the Roman baths. The church viewed attention to the body as time stolen from devotion to God. Many monks and clerics believed, with St. Francis of Assisi, that an unwashed body served as a badge of piety. When Thomas à Becket, Archbishop of Canterbury, died in 1170, the fact that his undergarments were "seething with lice" stood as evidence of his religious ardor. (Pope Gregory the Great, however, took a more lenient stance toward bathing as long as it did not turn into a "time-wasting luxury.")

Piety is in the eye—or the nose—of the beholder, and European attitudes toward cleanliness did not endear them to other cultures. Olaudah Equiano, a freed slave who wrote *The Interesting Narrative of the Life of Olaudah Equiano, or Gustavus Vassa, the African* in 1789, described the bathing and hand-washing rituals of his West African Ibo tribe and blamed Europeans for bringing physical and moral corruption. According to Virgil Vogel, in his classic *American Indian Medicine,* pre-contact Native Americans on the northern plains bathed daily in streams and lakes, even in winter. Katherine Ashenburg, author of *The Dirt on Clean: An Unsanitized History,* points out that cleanliness was central to both Islam and Hinduism from their beginnings, and Asian cultures, especially China and Japan, perceived Westerners as filthy.

But if pale-faced Westerners were slow to jump on the personal hygiene bandwagon for the first nineteen centuries of the Christian era, they have made up for it since. Americans on a broad spectrum of shades and religious persuasions now spend an average of $1300 per household each year on personal care and housekeeping products, and we are so clean that we may actually be making ourselves sick.

The hygiene hypothesis, which has been developing now for two decades, suggests that the sharp increase in developed countries of allergies, certain types of heart disease, and autoimmune inflammatory diseases such as MS and Crohn's disease may have resulted from the widespread use of antibacterial cleansers and the eradication of microbes, dirt, dust, and parasites such as hookworms. The theory suggests that the immune system turns on itself if it has nothing else to tackle. Excessive cleanliness may even slow the healing of cuts and bruises.

Over-sanitation did not trouble us on the ranch; a hot bath at the end of the day offered one of life's simple pleasures. Winter on the high plains is brutal. A windchill factor of thirty or forty below can sustain itself for weeks at a time. Snow doesn't melt, the locals say, it just wears out blowing from place to place. I remember my father coming in from feeding the cattle, icicles frozen from his mustache to his shearling collar. My mother would draw him a steaming bath and deliver a shot of chartreuse, a thick green liqueur revered for its warming properties.

Housekeeping itself can have its rewards, especially when it signals the completion of a big project or the end of a long winter. I remember one spring when my mother and I decided to do a particularly thorough job, and we hired a woman from town to help us. We pulled out every appliance and piece of furniture to clean behind it, polished the baseboards and window casings, and even took all the books off the shelves, using paint brushes to banish the dust that had accumulated over the years.

Our helper would have no part of this last task. I suppose it seemed not only pointless but also daunting, as every room in the house had at least one bookcase, including the bathroom. But this was the chore Mom and I enjoyed most, savoring the heft of each book and the pleasure of realigning the spines in perfect order. I suppose we indulged in something of the miser's glee, for we reveled in the riches at hand: the collected works of Shakespeare, unabridged volumes of Kipling's poetry and prose, the Nobel Prize Library, the Encyclopaedia Britannica, a series from the Metropolitan Museum of Art, and an endless array of popular literature: Nevil Shute, Ayn Rand, John Fowles, Rex Stout, Raymond Chandler, Mari Sandoz, Willa Cather, James Michener, Erica Jong, and Paul Ehrlich's *The Population Bomb*, to name just a few. We didn't indulge in any significant housekeeping for a long time after that. How could we? We had so much to read.

SILENCE

Making Space for Conversation

Speak not but what may benefit others or yourself;
avoid trifling conversation.
—Benjamin Franklin

It's good to shut up sometimes.
—Marcel Marceau

On a perfect September afternoon in 2003, I found myself walking along the Charles River in Boston. Headed downtown from my hotel, I was in a glorious mood. I had come a day early for a conference at MIT, "Investigating the Mind," the eleventh in a series of exchanges convened by the Dalai Lama between Buddhist scholars and western psychologists, neuroscientists, and philosophers. I had long been fascinated by cognitive science, and I had recently begun a practice of Zen meditation. I wanted to know what this collaboration between the 2500-year-long Buddhist meditative tradition and cutting-edge science had to say about the capacity of the mind.

Now, as I strode along Memorial Drive, I came closer and closer to a huge construction project. As I approached, what from a distance rang out as a faint industrial clanking turned into a din. I didn't know what caused it—perhaps they were driving pylons—but the noise assaulted me, and I remember thinking: I can't bear this. How can this happen on such a beautiful day?

And then something shifted. I started to listen, to open up to the sound instead of trying to resist it, and I stepped inside it. Or maybe it stepped inside me. But it became as complete and whole and satisfying as the warmth of the sun, the feeling of the sidewalk beneath my feet, and the movement of my body. This feeling of perfection stayed with me well beyond the construction site, and at some point I thought: Oh, so this is what they mean about becoming one with the universe (a thought, of course, that immediately separated me from the universe, but that's another topic).

If I assumed, however, that enlightenment was near, I had a rude awakening the following day when a friend joined me for the conference. This friend—I'll call her Melia—is funny and brilliant and warm. She also talks nonstop, a human response-o-meter, as if in order to process the world around her she has to offer a running commentary. As the first few speakers greeted us, she whispered continuously in my ear. Increasingly annoyed, I didn't want to embarrass her with an audible "shhh," so I made the small waving motion a traffic cop makes when he has your eye and wants you to slow down, a gesture that she either missed or chose to ignore. Then the Dalai Lama himself took the podium. She continued to talk, and I finally shushed her, but what I really wanted to do was snarl: "Would you SHUT UP? Can't you see I'm trying to learn about COMPASSION?!!"

We tend to respond most strongly against traits in others that most disturb us about ourselves. I'm a talker. It's my most persistent fault—winner of a lively competition, to be sure—and I get tired of my own voice. At times, I listen well: when I teach or sit with a troubled friend or settle into deep meditation. But when I'm excited or anxious or happy or insecure or defensive— in other words, most of the time—I babble on. And, like Melia, I have a tendency to narrate the world around me.

When Benjamin Franklin devised his list of thirteen virtues, he set them out in a particular order: temperance first, as it would support the discipline the other virtues required, followed by silence because knowledge is "obtain'd rather by the use of the ears than of the tongue." He wished to break his habit of "prattling, punning, and joking, which only made [him] acceptable to trifling company." In an essay titled "On Conversation," he listed what he saw as the most common transgressions:

- talking overmuch
- seeming unconcerned
- speaking too much of yourself and your own affairs
- impertinent inquisitiveness into the business of others
- long-winded storytelling
- wrangling and disputing
- ridiculing or railing against things except in small witty doses
- scandal mongering

The list points to the underpinning of prattle, a hunger or greed to be the center of attention, acknowledged or admired or right or simply in control. But Franklin's desire for silence can seem almost as manipulative: "Would you win the hearts of others," he wrote, "you must not seem to vie with them, but to admire them. Give them every opportunity of displaying their own qualifications, and when you have indulged their vanity, they will praise you in turn and prefer you above others."

The biographer Walter Isaacson notes that Franklin employed silence skillfully, "making him seem wise or benign or serene." Franklin, the ultimate pragmatist, has been called the patron saint of getting on, but to focus too much on that part of him is to deny the essential magnanimity that made him beloved as a great conversationalist and a generous listener.

Perhaps, at least in the realm of conversation, it makes sense to focus more on listening than on silence. Silence is a withholding. Ideally, it creates an emptiness, an invitation. But it can also be used to brutal effect, the iceberg in an arctic marriage. As shunning, silence has been used for social control as far back as we can discern, and its ultimate practice, solitary confinement, is an effective means of torture.

Listening, on the other hand, is almost always active and generous. The best listener I've ever known was Terence O'Donnell, a dear friend and mentor whom I met when I lived in Portland, Oregon. He was my father's age and had spent many years in the Middle East. He lived for over a decade on a pomegranate plantation in rural Iran before the revolution, and the book he wrote about it, *Garden of the Brave in War*, stands with Isak Dinesen's *Out of Africa* as one of the great cultural memoirs.

I always felt heard when I talked to Terry. He had a deep respect for his friends, and he liked seeing the world through their eyes. He also shared his own experiences with generosity, and in his calm presence, I listened well. Afterward, I understood the world better, but I also felt like he got something in return.

Many scenes in his book capture the spaciousness I felt in our own conversations. Once, crossing the desert, his radiator overheated, and he made his way to a tribal encampment to ask for water. The men who came out to greet him had,

> like so many tribesmen, that look which I have only seen before in Byzantine icons and in the faces of the Aran Islanders—a kind of stunned staring like men caught dreaming of eternity. I do not know the reason for this look—perhaps the saints saw God—but with the tribesmen and the Aran Islanders, it may be that men who all their lives have before them great unbroken sweeps of sky and land are left wide-eyed and somehow dazed.

They led him to the kalantar, the chief, who invited Terry into his tent and saw that he was fed—a skewer of kabobed liver, sheep's milk, bread. Then he asked Terry a question:

> Since my countrymen were rich, was it not possible for them to sit all day and think? I told him they did not. He was puzzled. Then he went on to say that he was certain that if he sat thinking for a year or two—it might take

three—he would be able to conceive the construction of a radio. Having done so, he would simply go to town, buy wire and metal, and make it. He added that sometime, as a kind of experiment, he might do this.

They chatted for a while, and then Terry took a nap. He woke at dusk and lay still a moment longer, watching the sparks rise from the evening fires and the shadows of the women tending food in the dusk. The moon had started to rise. "I wanted to stay," he wrote, "but I knew I must go."

> The kalantar and some of the others came up to me. The food, they said, would soon be ready, and after that I could sleep again. I looked at their faces and at the fires and again I was tempted. But I had made certain promises. They did not say that I should break the promises, but only that I should put them off for another day. I started walking to the Land Rover. They came along with me, looking puzzled and hurt. "Why?" the kalantar asked. "After all there is time—time," and he motioned toward the plain, the mountains, and the sky.

Perhaps Terry's years in Persia made him a good listener. He spoke fluent Farsi, but it was a street Persian sprinkled liberally with slang. He learned by observation rather than classroom study. He won his facility through great interest, patience, and a total lack of fear.

Interest, patience, and the lack of fear: those qualities make good communication possible. They are the qualities, come to think of it, that I experienced so many years ago in Boston when an industrial cacophony washed over me like a symphony, qualities I settle into in my best meditations. Sometimes, I even remember to listen like this, with my whole being, when I am with friends.

COURAGE

The Truth of the Land

The opposite of courage in our society is not cowardice, it
is conformity.
—ROLLO MAY, *The Courage to Create*

Courage is being scared to death but saddling up anyway.
—JOHN WAYNE

Many years ago, I heard a story about a woman homesteader so lonely that she wrote poems on scraps of paper, sewed them onto tumbleweeds, and released them to the prairie wind. I suspect this is apocryphal—I've since heard several variations— but, as my grandfather used to say, "If it ain't true, it oughtta be." The story touches that part of the human spirit that not only struggles to understand its deepest concerns, but also wants to share them.

I've just returned from the National Cowboy Poetry Gathering in Elko, Nevada, an event I have attended for twenty-two of its twenty-seven years. Even after all this time, it surprises me. On the one hand, it's just plain fun. Poetry and music start early in the morning and last into the wee hours, and by the time I get to bed most nights, my ribs hurt from laughing and hugging. On the other hand, something more serious bubbles under the surface, and each year I come away with renewed respect for the courage it takes to speak.

I didn't attend the Gathering until its sixth year, in 1990, when

I was invited to take part in a panel of prose writers. To tell the truth, when I first heard about the event, I'd had no interest. My family's fourth-generation Wyoming ranch had been sold a decade earlier, in the midst of the agricultural crisis of the 1970s and '80s. I was trying to become a writer, in part to keep a hold on the land through its stories if not through its soil, but I had little interest in nostalgia or romanticizing the past. I knew firsthand the complicated family dynamics that combine with economics and harsh weather to push people off the land. I assumed that the event attracted a bunch of dressed-up Hollywood pretenders, all hat and no cattle, spouting doggerel about a mythic West they thought they knew from watching Westerns on TV.

These assumptions disappeared the minute I walked through the door of a hospitality room at the Salt Lake City Airport, where I had been directed to wait for a charter bus to Elko. The room buzzed with the voices of working ranch people, familiar to me as my own DNA, and yet the context was entirely new. I took the only empty chair available and joined two older men, beat up by years of hard work, their canes tucked under the table, bent toward each other in intense conversation. As I settled in, I realized that they were passing poems back and forth, arguing line breaks and metaphors.

When the Gathering started the next day in Elko, I enjoyed recitations of poems by old-time cowboy poets familiar to me from childhood such as Bruce Kiskaddon, S. Omar Barker, and Badger Clark, and I heard well-crafted new poetry telling familiar stories of hard rides, big wrecks, and favorite horses. But other work took me completely by surprise: Paul Zarzyski's free-verse tribute to a bull rider who lost his life to the "sheer / peril of living with a passion / that shatters all at once . . ."; John Dofflemyer's environmental sonnets; and Buck Ramsey's "Anthem," which infused traditional themes with contemporary insight:

And in the morning I was riding
Out through the breaks of that long plain,

And leather creaking on the quieting
Would sound with trot and trot again.
I lived in time with horse hoof falling;
I listened well and heard the calling
The earth, my mother, bade to me,
Though I would still ride wild and free.
And as I flew out in the morning,
Before the bird, before the dawn,
I was the poem, I was the song.
My heart would beat the world a warning—
Those horsemen now rode all with me,
And we were good, and we were free.

We were not told, but ours the knowing
We were the native strangers there
Among the things the land was growing—
To know this gave us more the care
To let the grass keep at its growing
And let the streams keep at their flowing.
We knew the land would not be ours,
That no one has the awful pow'rs
To claim the vast and common nesting,
To own the life that gave him birth,
Much less to rape his mother earth
And ask her for a mother's blessing
And ever live in peace with her,
And, dying, come to rest with her. . . .

To my surprise and disappointment, I wasn't as impressed with the women's work: most poems seemed little more than attenuated versions of traditional male verses, both in style and content, or they were humorous and self-deprecating renditions of a woman's particular folly in a mostly male domain. But that year, a group of Australian bush poets came to the Gathering, and Nerys Evans, a soft-voiced woman from Alice Springs, recited a

poem titled "Past Carin'" that changed things forever. To cite
two of its five verses:

Through Death and Trouble, turn about,
Through hopeless desolation,
Through flood and fever, fire and drought,
And slavery and starvation;
Through childbirth, sickness, hurt, and blight,
And nervousness an' scarin',
Through bein' left alone at night,
I've got to be past carin'.
Past botherin' or carin',
Past feelin' and past carin';
Through city cheats and neighbors' spite,
I've come to be past carin'.

Our first child took, in days like these,
A cruel week in dyin',
All day upon her father's knees,
Or on my poor breast lyin';
The tears we shed—the prayers we said
Were awful, wild—despairin'!
I've pulled three through, and buried two
Since then—and I'm past carin'.
I've grown to be past carin',
Past worryin' and wearin';
I've pulled three through and buried two
Since then, and I'm past carin'.

Nerys recited this poem in the plenary session that kicked off
the event, and I'll never forget how quiet the auditorium had
become by its conclusion. The poem told a story close to the
ancestral experiences of many families in the audience, and men
and women both sat moved to tears. But we also experienced gratitude, relieved to hear something we knew finally spoken out loud.

To our surprise, we learned that a woman did not write "Past Carin'"; rather, it came from Henry Lawson, Australia's version of Rudyard Kipling or Robert Service. Lawson knew whereof he wrote; he had grown up one of seven children in the goldfields, and his parents split when he was sixteen, riven by hopelessness and poverty.

For the women at the Gathering, I imagine that part of the poem's liberating magic came through the very fact that a man wrote it. No accusation wounds a countrywoman more than to be called a whiner; in the particular vocabulary that attaches to gender, women whine but men state facts. These words, penned by a man's hand, allowed the truth of women's experience to surface without self-censoring prejudice.

The next year saw a startling change in the women's poetry. I don't want to put too much emphasis on the power of Nerys Evan's recital; there were many forces aborning nationwide that released women's storytelling about that time. But ranch women both inside and outside of the cowboy poetry movement were finding their authentic voices, and by 1994, when I had the pleasure of gathering many of them together in an anthology titled *Graining the Mare: The Poetry of Ranch Women*, they spoke with an honesty and raw intensity that comes when voices emerge where there has been largely silence before.

In "When Cowboys Cry," Judy Blunt wrote of her grandmother's funeral where

> *. . . the whole*
> *of my father's face simply turned*
> *and came apart, like an old wall*
>
> *falls one hard brick at a time. . . .*
>
> *at the big supper they all said*
> *they thought the better of him*
> *for a few tears, and if not here*
> *for chrissake, among friends, then where?*

Peggy Godfrey wrote about "Old Vogal" and his response to her successful contract-haying business:

He assured me I was lucky
That my bales were done up tight
Lucky that I caught the dew
And chanced to bale it right. . . .

I clenched my jaw and held my tongue
Red anger 'round me swirled
If I was a man, he'd say I was good,
But "lucky" 'cuz I'm a girl.

Joan Hoffman captured her love of the land in "The Lonely, Empty, Prairie Sky":

In the midst of everywhere I know this place
as I know my own voice calling echoes up and down
the valley, as I know my eyes looking into a close-held
mirror, as my tongue knows the inside of my mouth.

I know the wind as intimately as I know love,
its mark and signature upon the fragile land,
and I know the smell of rain riding down the gale
across the hills, across the meadows, across the river.

When seeping cold makes my bones
brittle inside my skin,
when relentless summer beats
my face with a gold hammer,
I am at home beneath the lonely, empty, prairie sky.

In "leaving," Doris Bircham recalled a neighbor who left an abusive husband in the middle of the night:

. . . sadness folds around me
while I search for you   for ways to reach out
and find the ragged edges
of your pain

I continue this simple task
of hanging clothes thinking
how little I know
about where they go
between one wash and the next
how there's no place to hide
the worn places, the three-cornered rips
how no bleach has been made
that can remove all the stains.

"How do we tell the truth in a small town?" asked the North Dakota writer Kathleen Norris in a piece in *The New York Times Book Review* in 1992. "Is it possible to write it?" She spoke of the pressure to "make nice," to write nothing that wouldn't be acceptable at a church picnic, and these ranch women poets ran up against the pressure to conform with each new poem. Yet one courageous voice empowered another, something as true for men as it was for women. About that time, Tom Sharpe used the metaphor of horse breaking in "The Round Corral" to work through the anger and brutality he inherited from his father; Joel Nelson, Rod McQueary, and Bill Jones wrote from their experiences in Vietnam.

Under any circumstances, it's hard to stand in front of a room full of people and speak your heart's truth; it's particularly terrifying to say out loud what has only been spoken in whispers before. I've seen the sweat bead on the upper lip, heard the voice quiver, and watched the page shake. "I hope you can hear me over the knocking of my knees," one woman said before she started. Another year, Vess Quinlan, a Colorado rancher, introduced

"Almost Home," his poem about a shell-shocked uncle who had frightened Vess as a child, by telling the audience, "Some people say this sort of writing has no place here, that it's not cowboy, but I'm beginning to rebel against the fact that I live in a box and you let me out to rope a calf or doctor a steer but the rest of the time I don't matter."

Writing is an investigative act. Serious writers quickly run through the clichés and arrive on new ground. What Vess and so many other poets at the Gathering have come to trust through the years is that the voice they give to the full complexity of rural life does matter. Their poems, along with workshops at the Gathering that deal with similar issues of changing politics, environmental collaboration, and family dynamics, have been resilient forces from within the culture that help it adapt and move forward. They comprise only one thread of the work presented at Elko each year, and they would not be nearly as effective if they weren't woven into a larger fabric vibrant with humor, tradition, and celebration.

I suspect that many writers feel like that woman homesteader who attached her poems to tumbleweeds: who knows where words from the heart might land? But sometimes, after a performance, you get an idea. I have recited the poem "Past Carin'" a few times, and twice—once at the Gathering in Elko and another time at a book fair in Casper, Wyoming—hard-bitten old ranch men have come up to me afterward. In both cases, the minute they started to talk, they began to weep. They were strong men, stoic, and they stood before me, tears rolling down their cheeks.

A while back, I asked Linda Hussa, a rancher whose poetry I admire, if she had ever experienced anything like that. Not exactly, she told me, but once, after she read "Homesteaders Poor and Dry," a woman made a beeline toward her at the end of the session. The poem tells the story of a little girl who had to be lowered down in the well to dip water with a cup for her family during a terrible drought:

I was lowered down in that well every day
'til the drought broke.
Every day.
I closed my eyes and sang myself songs
dipped the water raising down there in the pitch dark
all by the feel.

But there was no time I'll remember
like that first time.

After, when the water came back up in the well
I went and looked down into the water
and imagined myself on the bottom
and sometimes I wanted to go back down
to the quiet of the dark.

"You know how people will come up afterward," Linda said, "and tell you how well you did, or what they liked? Well, this woman didn't introduce herself, she didn't waste any compliments. She just looked me in the eye and said: 'Was that you in the well?' I started to explain: no, it was something that happened to a friend of my grandmother's. 'Well,' she interrupted, 'it was *me*.'

"You think you are writing a story about the past," Linda continued. "You think it's your story, or that of someone you know. But these stories are alive. They live in people right now."

But they can only live when we summon the courage to tell them.

CONCEIT

Conceit means having a particularly high opinion of oneself, but it can also refer to a notion or idea. The magpie is a rascal in a tuxedo whose central conceit might well be that as long as he dresses well, he can get away with anything.

PRIDE

The Pride of Work, The Work of Pride

There is this paradox in pride: it makes some men ridiculous, but prevents others from becoming so.

—CHARLES CALEB COTTON

If you practice an art, be proud of it and make it proud of you. It may break your heart, but it will fill your heart before it breaks it; it will make you a person in your own right.

—MAXWELL ANDERSON

Back when I was small and my father was a giant and always in a hurry, I remember trotting along at his side, trying to keep up with his long-legged stride. The father in such a scene might be not only a giant but also a bully, oblivious to his little girl's needs, or consciously insensitive, or downright cruel. But in my own memory, the sun shines on a slant, and the grass shimmers with dew. The day vibrates with purpose, and I feel a strength in my legs, a capacity in my lungs, a competence that, looking back now, I realize was completely at odds with my age. My father is going to work, and he has asked me to come along.

Perhaps we are heading for the shop, where my little hands will fit the grease gun to a nipple deep in the baler, a task that had left my father in a sputtering rage the night before. Or maybe we are on our way to the pickup to take salt and mineral to the cattle. I'll "ride shotgun" to get the gates, and I'll use my own pocketknife to open the sacks of supplement. Or perhaps I am older, ten or twelve, and we saddle up and head out for the high country to find a bull missing from the roundup. We don't find the critter in the first pasture we check, or the second, or the third.

By the time we locate him, sick with foot rot and on the fight, my father's colt has played out and is no longer useful. He stands to the side as I do the hard and dangerous work of getting the bull headed home. The bull tries to take me, sometimes feinting and other times charging. Twice he hits my stirrup, but my horse pivots out of the way, and we escape unharmed. If he becomes too dangerous, my father will suggest we leave him for another day, but my horse works well. Finally, the bull turns down the trail and limps off like it was his own idea all along. We arrive at a neighbor's corral at dusk, after having ridden thirty miles or more.

We call my mother to pick us up. A cloudburst explodes just as she arrives, and we slip-slide the gumbo road home through thunder and lightning and blinding rain as my father tells her that he couldn't have gotten the bull out of the hills without me. It's true. If I hadn't been along, he would have come home empty-handed. We both know this, and it makes us feel good.

———◦———

Of all the vices, pride is most likely to invite debate about whether it is a sin at all. "Pride [goeth] before destruction, and an haughty spirit before a fall," reads the Bible, and yet we want to take pride in our work, be proud of our loved ones, and raise our children with a sense of pride in themselves. We disdain the haughty, the arrogant, the vain, or the smug, but we admire those who move in the world with confidence, dignity, and self-respect. Among the seven deadly sins, pride may be the one whose chips fall most equally on either side of the line.

In the sixth century, when Pope Gregory the Great codified the deadly sins, he deemed pride the mother of all vices because it so often gave birth to the others. A proud man puts himself before God. Expecting deference, he angers quickly. Assuming superiority, he is prone to envy. Spiritually slothful, his sense of entitlement leads him to indulge gluttony, greed, and lust at others' expense.

Pride and its attending sense of entitlement figure almost daily in the scandals that rock Wall Street, Congress, and other fonts of power. Several years ago, in 1995, the public got an unusually intimate view into the thought processes at work when Oregon Senator Bob Packwood's 8,200-page diary came to light after he was accused of sexual harassment. Lurid excerpts filled the news. "Grabbed Tracy Gorman behind the Xerox machine today and she got a little pissed," Packwood wrote in one entry. "What's the big deal? I was smiling while I did it." In another, he confided that a woman's bridge game had so impressed him that he could "hardly concentrate on [her] breasts." Packwood resigned after the bipartisan Senate Ethics Committee voted to expel him not only because the diary proved the original charges but also because he attempted to delete incriminating evidence.

But the diary exposed more than lust and boorishness. In the words of the *Washington Monthly*, it also revealed "how money, friendships, and politics mix in Washington to produce policy; how politicians openly skirt campaign finance laws and abuse their power for personal gain; how even the most powerful can be desperately insecure."

Some would say that Packwood's tragic flaw was not his pride so much as self-doubt and an insatiable hunger for validation. A synonym for *pride*, *vainglory*, captures a sense of the relationship between destructive pride and insecurity. Overcoming low self-esteem became something of a national obsession in recent decades, with the hope of eradicating everything from teen pregnancy and bullying to pollution and domestic violence. Experts told us to praise our children's smallest efforts; preschoolers learned to sing, "I am special, I am special, look at me," to the tune of *Frère Jacques*; and their older brothers and sisters read, "I'm looking at the most important person in the world," engraved on the washroom mirror.

But efforts to raise self-esteem failed to cure society's ills. In 2005, Roy Baumeister, a psychology professor at Florida State University and an early advocate of enhancement programs, led a team of researchers in the review of fifteen thousand studies. They found that high self-esteem didn't lead to better grades: "Kids with high self-esteem do have slightly better grades in most studies, but that's because getting good grades leads to higher self-esteem, not the other way around." Nor did it reduce bullying: "Violent individuals, groups, and nations think very well of themselves. They turn violent toward others who fail to give them the inflated respect they think they deserve." It didn't even make kids better behaved. In fact, the review found that kids with high self-esteem may actually be more likely to experiment with drugs and sex than their less-confident peers.

Baumeister and his group found that high self-esteem did correlate with greater happiness and initiative as well as a lower incidence of eating disorders, but in many cases, they could not discern whether self-esteem was a cause of these conditions or a consequence. The study suggests that instead of focusing on self-esteem as an end in itself, we would be better off to concentrate on developing skills and a sense of integrity.

Aristotle embedded pride, *megalopsuchia,* in his system of ethics and named it the crown of all the virtues. *Megalopsuchia* is also translated as "greatness of soul" or "magnanimity," something that *Webster's Unabridged Dictionary* defines as "a loftiness of spirit enabling one to sustain danger and trouble with tranquility, firmness, and courage . . . a nobility of feeling that is superior to meanness, pettiness, or jealousy and that disdains revenge or retaliation . . . [a] generosity of mind."

Implicit in *magnanimity* is another element that is—finally—making its way into the highest echelons of leadership training: humility. Writing in the *Harvard Business Review,* management researcher Jim Collins describes the most successful leadership as a "triumph of humility and fierce resolve," and Harvard Business School professor Clayton M. Christensen emphasizes the importance of humility, combined with clearly delineated values and a sense of purpose, for those who want to succeed not only in their careers but also in their personal lives.

In "How Will You Measure Your Life?" Christensen notes that he began to understand the importance of humility after he asked students to describe the most humble person they knew:

> One characteristic of these humble people stood out: They had a high level of self-esteem. They knew who they were, and they felt good about who they were. We also decided that humility was defined not by self-deprecating behavior or attitudes but by the esteem with which you regard others. Good behavior flows naturally from that kind of humility. For example, you would never steal from someone, because you respect that person too much. You'd never lie to someone, either.
>
> It's crucial to take a sense of humility into the world. . . . if your attitude is that only smarter [or more experienced] people have something to teach you, your learning opportunities will be very limited. But if you have a humble eagerness to learn something from everybody, your learning opportunities will be unlimited.

He sees self-esteem as a central element in a satisfying life, but only when built on an unshakeable foundation of integrity.

Our experiences with work influence how we see the rest of our lives. In 1974, the Chicago radio host Studs Terkel published *Working: People Talk About What They Do All Day and How They Feel About What They Do*, a collection of interviews with over a hundred people from every walk of life. "The book," he writes in the introduction, reveals a search for "daily meaning as well as daily bread, for recognition as well as cash, for astonishment rather than torpor; in short, for a sort of life rather than a Monday through Friday sort of dying." Almost every interview addresses the degree to which work either encourages a sense of pride or destroys it.

> A farm equipment worker in Moline complains that the careless worker who turns out more that is bad is better regarded than the careful craftsman who turns out less that is good. . . . Why, in these circumstances, should a man work with care?

> Others . . . murmur of a hunger for "beauty," "a meaning," "a sense of pride."

> [The parking attendant] sings out, "I could drive any car like a baby, like a woman changes her baby's diaper. . . .

> [The waitress] describes the trials . . . in a fashionable restaurant [and how] pride . . . helps her make it through the night. "When I put the plate down, you don't hear a sound. When I pick up a glass, I want it to be just right. When someone says, 'How come you're just a waitress?' I say, 'Don't you think you deserve being served by me?'"

I read *Working* in college, stunned by the extraordinary eloquence of ordinary people as they spoke about what mattered to them most. The book inspired me to seek out such voices on my own, and I soon began interviewing women who worked on the land. Their stories made me grateful for my own early work experiences, where adults took me seriously and gave me the opportunity to develop skills I could be proud of.

Now, as I revisit Terkel's legacy and the model of his own approach to work, I recognize another aspect of healthy pride: a good sense of humor. Once, after several of Terkel's books had become bestsellers and he had won the Pulitzer Prize, a reporter asked him about his increasing renown. "You've always been the voice of the noncelebrity," the reporter said, "but now you are a celebrity yourself. Does that cause problems?"

"You can get the big head," Terkel responded, "but something always brings you back to earth." Just that day, his publisher had read him a letter from an irate librarian: "Ours is a family library," the librarian wrote, "and we're not about to put a book on our shelves about working studs by some man named Terkel."

SLOTH

Everything I Need to Know About Sloth I Learned from Critters

I must lose myself in action, lest I lose myself in despair.
—Alfred, Lord Tennyson

Man is the only animal for whom his own existence is a problem which he has to solve.
—Erich Fromm

Mr. Big, one of my two cats, subscribes to the notion that the primary secret to success is just showing up. He puts in the hours, arriving on my desk each morning as I turn on my computer and often remaining there after I have quit for the day, if only because he is sound asleep. He takes his job as the largest living paperweight seriously, and if I try to access a book or stack of notes he has settled himself upon, he hisses and bites my hand. Whether this behavior derives from commitment or just plain grumpiness, I'm not sure; nor do I know why I get such a kick out of it, but I do.

At eighteen pounds, he is only slightly larger than his house-mate, Elroy, a big orange cat who spends his day chasing his tail, jumping on my desk with his ball to play fetch, climbing the curtains, crawling into the refrigerator, playing slinky on the stairs, or pawing at the door and complaining that we won't let him out or we won't let him in. Mr. Big is Sloth and Elroy is Industry; other than their size, I can't imagine two cats with less in common.

But critters of the same species often have distinct personalities. Take, for instance, the biker robin and the Junior League robin who built nests on our porch one spring when Hal and I lived on a small ranch on the edge of the Ruby Mountains in Nevada.

The Junior League robin arrived first and in a single day had constructed the neatest, tightest nest we had ever seen. We watched from inside the house as she assessed its perfect symmetry and then settled in with a measure of pride. Her satisfaction ended quickly, however, when we stepped out to enjoy our nightly cocktails on the porch and she had to confront the unsavory nature of the neighborhood she had just adopted. She started nattering and scolding and flitting about with such anxiety that Hal and I moved our chairs as far as away as we could without falling off the end of the porch.

Things went from bad to worse for her the next day when the biker robin arrived. This new neighbor had a spiky hairdo and ruffled appearance and started jerry-rigging a nest that was—well, a mess. Splattered with coughs of mud, it had twigs and leaves and grass sticking out every which way. The Junior League robin complained the entire time of its construction. By day's end, more of it had ended up on the floor of the porch than had stayed in place, and the biker robin abandoned it.

She returned the next day to start all over again, this time a bit further away from her neighbor. Hal and I assumed this would please Ms. JL, but she seemed as agitated as ever. We'll never know what words passed between the two while we were at work, but when we returned that evening, nest number two, an even sorrier construction that the first, sat abandoned, and Ms. JL had the porch to herself.

Day three: The biker robin came back. By the time we returned that evening, she had completed her abode and moved in. She built this one in the far corner of the porch, using the junction of roof and corner post to supply the back wall. Her new home had a certain hobo-jungle chic about it, and the amount of building supplies that littered the porch set a new record, but she seemed entirely pleased with herself and in fact was entertaining a gentleman caller, a rough-feathered friend of impressive girth who I'm sure had "Fly Free or Die" tattooed beneath his bright red breast feathers. We were to see a lot of him over the next few weeks, and he proved to be a generous and tender provider. To our delight, they both seemed to enjoy our company, and each night the four of us gathered to watch the sunset show us how the Ruby Mountains got their names.

Ms. Junior League, on the other hand, apparently disdained the male sex except for the minimal contact required to initiate a brood. And broods we soon had on both sides of the porch, four chicks in each nest, ever hungry and vocal when their providers were away. We watched them grow, and we applauded their first ventures from the nest until one afternoon we came home to find both nests abandoned. We never heard from any of them again.

This tale ends on a note of sorrow, for we found a dead chick on the porch. It lay exactly centered between the two nests, so we can't draw any moral conclusions beyond our own prejudices about the merits of perfection versus affection in the raising of young.

I feel a great fondness for both Mr. Big and the biker robin even as they exhibit traits of sloth and slovenliness that drive me crazy in myself. My pleasure in them comes, I think, from the complete abandon, even glee, with which they comport themselves. They are, after all, just being themselves, and doing a damn good job of it.

And it's that quality of being themselves that separates their behavior from what disturbs us about our own sloth or *acedia*, with its measure of apathy and depression. When we are being truly slothful (as opposed to enjoying rest and recreation or succumbing to a spate of simple laziness), we feel removed from ourselves and from the world. This sense of despair underlies the concept; in the sixth century, when Pope Gregory condensed an earlier list of *pietas* into what we now know as the Seven Deadly

Sins, he folded *tristitia,* sorrow and despair, into his definition of *acedia,* the sin of failing to enjoy the goodness of God and his creation. Over time, in both religious and secular thought, we have come to view sloth as a paralyzing despondency that comes from the failure to use one's talents and gifts.

In *The Divine Comedy,* Dante viewed the seven sins as aberrations of love and organized them accordingly on his Mountain of Purgatory. The bottom three levels—pride, envy, and wrath—represented love directed toward evil. The top three levels represented excessive love for what is inherently good—greed, gluttony, and lust. Sloth took up the middle level, and it alone came from an absence of love; in Dante's view, sloth manifested from the "failure to love God with all one's heart, all one's mind, and all one's soul."

Sloth in animals gives us a view into another dimension of broken love, for a critter rarely exhibits genuine sloth, an inactivity born out of hopelessness and despair, unless it has been badly abused. In the human realm, if sloth demonstrates itself in an inability to love the beauty of the world and its creator, it surely originates in an inability to feel loved or worthy. The pit of self-doubt at the core of sloth makes it more of an affliction than a sin.

Critters don't worry about essential worthiness, which is one reason we take such comfort from them. It's also something we can learn from them. Perhaps what I blithely called sloth in Mr. Big is actually closer to the Taoist concept of *wu wei,* natural action or effortless action. Planets revolve around the sun, ice melts, seeds germinate; Mr. Big eats when he's hungry, cleans himself when he needs grooming, and sleeps when he grows tired. The rest of the time he rests quietly with a slight grin on his face, meditating.

I don't mean to make light of this. When we slide into laziness, we need to be reminded to get off our butts. But I come from a family with a long history of depression, and I have endured my own dark nights of the soul. The sloth that accompanies such periods rarely yields to sternness and condemnation, though I have employed plenty of both. What brings me around in the end I can only call love: a sense of belonging on this earth, as unquestionably as Mr. Big and the biker robin do.

Perhaps the animal that can teach us most about natural action is, ironically, the sloth, a creature that seems to move through the world in slow motion. While its scientific designation is nonjudgmental—its suborder, Folivora, means simply "leaf eater"—it earns little respect in its native habitat in central and South America. Ecuadorian tribes call it *ritto*, *rit*, and *ridette*: "sleep," "eat," and "dirty"; in Brazil, it's known as *bicho-preguiça*, "lazy animal."

In fact, the sloth is highly industrious, digesting otherwise inedible leaves through the combination of a large, slow-acting stomach, a slow metabolism, and low body temperature with such success that in some places it accounts for as much as two-thirds of the mammalian biomass. And however you have pictured sloths in your imagination, they are endearing in person, big-eyed, long-haired, and serene. As beautiful—and as lovable—as Mr. Big.

INDUSTRY

The Hard Work of Staying Still

Lose no time; be always employ'd in something useful; cut off all unnecessary actions. —BENJAMIN FRANKLIN

"You know that the antidote to exhaustion is
not necessarily rest?"
"What is it, then?"
"The antidote to exhaustion is wholeheartedness."
—DAVID WHYTE,
*Crossing the Unknown Sea:
Work as a Pilgrimage of Identity*

Last fall, one morning just after 3:00 AM, I found myself on a country road in the high Ogden Valley near Huntsville, Utah. It was the first morning of a three-day retreat at the Abbey of Our Lady of the Holy Trinity, a Trappist monastery, and I was walking the half mile from the guest house to the church for Vigils, the first of seven times each day that the monks gather to chant and pray.

I am not Catholic. As a child, I did not attend church of any kind, and my adult observance can best be described as Cafeterian, drawing nourishment from many spiritual traditions. But the Abbey offers retreat to anyone who seeks renewal, and for three days I had an apartment in the guesthouse to myself and an invitation to use my time for contemplation in whatever form I chose.

At 3:00 AM on a moonless night, the earth was an inky black and the sky a field of diamonds. I did not, however, find myself in a world of ethereal quiet. I might have expected the chirp of night birds, the strange wooden cooing of Sandhill cranes, the bark of town dogs a few miles away, or even a truck groaning up a distant grade. All of these were present but only as bass tones to a more pervasive racket, an eerie, high-pitched call-and-response back and forth across the valley from high up in the hills. I didn't recognize the sound: certainly not coyotes; too high-pitched for donkeys; unlike any birdcall I could imagine. The sound wrapped me in its mystery, and a thought occurred that often arises when I stop to really listen, even in midday: a world exists outside my knowing because I am asleep.

Later, Father Charles, who coordinates the retreats for women, told me I had arrived at the height of elk mating season. Of course. I should have known. I had heard bugling once or twice in my childhood, but I remembered it as much lower in pitch, and in fact elk make many different sounds. On subsequent mornings on my predawn trek to the chapel, I heard a range of calls as well as other signs that the animals were near: the sound of hooves running in the field beside the road as I walked, the stick-on-stick clatter of antlers as two bulls sparred. All this in the pitch dark. By day, the elk were nowhere to be seen, but I took comfort in knowing they were about, taking refuge, as was I, at the Abbey.

The Abbey of Our Lady of the Holy Trinity was founded in 1947 with thirty-four monks from Gethsemani Monastery in Kentucky and is one of twelve monasteries of Cistercians of the Strict Observance in the United States. (There are also five convents.) More commonly known as Trappists, the monks observe seven periods of Scripture, prayer, and song throughout the day known as the Liturgy of the Hours: Vigils, Lauds, Terce, Sext, None, Vespers, and Compline. The ancient chants—historically in Latin but now in English—are sung in unison. In addition, the monks devote their lives to private prayer and manual labor.

Monks who enter a Trappist monastery live out their lives in community. Today, fifteen monks live at the Huntsville Abbey, and their average age is eighty; there have been four funerals in the past year. There are more stones in the graveyard than plates on the table. They have no novices. "We are praying for that to change," Father Charles told me.

The Abbey is self-supporting on 1800 acres of crop and range ground. Traditionally, the monks did all the ranch work themselves. Now, in deference to their ages, they lease out the land but still do the maintenance and housekeeping themselves as well as process creamed honey and run a bookstore and gift shop. One monk, a fine woodworker, builds grandfather clocks.

I had been under the impression that Trappist monks observe a vow of silence, but that has never been true. They follow rules of silence, but they have always believed, as they explain on their website, that silence "is a form of charity to others, but it is not absolute. Charity may sometimes oblige persons, including monks, to speak at the right time and in the right way." The words have stayed with me. Often I am so distracted that I feel far removed from a world in which I know how to speak—or do anything else, for that matter—"at the right time and in the right way."

Last week, in response to my thoughts about sloth and industry, a reader commented:

> This reminds me of a memorable quote from the world of advertising: "I know half my advertising dollars are completely wasted; the problem is, I don't know which half." I feel this way sometimes about my busyness—it's usually only in retrospect that I can see things that really didn't need to be done, or at least not done in the frenzy with which I approached them, or indeed would have been much better left undone.

She identifies a quandary that many of us feel. We are dancing so fast that we hardly hear the music. We fall in bed each night too exhausted to imagine that the ceaseless tasks that engage us might be a form of what the Tibetan Buddhist master Sogyal Rinpoche calls "active laziness."

"Eastern laziness," he writes in *The Tibetan Book of Living and Dying*, "is like the one practiced to perfection in India. It consists of hanging out all day in the sun, doing nothing, avoiding any kind of work or useful activity, drinking cups of tea, listening to Hindi film music blaring on the radio, and gossiping with friends. Western laziness is quite different. It consists of cramming our lives with compulsive activity, so that there is no time at all to confront the real issues."

Many of us want to confront the real issues—how to live responsibly on this earth, practice love for one other, and live in gratitude for the miracle of our existence—but we have forgotten how. It is one reason I went to Huntsville: to grow quiet enough to remember. It was not a complete retreat. I was "too busy" not to bring a writing deadline with me, and I spent a few hours each day in the Huntsville Library. But for a little sliver of time, my days were not so very different from those of the monks, in form if not in depth: I attended many, though not all, of the hours; I spent time in private meditation; I worked quietly with little outside distraction.

The Trappists are not teachers in the active sense; they do no ministry outside the monastery. In their words, they devote their lives "to live the gospel in our particular way for the sake of our brothers and sisters throughout the world." They pray for us, and they provide a model of commitment and reverent industry through the quiet order of their day.

The monks live the strength of their vows to a degree that few of us can imagine. But as they observe the hours, they remind us that we all make vows with time, something which David Whyte eloquently explores in his book *Crossing the Unknown Sea: Work as a Pilgrimage of Identity*:

When we make a good marriage with time, . . . whatever sanity, patience, generosity, and creative genius we are able to achieve in life is not solely within our own remit. It comes from a real conversation with something other than ourselves. . . . The closer we are to the productions of time—that is, to the eternal—the more easily we understand the particular currents we must navigate on any given day. . . .

To say yes . . . to [something] that we know we cannot do with any sanity given all our present commitments . . . would be the equivalent of promiscuity, of faithlessness and betrayal. Stress means we have committed adultery with regard to our marriage with time. If we want to understand the particulars of our reality, we must understand the way we conduct our daily relationship with the hours.

I did not come home from Huntsville having entirely healed my marriage with time, and I know myself well enough to doubt I can completely resist the seduction of unnecessary busyness. But the retreat reminded me of the power of contemplation to create a spaciousness where our larger commitments can come into view. This seems a simple truth, and in fact the Greek word for truth, *aletheia*, means "a clearing." No matter how full the hours, I need to clear time to hear the elk bugling in the hills, the monks chanting in the chapel, and the still, small voice within.

LISTENING

Listening to the Devil's Trill

Stare, pry, listen, eavesdrop. Die knowing something. You are not here long.
                                        —WALKER EVANS

Long before I wrote stories, I listened for stories. Listening for them is something more acute than listening to them. I suppose it's an early form of participation in what goes on.
—EUDORA WELTY, *One Writer's Beginnings*

At its purest, silence makes space for stillness and receptive emptiness. Listening, on the other hand, is active. A couple of nights ago, when I heard the story behind Giuseppe Tartini's haunting sonata "The Devil's Trill," I found myself thinking about how both silence and listening play out in a creative life.

Tartini had a dream one night that the devil sat on the foot of his bed, begging to learn to play the violin. Tartini agreed to teach him, and then the devil performed a melody so beautiful that it broke Tartini's heart. When he woke in the morning, he tried to write it down, but he could never recover what he had experienced in the center of the night. Later he said that his own composition was "so inferior to what I had heard, that if I could have subsisted on other means, I would have broken my violin and abandoned music forever." At the end of his life, he still grieved for what might have been, and I imagine him through all those years listening, listening, trying to hear the music out there somewhere in the ether.

Many creative people talk about the role of listening in their art. Once, while I struggled with a short story, I asked the novelist Judith Freeman how she approached dialog. She told me she didn't make it up so much as listen to it. The composer Philip Glass described his own process in the documentary film *Glass: A Portrait of Philip in Twelve Parts*:

> Where does music come from? My experience with music is that it's like an underground river that is always there. And like an underground river, you don't know where it comes from, you don't know where it is going. The only difference is whether you are listening to it or not. . . .
>
> I begin by hearing very little. I hear something, and I train myself to follow the sound, follow the thought of the sound, follow the sound of the sound. And eventually I'll hear what it is. . . .
>
> With Symphony no. 8, I had great difficulty. . . and [Dennis Russell Davies, the conductor]. . . started looking at it, and he was questioning: "Is this an E-flat or E-natural? Is this a B?" And I said to him, "Dennis, when I wrote this, I was at the limits of what I could hear. . . . I am writing down what I think I heard, but I'm not really sure."

Artists paint so others can see; composers listen so we can hear. Whether our taste runs to rock or folk or classical, many of us will travel a long way and pay a dear price to attend a great concert. But sometimes we are deaf to the music that is right in front of us.

In 2007, *Washington Post* writer Gene Weingarten and classical violinist Joshua Bell undertook an experiment. Bell, considered one of the greatest violinists in the world, played for forty-five minutes in a Washington, D.C., subway station during rush hour, incognito in jeans and a Washington Nationals baseball cap. *Interview* magazine said that Bell's playing "does nothing less than tell human beings why they bother to live," but almost no one stopped to hear. A hidden camera videotaped Bell's performance, and in forty-five minutes, though more than 1,100 people passed by, only twenty-seven tossed money in Bell's violin case for a total of less than thirty-three dollars; only seven people actually stopped, most of them for less than a minute.

As Weingarten described it:

> There was no ethnic or demographic pattern to distinguish the people who stayed . . . or the ones who gave money, from that vast majority who hurried on past, unheeding. Whites, blacks, and Asians, young and old, men and women, were represented in all three groups. But the behavior of one demographic remained absolutely consistent. Every single time a child walked past, he or she tried to stop and watch. And every single time, a parent scooted the kid away.

I think I would have noticed the music. I think I would have recognized its virtuosity. I even think I would have stopped for a moment. But I know the power of momentum, and I'm sure that I, too, would have soon rushed on. Later in the day I would tell a friend about it and bemoan the fact that I thought I was too busy to stay. Sadly, I would take more time telling the story than I had spent listening to the music of the spheres.

ORDER

A Pomegranate of Impossible Tasks

Let all your things have their places; let each part of your business have its time. —BENJAMIN FRANKLIN

I just kept on doing what everyone starts out doing. The real question is, why did other people stop? —WILLIAM STAFFORD

Each morning, the poet William Stafford woke at 4:00 AM, made a cup of instant coffee and ate a piece of toast, and then went to the living room, where he turned on a small lamp, lay down on the sofa, and began to write.

Each morning, he wrote a poem. It didn't have to be a good poem—it could even be a very bad poem—but he was a poet, and his job was to write poems. He worked until the words found their shape, and then he rose from the couch, placed the hand-written draft into his writing box for later consideration, and began the day.

You might think he had already begun the day, lying prone on the couch, inviting the poem. But his son, Kim Stafford—himself an elegant and prolific writer—will tell you that his father inhabited two realms: the deep, dark waters before dawn where nothing stood between him and the poem; and the light of day, where he did everything else to meet the responsibilities of his life as father, husband, teacher, friend, and public persona.

By this habit, he published fifty-nine books and thousands of poems by the time he died in 1993 at the age of seventy-nine. He corresponded with a vast network of friends. And he touched the lives of literally thousands of students at colleges and writing workshops all over the world. When someone asked him how he got so much done, he'd answer simply: Do the big thing first.

I met Bill—everyone who knew him even slightly called him Bill; something in his plainspoken directness seemed to require it—through his son Kim. Kim and I had become friends after he hired me to teach workshops for the Northwest Writing Institute that he directed at Lewis and Clark College in Portland, Oregon, the same school where his father taught.

The son of a famous man faces challenges as he tries to carve out his own work life, especially if he pursues the same craft. Bill cleared his desk every night so that he could rise before dawn undistracted, and there were times Kim railed against the expectations of such a model: he was a young father, going through a divorce, managing a staff, and juggling fundraising and academic politics to keep the Institute alive. Sometimes, he said, life felt like "a pomegranate of impossible tasks."

I've never forgotten that phrase, with its grant of sweetness and structure to the overwhelming chaos of contemporary life. Somehow, out of those infinite seeds, Kim nurtured his own daily practice. "Everything I have to write," he told me once, "will include something I want to write." In the years I worked with him in Portland, 1986 to 1991, he published four books, and he has since written ten more.

One of those books is *Early Morning: Remembering My Father*. In it, he tells the story of the day his father died.

> He rose early, settled on the couch before dawn to write a great poem, shared breakfast with my mother, went to his desk to "do the hard things first"—in this case a book review . . . —took a glorious nap after lunch and responded to a flurry of letters. (One friend received not one but two letters

my father wrote that day.) Then my mother called him to the
kitchen. She had been making a cream pie when the blender
exploded, scattering lime pie filling everywhere. She called,
and in a moment he came in from the study. In good spirits,
he went to work cleaning up the mess and turned to her.

"Better get another spatula," he said. Then, without another
word he fell backward to the floor. When my mother heard
how hard his head hit, she knew he was gone.

Kim's mother called Kim's sister Barb, who lived in Portland
and rushed over. Kim was in central Oregon and picked up his
other sister, Kit; they came as quickly as they could. The next
day, they read Bill's last poem. He often started his poems with
something out of recent experience, and the day before he died,
an insurance agent had called, trying to track down what proved
to be a different William Stafford:

"Are you Mr. William Stafford?"
"Yes, but . . ."

Well, it was yesterday.
Sunlight used to follow my hand.
And that's when the strange siren-like sound flooded
over the horizon and rushed through the streets of our town.
That's when the sunlight came from behind
a rock and began to follow my hand.

"It's for the best," my mother said —"Nothing can
ever be wrong for anyone truly good."
So after the suffering
So later the sun settled back and the sound
faded and was gone. All along the streets every
house waited, white, blue, gray; trees
were still trying to arch as far as they could.

You can't tell when strange things with meaning
will happen. I'm [still] here writing it down
just the way it was. "You don't have to
prove anything," my mother said. "Just be ready
for what God sends." I listened and put my hand
out in the sun. It was all easy.

Well, it was yesterday, and the sun knows
Why
It came.

Published in *Early Morning*
Remembering My Father, William Stafford,
by Kim Stafford, (Greywolf Press, 2002)

A few days later, Kim returned to his familial home to spend the night. His mother was staying with friends, so he was alone when he woke at 4:00 AM, his father's time but not, usually, his own. He rose, made a cup of instant coffee, and ate a piece of toast. When he had finished, he went to the living room to lie down on the sofa with paper and pen. He rested his head on his father's worn pillow and gave patience to the words that he knew would rise, in their own time, until he could catch one line and then another:

pause at the gate to take off the one big shoe
of his body, step forward light as wind.

"In the uninterrupted abundance of my own time," Kim wrote, "I finished a page, closed my notebook, and rose for the day. As my father would say at such a time, there was much to do, but I had done the big thing already."

HABIT

Some Thoughts on In-habitation

We are what we repeatedly do. Excellence, then, is not an
act, but a habit."
—ARISTOTLE

Bad habits are like a comfortable bed, easy to get into,
but hard to get out of.
—PROVERB

When I was a child growing up on an isolated ranch, each
day started with the last gesture at night, the thermos of
coffee my mother made and took up to her bedside table in preparation for the morning to come. When the alarm rang at 5:00 AM,
she woke to light a cigarette and drink a cup of coffee in the dark
before she dressed quietly and headed downstairs to put the kettle
on and let out the dog. When the dog came back in, he bounded
upstairs to wake my father, who gave him a biscuit before rising
to pull on his jeans, his boots, his snap-fastened shirt. On his
way to the bathroom, he would turn on the light in my room and
stand at the door saying, not unkindly, "Hon, it's time," over and
over, until I finally, reluctantly, acknowledged him so he could
move down the hall to my brother's room and do the same thing.

These were the first motions in the daily habit of my family.
By the time we all got downstairs, Mom would have breakfast on
the table, five thirty, sharp, and though the menu would change,
the accoutrements would not, most especially my father's tea
in a yellow china pot with a graceful spout and a twirled finial

that made me think of Aladdin's magic lantern. My father had a tender mouth, and before he drank his tea he cooled it with a heavy cylinder of stainless steel that rested in a bowl of ice cubes until he put it in his cup, a gesture that said time was too important for tea to cool on its own.

When we were not in school, my brother and I took turns wrangling the horses, and whoever was on call ate quickly to get out to the barn. The barn was the heart of it all, the cathedral, the place where the day truly began, a hall you entered with a sacred tone—"whoa"—to avoid startling the horses. Whether there were horses in the barn or not, you spoke the word, a rule as inviolate as never pointing a gun, not even a toy, at a human being.

I loved stepping into the fragrant dark, the timbre of "whoa" vibrating in my chest. I would flip on the yellow light, dip oats out of the wooden bin with a three-pound coffee can, grab the halter to catch the wrangle horse from the corral, and then speak softly, almost humming, as I groomed him with currycomb and brush. Something about the firmness and gravity of a horse's body and its sharp yet strangely floral scent is almost holy. I'd smooth the blanket over the line of his spine, swing the saddle across, clip on the breast collar, snug the cinches, warm the bit in my hands before I invited him to take it in his mouth. Then I'd lead him outdoors and give the cinches a final pull before I walked him a few more steps to let the saddle settle. Finally, I'd swing on and head out to ride the ridges and find the horse herd.

You always move horses on the run; they won't stay bunched at slower speeds. Our horse pasture was a mile square, more or less, and hilly with its share of rocks. Wrangling had its thrills. In the early morning chill just past first light, I would find the horses bunched up along the creek or tucked in the far corner, steam rising off their backs, snorting out in chuffs of recognition. I didn't have to get too close before they would start to run— we all knew the drill—and usually they would start to the barn, though sometimes they took me on a romp around the fence lines first. Then, as we crested the last hill above the home place, they would line out to run through the gate into the corral in ones and twos. One of the men would swing the big wooden gate shut behind them, and we would gather in the barn to get our day's marching orders from my dad.

With these rituals, we inhabited this place, and I doubt the rhythms changed much over our four-generation tenure on the land. The ranch passed out of our hands in 1979. I still find it hard to say that we sold it, though we did, a necessity born by estate taxes after my grandfather's death and an economy in worse shape than it is right now.

I've been thinking a lot lately about what it means to inhabit a place, or a life, or one's work. Inhabit: in-habit. Habit can be mindless and deadly, a thoughtless routine. But cultivated with attention, it can allow us to "do the big thing first," carving out the non-negotiable space where the real work happens, whether it is wrought of the imagination or of the hands or—as is often the case—of both.

Saying good-bye to the ranch was one of the hardest things I ever did, though over time, I have come to realize that a part of me remains in that place. Perhaps it is more accurate to say that the place remains in me. It in-habits me, available on call, a realization that figures in a poem I wrote more than a decade later.

LOOKING BACK

The secret place is gone.
Picked up like a tenant
in the middle of the night
after a bad run of luck
it trudges down the dark lone road
with the meadow
and the barn
and a long line of cows,
tails bedraggling behind them.
I loved

that secret place
down by the riverbed
hidden by a bank. I whittled
dolls from willows there, made whistles
out of broad bladed grass, told my big bay
Buddy how I'd never leave.
I lied

though not from will.
Let me be salt
sculpted by cow
tongues until I am lace
and then I am gone.

I want to belong to the ground
again. It is the barn

that breaks my heart
trudging soddenly along, bedsteads
and broken harnesses rocking
softly in the loft, lost
beneath great drifts of
guano. A spavined horse-
collar mirror hangs
cockeyed on the ladder
and that other me looks back
amazed. In the darkness
only one of us is
gone.

FRUGALITY

Stepping Off the Hedonic Treadmill

Make no expense but to do good to others or yourself;
i.e., waste nothing. —Benjamin Franklin

If you want to be richer, make more money or need less.
 —Unknown

Around 1980, when I was just out of college, I spent two years driving back roads across a dozen Western states, searching out women who worked on the land for what would become my first book, *Cowgirls: Women of the American West.* I had a $20 backpacking tent and a Honda Civic, and I drove close to sixty thousand miles. I interviewed over eighty women and a lot of men, and hardly a week goes by that I don't think of something one or another of them told me.

Once, in northern Wyoming, after I helped a ranch woman and her crew gather cattle, we sat down to a feed of hamburgers. As the ketchup and mustard made their way around the table, she told me that she had never tasted ketchup until she got married. Her father didn't allow condiments of any kind. He saw them as an unnecessary expense. Sometime later, at another ranch feed—this one after a branding in Montana—I told this story to the cowhand who sat next to me. Glenn (I hope I am remembering his name right after all these years) and I had worked together all morning, and I admired how quiet and competent he was around the calves. Now he shook his head. "Boy," he said, "some people work awful hard to make life harder."

As I remember those stories now, they seem like relics of another age. It's hard to imagine anyone in America today wanting for condiments. Junk food, the cheapest source of calories around, comes loaded with condiments. Sometimes it seems to be nothing *but* condiments. But what Glenn was responding to was what he saw as a rigid and mean-spirited frugality. He knew enough about scarcity to know how small things, even rarely enjoyed, can make life sweeter. But that was before advertising reached the most remote spots on the globe. Today, in the parade of ever-escalating enticements, ketchup ranks low on the list of perceived deprivations.

I only met Glenn once and then for only half a day, so the assumptions I make about him are drawn from the hundreds of ranch people I've known through the years: that he was naturally frugal but generous within his means, and that he savored small sweetnesses, such as the shared work of a branding and the barbecue afterward, because they made a hard life not only bearable but rich.

Such moments were already becoming rare. In 1993, only thirteen years after I met Glenn, the Census Bureau would stop counting people who lived on farms and ranches in a separate category: numbering less than 2 percent of the population, they were deemed "statistically insignificant." Industrial agriculture required a fraction of the workforce and inspired an exodus from rural communities. Even those who still worked in agriculture rarely lived on the land: one third of those who owned or managed farms and ranches lived somewhere else, as did nine out of ten hired hands. Most drove to work from houses in town or trailers on the edges of urban sprawl. The evenings they once enjoyed with neighbors playing poker or pinochle were now devoted to TV.

Of course TV had come to those who remained in the country as well: by the 1990s, satellite dishes were so ubiquitous in rural

Montana that some called them the new state flower. And even though industrial agriculture had brought material improvements—electrification, telephone, TV (and eventually Internet), better roads, better access to medical care, and generally higher incomes—many people felt poorer than they ever had before. More and more took on multiple jobs just to keep up. (And this doesn't take into consideration the terrific pressure to buy more land and machinery on credit, a subject all its own.)

A commute to work, multiple jobs, long nights in front of the TV or the computer, and the incessant drumbeat that you have to buy things in order to be happy: rural people have increasingly had these experiences in common with their urban cousins. No matter where we live, we've seen consumption become something of a patriotic duty, a way to demonstrate our indomitable spirit to the terrorists or to spend ourselves out of the current recession.

MIT management professor John Sterman calls it the "hedonic treadmill." In his words, "The ironic thing is that the pursuit of more, so stunningly successful so far, has not increased our happiness. . . . Consumption per capita in the developed economies has increased dramatically over the past half century, yet reported life-satisfaction is no higher. . . . We find ourselves in a no-win situation in which no level of income or consumption remains satisfying for long—the hedonic treadmill. The more people seek to boost consumption, the more income they require and the harder and longer they must work, undermining those activities that are actually fulfilling and satisfying."

But a lot of people, rural and urban, aren't buying it anymore. The silver lining to this deep, dark recession is that many of us are discovering the sweetness in small things. We are saving four to five times as much as we did before the downturn, and we are spending what money we have on memories rather than stuff. As Stephanie Rosenbloom reports in *The New York Times*, "consumers have gravitated more toward experiences than possessions over the last couple of years, opting to use their extra cash for nights at home with family, watching movies and playing games—or for 'staycations' in the backyard. Many retailing professionals think this is not a fad, but rather 'the new normal.' . . . Analysts say consumers may be permanently adjusting their spending based on what they've discovered about what truly makes them happy or fulfilled."

I'd like to think that part of this change, with its appreciation of relationships over material goods, will be good not only for our souls but also for the rural economy. The extraordinary proliferation of farmers markets hints that "slow food" from local producers figures among the experiences we increasingly rely on to give life savor. And many of the producers have turned away from industrial agriculture in order to have a more hands-on experience with both the land and the people who enjoy its fruits. As Glenn might put it, we've been working awful hard to make life harder. The new frugality might help us find a way to turn that around.

HOMECOMING

Rethinking Nostalgia

It's surprising how much memory is built around things
unnoticed at the time.　　—BARBARA KINGSOLVER

Nostalgia is like a grammar lesson: you find the present
tense, but the past perfect.　　—OWENS LEE POMEROY

The readers who commented on the previous post about frugality have got me thinking. Several people recalled childhood
pleasures of homegrown or hand-prepared food. It's easy to
dismiss such thoughts as nostalgia, the roseate haze of time, and
it's true that we tend to remember pleasure more than pain (an
evolutionary advantage that allowed the concept of "siblings"
to come into the world). But other readers offered memories no
more than a few days or hours old, such as making jam from
Concord grapes that very afternoon.

Nostalgia, at any rate, is highly underrated, as the late Paul
Gruchow reminded us in his book *Grass Roots:*

> It is the fashion just now to disparage nostalgia. Nostalgia,
> we believe, is a cheap emotion. But we forget what it means.
> In its Greek roots it means, literally, the return to home. It
> came into currency as a medical word in nineteenth-century
> Germany to describe the failure to thrive of the displaced
> persons, including my own ancestors, who had crowded
> into that country from the east. Nostalgia is the clinical term
> for homesickness, for the desire to be rooted in a place. . . .

This desire need not imply the impulse to turn back the clock, which of course we cannot do. It recognizes, rather, the truth—if home is a place in time—that we cannot know where we are now unless we can remember where we have come from. The real romantics are those who believe that history is the story of the triumphal march of progress, that change is indiscriminately for the better. Those who would demythologize the past seem to forget that we also construct the present as a myth, that there is nothing in the wide universe so vast as our own ignorance. Knowing that is our one real hope.

One reader worried that "when business gets back to normal, we will forget this newfound pleasure in experience and go on consuming, consuming, consuming." His concern has historical precedent: every energy crisis has seen us dump our big cars only to go out and buy new guzzlers as soon as the price of gas came down. But I'd like to think a deeper change is afoot, and my optimism is rooted in the slow-food movement that was well underway before the current economic crisis and has gained such momentum that every time I turn around another major magazine is featuring it on its cover. (In October 2010, *The New York Times Magazine* devoted an entire issue to it under the title "Eating Together: How the food revolution—from farm to table—is really a story about seeding and savoring communities.")

It is easy to have doubts about a new frugality when almost every page of a feature about slow food features an ad for a kitchen appliance that costs as much as the down payment on a modest home. But I see lots of encouraging signs on the grassroots level right here where I live, Salt Lake City. When Novella Carpenter came to the Salt Lake City Public Library a couple of months ago to talk about *Farm City*—her very funny memoir of turning an abandoned lot in Oakland, California, into a farm—the auditorium was packed, and folks stayed afterward to share their own urban farming stories.

The Saturday Downtown Farmers Market here has expanded

to Tuesday afternoon, and there are at least four other farmers markets around the metropolitan area. Most accept food stamps, which gives low-income families access to nutritious food. (One symptom of our out-of-balance food system is that nutritious calories are so much more expensive than junk food.)

Those who want to garden but don't have land have increasing opportunities as well. Wasatch Community Gardens has five locations where people can grow their own food, and over 4,500 people a year participate in one way or another. Other community gardens are springing up all over, including one in South Salt Lake for refugees from Myanmar.

But perhaps one of the most encouraging signs I see in urban culture is the interest among young people in food production. It's not idle talk. Within our own circle of friends, my husband and I know at least six people in their twenties and thirties who are working or have recently worked on farms and ranches in the American West and in Mexico and Central America.

If grassroots agriculture is connecting a lot of urban kids with food production for the first time, it is also allowing a lot of rural kids to stay on the home place. One of the success stories I've followed for a very long time is that of Country Natural Beef, which Doc and Connie Hatfield started in eastern Oregon thirty-five years ago after they got tired of going broke raising hormone- and antibiotic-dependent cattle that suffered from illness and birthing problems. In 1976, they formed a cooperative with thirteen other ranchers to raise drug-free, range-raised beef and sell it directly to the consumer. Today, the group includes over 120 ranches in thirteen states and has proved so economically viable that many of the original partners who thought their kids had no future on the ranch are now watching their grandkids grow up there.

Hal and I get our grass-fed beef from Bar 10 Beef, a one-hundred-year-old ranch located in southern Utah and northern Arizona. For decades, the Heaton family followed the industrial model, selling their calves to feedlots, where they were corn-fed and then commercially slaughtered and packed. But as they say on their website, they became concerned that "from the time it was sold at auction to the time it reached the consumer's plate, [we] didn't ever know where that calf went, or how it was treated. In recent years, with the industrialization of beef and the distrust created by inhumane animal treatment and food-borne illnesses, the decision was made to start providing consumers directly with safe, high-quality, gourmet, all-natural, grass-fed beef. Now, the Bar 10 Ranch controls how the cattle are treated from beginning to end."

The family likes to connect directly with consumers. As marketing director Ryan West told me, most of us know our doctors and our lawyers. It's time we knew our ranchers as well.

One of the most eloquent voices for the need to reconnect with our food supply is Wes Jackson of the Land Institute in Salina, Kansas. In his 1994 book *Becoming Native to This Place*, he wrote:

> The universities now offer only one serious major: upward mobility. Little attention is paid to educating the young to return home, or to go some other place, and dig in. There is no such thing as a "homecoming" major. But what if the universities were to ask seriously what it would mean to have as our national goal becoming native in this place, this continent? We are unlikely to achieve anything close to sustainability in any area unless we work for the broader goal of becoming native in the modern world, and that means becoming native to our places in a coherent community that is in turn embedded in the ecological realities of its surrounding landscape.

In the past few years, as the universities have begun paying more attention to sustainable agriculture, the rest of us have also been getting a grassroots education in homecoming from the school of hard knocks that is the current recession. I hope so, anyway. I'm probably a hopeless romantic and nostalgic to boot. But perhaps nostalgia is the spirit's way of showing us the road home.

GOVERNANCE

What George Might Say

Congress Continues Debate Over Whether or Not Nation should be Economically Ruined.

> —Headline in the satirical paper
> *THE ONION*, July 20, 2011.

One of the expedients of party to acquire influence within particular districts is to misrepresent the opinions and aims of other districts. You cannot shield yourselves too much against the jealousies and heartburnings which spring from these misrepresentations. . . .

> —GEORGE WASHINGTON, Farewell Address, 1796

[This chapter originated as a blog entry in July of 2011 as Congress bickered so bitterly over raising the debt ceiling that our national credit rating was lowered. Because it was so timely, I never expected to include it in the book. Alas, as I readied the book for publication two years later, not much had changed.]

When I set upon this project, I vowed to refrain from commenting on current events, most especially political ones. But as we slouch toward national default, which brings with it not only the specter of economic chaos but also of national disgrace, I am sick at heart. As I write, both parties are working toward an eleventh-hour deal that will raise the debt ceiling before we begin to renege on our obligations on August 2. And both parties are threatening to act independently if they don't get their way.

However this plays out, there is plenty of blame to go around. Even so, as there has been at least some willingness to negotiate by nearly all the players except for the Tea Party legislators who have taken the Taxpayer Protection Pledge, my ire of the moment lands primarily upon them. Those who take the pledge promise not to vote for a net increase in revenue under any circumstances. I respect people who keep their promises—when those promises are honorable. I do not, however, respect those who pledge their votes in advance, regardless of circumstances, even if it means defaulting on what both parties have deemed "the full faith and credit of the United States."

What does it mean for nationally elected officials, whose first commitment should be the oath of office—which states, in part, to "faithfully discharge the duties of the office on which I am about to enter"—to pledge their higher allegiance to a position that translates in plain language as, "My mind is made up. Don't confuse me with facts." Surely, one of the duties of office is to respond to the needs of the nation by entering into open-minded debate in good faith. After intense research, both the bipartisan Gang of Six and the bipartisan National Commission on Fiscal Responsibility and Reform concluded that a workable, long-term solution will include revenue increase alongside deep cuts in spending. To refuse to at least consider such recommendations is the equivalent of sticking one's fingers in one's ears—or perhaps more to the point, extending the middle finger of one hand to those who don't agree.

Jacob Needleman, author of *The American Soul: Rediscovering the Wisdom of the Founders*, writes at length about the responsibilities that come along with the rights we enjoy as American citizens. As he said in a recent interview, "If I have the right to speak, I have the duty to let you speak. Now, that's not so simple. It doesn't mean just to stop my talking and wait until you're finished and then come in and get you. It means I have an obligation inwardly . . . to work at listening to you. That means I don't have to agree with you, but I have to let your thought into my mind in order to have a real democratic exchange between us."

It is exactly this "democratic exchange" that the Tea Partiers have vowed to eschew. In the words of conservative columnist David Brooks, these sorts of "rigid ultimatums . . . make governance, or even thinking, impossible."

The Taxpayer Protection Pledge came into being in 1986, written by Grover Norquist at the behest of Ronald Reagan, who has come down to the Tea Party as the patron saint of tax cuts. It's true that Reagan slashed taxes, but when it was clear that the drastic tax cuts he signed into law in the Economic Recovery Tax Act of 1981 would create record peacetime deficits, he reversed himself and agreed to a number of tax increases. Norquist, now head of the anti-tax Americans for Tax Reform that administers the Taxpayer Protection Pledge, says that "every one of those was a mistake." As Brian Faler reports in *Bloomberg,* Norquist complains that "Reagan was 'pushed' into [the tax increases] by the Democrats who then controlled the House and the 'liberal' Republicans who ran the Senate." David Stockman, Reagan's first budget director, remembers it more pragmatically: "We were scared out of our wits because the [deficits resulting from the tax cuts] seemed to be unimaginable."

The bottom line for Reagan was that he was committed to governance—to making the country work for all its people. He refused to be locked into an immutable position predetermined by his party or any other faction.

As I, along with the rest of the country, have been watching partisan politics turn into a slow-motion train wreck, I have been thinking about an earlier American whose life's work is a testament against intransigence. During the past few days, I have run across many references to George Washington's warnings in his 1796 Farewell Address against "the baneful effects of the spirit of party." To read this address now is to think that he wrote it for our day.

Washington believed in the sacred duty of negotiation. "He deplored the adversary theory which sees government as a tug-of-war between the holders of opposite views, one side eventually vanquishing the other," wrote James Thomas Flexner, one of

Washington's most-respected biographers. "Washington saw the national capital as a place where we came together not to tussle but to reconcile disagreements. Washington's own greatest mental gift was to be able to bore down through partial arguments to the fundamental principles on which everyone could agree."

Politics is an imperfect art, and we will never be in complete agreement. It is important to remember that the Constitution, which has served us so well and for so long, was born out of huge divisions and signed by only thirty-nine of the fifty-five delegates to the convention. Those who had the courage to bequest us this gift were not locked immutably into positions they held before the negotiations began.

I hope you will take the time to read Washington's entire address, but I have chosen some excerpts that seem especially relevant today. Each of us will read our own politics into his advisements. Because I am so disgusted with the Tea Party right now, I of course read them into Washington's caveats. Today, as always, it is easy to point a finger. But I hope each of us can recognize our own blind spots, our own ruts of intransigence. George Washington is speaking to us. All of us. The good in us, as well as the parts of us we try to foist on others.

GEORGE WASHINGTON ON
"THE BANEFUL EFFECTS OF THE SPIRIT OF PARTY"

The unity of government which constitutes you one people is also now dear to you. It is justly so, for it is a main pillar in the edifice of your real independence, the support of your tranquility at home, your peace abroad; of your safety; of your prosperity; of that very liberty which you so highly prize. . . .

One of the expedients of party to acquire influence within particular districts is to misrepresent the opinions and aims of other districts. You cannot shield yourselves too much against the jealousies and heartburnings which spring from these misrepresentations; they tend to render alien to each other those who ought to be bound together by fraternal affection. . . .

All obstructions to the execution of the laws, all combinations and associations, under whatever plausible character, with the real design to direct, control, counteract, or awe the regular deliberation and action of the constituted authorities, are destructive of this fundamental principle, and of fatal tendency. They serve to organize faction, to give it an artificial and extraordinary force; to put, in the place of the delegated will of the nation the will of a party, often a small but artful and enterprising minority of the community. . . .

However combinations or associations of the above description may now and then answer popular ends, they are likely, in the course of time and things, to become potent engines, by which cunning, ambitious, and unprincipled men will be enabled to subvert the power of the people and to usurp for themselves the reins of government, destroying afterwards the very engines which have lifted them to unjust dominion. . . .

The alternate domination of one faction over another, sharpened by the spirit of revenge, natural to party dissension, which in different ages and countries has perpetrated the most horrid enormities, is itself a frightful despotism. But this leads at length to a more formal and permanent despotism. The disorders and miseries which result gradually incline the minds of men to seek security and repose in the absolute power of an individual; and sooner or later the chief of some prevailing faction, more able or more fortunate than his competitors, turns this disposition to the purposes of his own elevation, on the ruins of public liberty. . . .

[The spirit of party] serves always to distract the public councils and enfeeble the public administration. It agitates the community with ill-founded jealousies and false alarms, kindles the animosity of one part against another, foments occasionally riot and insurrection. It opens the door to foreign influence and corruption, which finds a facilitated access to the government itself through the channels of party passions. Thus the policy and the will of one country are subjected to the policy and will of another.

GEORGE WASHINGTON ON
OUR GOOD NAME AND THE ROLE OF TAXATION
(ESPECIALLY DURING WARTIME)

As a very important source of strength and security, cherish public credit. One method of preserving it is to use it as sparingly as possible, avoiding occasions of expense by cultivating peace, but remembering also that timely disbursements to prepare for danger frequently prevent much greater disbursements to repel it, avoiding likewise the accumulation of debt, not only by shunning occasions of expense, but by vigorous exertion in time of peace to discharge the debts which unavoidable wars may have occasioned, not ungenerously throwing upon posterity the burden which we ourselves ought to bear. The execution of these maxims belongs to your representatives, but it is necessary that public opinion should co-operate. To facilitate to them the performance of their duty, it is essential that you should practically bear in mind that towards the payment of debts there must be revenue; that to have revenue there must be taxes; that no taxes can be devised which are not more or less inconvenient and unpleasant; that the intrinsic embarrassment, inseparable from the selection of the proper objects (which is always a choice of difficulties), ought to be a decisive motive for a candid construction of the conduct of the government in making it, and for a spirit of acquiescence in the measures for obtaining revenue, which the public exigencies may at any time dictate. . . .

GEORGE WASHINGTON'S HOPE FOR US

In offering to you, my countrymen, these counsels of an old and affectionate friend, I dare not hope they will make the strong and lasting impression I could wish; that they will control the usual current of the passions, or prevent our nation from running the course which has hitherto marked the destiny of nations. But, if I may even flatter myself that they may be productive of some partial benefit, some occasional good; that they may now and then recur to moderate the fury of party spirit, to warn against the mischiefs of foreign intrigue, to guard against the impostures of pretended patriotism; this hope will be a full recompense for the solicitude for your welfare, by which they have been dictated.

SINCERITY

Giving Voice to Untold Stories

Use no hurtful deceit; think innocently and justly, and, if you speak, speak accordingly.

—BENJAMIN FRANKLIN

It's only as we engage in truthful dialogue and in a quest for building a relationship that we can grow as individual people. So to the extent that I am estranged from you, I am less than human.

—CHARLES VILLA-VICENCIO,
executive director of the Institute for Justice
and Reconciliation, South Africa

How do we reach each other across a great divide?

The question has been much on my mind since hearing Logan Hebner and Forrest Cuch, director of the Utah Division of Indian Affairs, discuss Hebner's just-released book, *Southern Paiute: A Portrait*, at the Utah Humanities Book Festival this past weekend. In the book, thirty-two members of the various Southern Paiute tribes and bands across northern Arizona and southern Utah, Nevada, and California tell their life stories in their own words.

Hebner spent nine years collecting these interviews, often traveling with friends such as Vivienne Caron-Jake of the Southern Paiute Kaibab Band, or Arthur Richards of the Cedar Band. The photographer Michael Plyler went along, and his powerful black-and-white portraits lend visual weight to the dignity so evident in the stories themselves. The book is a landmark, the first time that

Southern Paiute have had their voices heard in depth beyond their own communities.

On the surface, Hebner is an unlikely conduit for these stories. He was born in Delaware and was fresh out of Vassar College in 1981 when he came out West with a friend looking for entre-preneurial opportunities. The two young men bought the Bit and Spur bar in Springdale, Utah, near the entrance to Zion National Park, and with not much more than a Mexican cookbook to guide them, they plunged into the restaurant business. For his first few years in Utah, Hebner's only interface with Native culture was its dysfunctional fringe, the alcoholics who would wander into the bar and too often, by night's end, cause serious trouble.

But he fell in love with the desert, and as he moved deeper into its heart, he became intrigued with the people who for cen-turies had been able to live there. Then he became involved with protesting the massive hazardous waste incinerator that Waste Tech Services, Inc., was negotiating with the Kaibab Paiute to place on their reservation on the Arizona Strip. The tribe almost unanimously supported the project, which they saw as their only chance for jobs and prosperity, but a few members did not, and Logan grew close to Vivienne Caron-Jake, her mother Lucille, and her nephew Verdell through their shared protest of the facility and an appreciation of each others' humor. Logan was often the only one who caught Vivienne's sharp puns, like her use of the term "honky dory" whenever white folk are oblivious to the fallout of their deeds.

The incinerator was on the verge of tribal approval when Bill Tom, Vivienne's uncle and a revered elder, died after a sudden and vicious bout of cancer. His last wish was that the tribe would "reject the incinerator to preserve the sliver of ancestral lands they still possessed." In a vote held the day after his death, the tribe voted unanimously against the project.

Vivienne and her family invited Hebner to the Cry ceremony honoring Bill Tom. Logan politely declined; he felt he had intruded enough already. But that night, on his way back to

Springdale, he stopped at a grocery store in St. George, Utah, and ran into Verdell, who was buying coffee cakes. "I asked if the Cry was over," Logan wrote in the book, "and he shot me a look of pity; how could I not know that they go all night?" For the second time, Verdell invited Logan; this time he accepted and drove to Kaibab, Arizona, on the edge of the Vermillion Cliffs, in the middle of the night:

> Attending a ceremony is always a step up in intruding on people, more so of course for a funeral. I sat inside my unheated Toyota pickup until it just got too cold. I slipped inside, headed right up the closest gymnasium bleachers, and was stunned by what was unfolding. The gathering shined with an astonishing density, alive with song, rattles, grief, dance, feasting, and reunion, all layered around Bill Tom's open casket near the center of the basketball court.

> That night they sang Bill Tom's dazed soul through the landscape of the dead, singing and dancing hard so he could hear them through death's confusion. Near dawn, they redoubled their efforts to help his soul leap the canyon to the next world. Just days earlier the tribe had been deeply split about the incinerator; they had just turned down hundreds of millions of dollars; that night they were all united in ceremony. . . .

> Somewhere in the night everyone collectively crossed a threshold, achieving the rarified ether of ceremony. You could feel grief spiral in, condense, and release through communal weeping.... It was the most elegant, unpretentious, and powerful ceremony I've yet experienced.

That night was a turning point for Logan. He recognized that he wanted to know, really know, his Paiute neighbors. And he began to trust that authentic friendship was possible across the great gulf of history and pain.

Sociologists tell us that prejudice is greatest between peoples who have never met, but the situation with Indian people is often reversed. As Forrest Cuch, an enrolled member of the Ute Indian Tribe and editor of *A History of Utah's American Indians*, pointed out, it's ironic but true that Europeans an ocean away, who have long been fascinated by Native American history, are likely to know more about the lifeways of America's desert Indians than the white Americans who live near them. Logan and Forrest discussed the background to that disconnect, aided from the audience by Lora Tom, former chairwoman of the Paiute Indian Tribe of Utah.

They talked about how non-Indians often see only the most dysfunctional edge of Indian culture, as Logan had when he first came to Utah. In addition, many non-Indians feel ancestral guilt for the history of Western settlement that robbed Indian people of their land, razed their culture, and in the case of the Southern Paiute, led to a population decline of more than 90 percent through a combination of disease and policy. Many Indians, on the other hand, keep their distance out of a blend of anger, distrust, and the deep sense of shame that inhabits the dispossessed.

The Paiute story is further complicated by the interface with Mormon theology that viewed indigenous people as Lamanites, a lost Abrahamic tribe that migrated to America in 600 BC. The Book of Mormon holds that the Lamanites were cursed by God but could regain His grace and become "white and delightsome" through conversion.

And then there is the festering wound of the 1857 Mountain Meadows Massacre, ". . . where Mormons blamed Paiutes for the slaughter of some 120 members of an immigrant train from Arkansas, even though the raid had been largely the work of the local Mormon militia, dressed as Natives." Only 150 years later, in 2007, did The Church of Jesus Christ of Latter-Day Saints officially acknowledge the scapegoating, noting that "an expression of regret is owed the Paiute people who have unjustly borne for too long the principal blame for what occurred." The statement acknowledged the wrong but did not explicitly apologize; the fact that throughout that century and a half, Paiutes had not been asked for their version of events added salt to the wound.

As I listened to these stories, I thought about an interview between Krista Tippett, host of the public radio show *On Being* (formerly *Speaking of Faith*), and Archbishop Desmond Tutu, who had chaired South Africa's Truth and Reconciliation Commission after the end of apartheid. "One of the hardest things for human beings to do is to say, 'I'm sorry,'" Krista said, and she asked the Archbishop what had surprised him most about the proceedings.

"I was amazed," he answered, "at how powerful an instrument it is being able to tell your story. . . . [For] people who for so long had been . . . anonymous, faceless nonentities, just being given the opportunity for something to rehabilitate them . . . was a healing thing. We had a black young man who had been blinded by police action in his township, and he came to tell his story. When he finished, one of the TRC panel asked him, 'Hey, how do you feel?' And a broad smile broke over his face, and he was still blind, but he said, 'You have given me back my eyes.'"

Southern Paiute: A Portrait gives a people back its collective voice. As thirty-two individuals speak the pain of unbearable loss and unthinkable injustice, a picture emerges of the very whole lives they inhabit. Historical events, such as the fallout from the Mountain Meadows Massacre, the devastating government policy of termination, or the removal of Indian children from their families to boarding schools are interwoven with the dailiness of life: footraces and bean harvests, peyote healings and Christian baptisms, weddings and divorces, births and funerals. And in the totality of these experiences, we begin to meet each other, one-on-one and face-to-face.

These stories help bridge the gap between Natives and non-Natives. Logan was sincere as he searched out each individual;

the people he met spoke with sincerity; and my hope is that non-Indians will hear these experiences not only with sincerity but also with lasting attention.

Of course these portraits are first and foremost for the families and tribes out of which they were born. "In the past, when asked the question, 'Who are you?'" Vivienne Caron-Jake writes in her foreword to the book, "I didn't always know how or where to begin. Today, I can tell you—not only based on my personal journey through this life, but also through these stories from my tribal elders, who tell it like it is." And then she addresses us all: "Open up these lives and let their truths speak to you."

Will Rogers, Shivwitz, is more blunt: "Are you listening to me? There's a lot of things that got to be told. There's things that shoulda been said that nobody said."

GREED

When we are victims of greed, it can feel as if the flesh is being ripped off our bones. Real vultures are not greedy, they are just hungry. They feed on the dead, on bodies that are no longer of use to their owners. They are efficient recyclers and our world is cleaner and healthier because of them. Vultures will gorge themselves: they never know when they will happen upon their next meal. But they will also dis-gorge. If they feel threatened, they will regurgitate to lighten their load and survive.

GREED

Is It Greed or Is It Gravity?

I conceive that the great part of the miseries of mankind are brought upon them by false estimates they have made of the value of things. —Benjamin Franklin

The desire of gold is not for gold. It is for the means of freedom and benefit. —Ralph Waldo Emerson

Some years ago, when my husband and I lived in northeastern Nevada, we joined Paiute friends at a powwow and found ourselves talking about ethnic stereotypes. "Of course stereotypes are generalizations," one Native friend told us, "but they have their value." She had a wicked wit and ran through unflattering characterizations of several groups, including Indians, before she got to Caucasians. "White people are greedy," she said. "Everybody knows that."

Ouch. But we all *do* know the statistics. According to the World Bank, the richest 10 percent of the world's population—composed primarily but not entirely of people on the paler end of the epidermal spectrum—consumes almost 60 percent of the world's resources.

We don't have to look far to find outrageous examples of overconsumption. Just today, I read that even as food banks in New York watch the number of first-time users double, high-end restaurants enjoy the trickle-down effects of record bonuses on Wall Street. After selling a bottle of 1982 Château Mouton Rothschild for $3,950, restaurateur John DeLucie noted that "we are seeing a lot of luxury purchases, like vintage Bordeaux, things that we haven't seen sell well in a few years."

Of course, Wall Street is not lily white nor is extravagance solely an American phenomenon. India's richest man, Mukesh Ambani, is about to move with his wife and three children into a twenty-seven-story single-family home in the national financial capital, Mumbai. With six floors of parking garages, nine elevators, a grand ballroom, and multiple helipads and swimming pools, it is, as another prominent citizen of the city told a reporter, "a bit show-offy."

Meanwhile, back at the ranch—or the suburban middle-class home—we don't live like that. We don't *want* to live like that, and I have to admit that I get a certain righteous satisfaction from pointing my finger at flagrant excess. As Congregationalist minister and rhetoric professor Robin Meyers has noted, "We file past the rogue's gallery of big-time sinners like gawkers at the state fair, curious to see nature's biggest mistakes: the world's smallest woman, the three-headed calf, the gluttonously greedy."

And yet, deep down, I know I can't blame everything on the high rollers. Many of us feel that something is amiss in our own lives, that we not only have more than we need, but more than we want. In the words of Rabbi Abraham Joshua Heschel, "Some are guilty, but all are responsible."

Greed is a powerfully judgmental word, a "deadly sin," and some economists make the case that overconsumption is born by more than a simple weakness of character. Most people don't feel like sinners if they assume extra work to buy a more expensive home so their kids can live in a better school district, if they take their kids to Disneyland to make up for all the late nights at the office, or treat their spouse to dinner in a nice restaurant as thanks for picking up the slack. "In a poor society," writes Richard Layard of the London School of Economics, "a man proves to his wife that he loves her by giving her a rose, but in a rich society he must give a dozen roses."

I have earlier referred to this syndrome as the hedonic treadmill, but Cornell University economist Robert H. Frank sidesteps such moralizing by analyzing the economic forces at work. In a 2009 article in *The American Prospect*, "Post-Consumer Prosperity: Finding New Opportunities Amid the Economic Wreckage," he points out that "higher spending by middle-income families is driven less by a desire to keep up with the Joneses than by the simple fact that the ability to achieve important goals often depends on relative spending"—buying that house that gives access to better schools, for instance, or the designer suit that will tell a prospective client that you are on top of your game.

Frank calls this "positional spending" and points out that it is not new:

> For example, as Adam Smith observed in *The Wealth of Nations*, local standards define how much people must spend on clothing if they are to appear in public "without shame." In eighteenth-century Scotland, he wrote, even the lowliest workers needed shirts made of linen, since the inability to afford a shirt of that quality generally signified indolence, incompetence, or worse.

We can understand such bread-and-butter reality, but how does it relate to the $4000 bottle of wine or the twenty-seven-story single-family home? Frank suggests that the "positional arms race" has trickle-down effects on us all.

> Although there is scant evidence that middle-income families in America resent the spending of top earners, they are nonetheless affected by it in tangible ways. Additional spending by the rich shifts the frame of reference that defines what the near rich consider necessary or desirable, so they too spend more. In turn, this shifts the frame of reference for those just below the near rich, and so on, all the way down the income ladder. Such expenditure cascades

help explain why the median new house built in the United States is now about 50 percent larger than its counterpart from thirty years ago, even though the median real wage has risen little since then. . . . Instead, middle-income families have opted to save less, borrow more, work longer hours, and commute longer distances than ever before, all in an effort to keep pace with escalating consumption standards.

This positional arms race causes huge waste in our economy, and Frank suggests that we can use basic economic forces—primarily the tax code—to turn things around. "Our current system taxes mostly useful activities, such as savings and job creation. Perversely, it also encourages us to build larger houses and drive oversize vehicles." Under our current system, for instance, we get a break if we take out a mortgage to build a new wing on our house, but we pay additional tax if we receive interest on a bond that allows a corporation to expand its work force.

Frank makes a case for changing our tax structure that makes horse sense. In fact, it reminds me of the sort of horse sense taught by Tom and Bill Dorrance, two brothers who revolutionized horsemanship and provided inspiration for *The Horse Whisperer*.

The Dorrances believed that if you understood a horse's instincts, you could work with its essential nature to get better results. "Make the right thing easy," they liked to say, "and the wrong thing hard," a concept Frank employs when he suggests we change the tax code to make saving and investment easy and over-consumption hard. But the Dorrance brothers also understood that fear causes a horse to act in ways that not only endanger the rider but also the horse itself. Only when that essential fear is allayed can a horse calm down and attend to the job at hand.

The positional arms race is fueled by fear—not of actual failure so much as the perception of failure. Until we recognize the essential insecurity at the core of positional consumption, no degree of material success will ever be enough.

EMPATHY

The Aftermath

Could a greater miracle take place than for us to look through each other's eye for an instant? —HENRY DAVID THOREAU

When we were children, we used to think that when we were grown-up we would no longer be vulnerable. But to grow up is to accept vulnerability. To be alive is to be vulnerable. —MADELEINE L'ENGLE

Child development specialists tell us that we begin to develop empathy by the age of two. A toddler, for instance, may try to comfort a crying baby. It is not until around the age of six or seven, however, that children start to imagine how others might feel. This, at least, was my own experience as I watched a younger friend lose everything. A memory for Mothers' Day, that, ironically, started on a day devoted to fathers.

———◇———

It was Father's Day, and we could hardly wait to give Dad his present: a new cribbage board, a slab of oak with colorful pegs big enough for him to maneuver with his callused rancher's hands. It would be an improvement from the wedge of delicate carved ivory we played on now, a souvenir from my father's service in Korea.

It was just after dawn, and Mom insisted that we finish breakfast before we give Dad the gift. My brother and I gulped down our fried eggs and rashers of bacon. We were almost done when we heard pickup tires crunch the gravel outside, followed by a quick knock on the door. Before Dad could get up, a neighbor stuck his head inside. "The house at the JT burned down. It must have been the lightning last night."

The chair scraped as Dad pushed back from the table. He grabbed his hat and was out the door while Blade and I sat stunned and stuttering: "But Dad—your present!"

Our mother had jumped up too, and now she watched through the window as the men skidded out of the driveway. I remember how thin she looked as she leaned over the sink to peer through the mottled glass. Blade and I took our places at her side, pestering: "Mom! What happened? Mom! Take us! Can't we go now? Mom! Are they okay? Were they trapped inside? When can we give Dad his present?"

The Hansen family lived at the JT. Jack Hansen was our ranch foreman. Natalie, his youngest daughter, was my nearest friend. Lynette, his wife, was in the hospital in Cheyenne, dying of breast cancer.

"I think Jack and the kids were in town," my mother said, a catch in her voice. "I hope so. I don't know." She had an arm on each of our shoulders, and now she drew us close. We'd never seen her cry before.

It was mid morning before she took us to the JT. All that was left of the two-story house was a smoldering pile of ash and timbers. Nothing was recognizable: not a door, not a window. Certainly, no trace of Jack's tall cowboy boots or Natalie's doll with the long blond hair. We got out of the car, and the air was awful. It didn't smell like fire, not fire as I understood it: not the wood smoke of a campfire, not the frightening but familiar smell of burning grass, not even the stench of singed hair and flesh at a branding. This was something else: black and thick and evil.

The rail fence that delineated the yard still stood, and a dozen pickups from the surrounding ranches were parked outside it in reckless disorder. The men gathered just inside, smoking cigarettes, leaning on their shovels with an air of helplessness. There was nothing they could do. Even as young as I was, I understood there was nothing they could do. The women hung back by the vehicles, speaking in low voices. I learned that Lynette's wedding rings had been in a china dish on the bedside table. Maybe, one woman suggested, when everything cooled, the men could sift through the ashes and find the engagement diamond. A needle in a haystack, I heard another woman say.

Mom was right. Jack and the kids had spent the night in town, visiting Lynette in the hospital where she would die a few weeks later. I thought about them, clustered around her bed that morning after someone had driven in to deliver the horrible news, and I gripped the unpeeled rails of the fence and let the rough bark cut into my hands, as if this discomfort could tell me something of what lay ahead for my friends. I wondered about their cat, a big, long-haired gray with sleepy yellow eyes, who was nowhere in sight. I found myself looking at the apple tree, its side closest to the house singed entirely black.

That night, both images converged in a nightmare: the cat, now nothing but a cat-shaped block of charcoal, sat in the scorched branches, smoldering. I woke, terrified, but instead of calling out to my parents or running to their bed, I walked through the house, sniffing for smoke.

It was a few minutes after two in the morning. I remember because I dragged the kitchen stool over to the big white range and climbed up to read the time on the clock with the luminescent face set into the splatter board behind the burners. For the rest of the night, I prowled the house, watching, sniffing, returning often to the stove to read the time, counting the minutes until Mom would come down and put on the kettle.

By the time she did, just after five, as always, I had fallen asleep on the sofa, and she took me in her arms and rocked me. I felt warm and safe and drowsy. For weeks after, she would hold me like this every night before I went to sleep, and I would ask if the house would catch fire that night. "No," she'd tell me. "The house won't burn down." Words so simple, so sure, I could sleep.

The community pitched in and helped Jack rent the K-9 Corral in Cheyenne, a boarding kennel with a house on the property. I don't know if he and the kids ever came back to the ranch, if they ever tried to find the diamond in the ashes.

A few weeks later, we visited them in their new home, and I recognized pieces of furniture donated by my folks and other neighbors. Natalie took me outside to play, and after we walked through the dog kennel, she took me into a back shed that was filled with chinchillas, something Jack hoped would supplement the family income. I remember standing in the dim light of the shed, my eyes adjusting to the shadows, and I don't know which was stranger: the rows of cages filled with soft, cuddly animals that cooed like pigeons and were so shy that a backfire from a truck could cause a dozen of them to die in fright, or meeting my friend Natalie in this changed universe—a new house, a new life, and most unfathomable of all, no mother to hold her safe against the terrors of the night.

———◦———

Names were changed for privacy.

JUSTICE

For the Horses

Wrong none by doing injuries, or omitting the benefits that are your duty. —BENJAMIN FRANKLIN

Cowards die many times before their deaths; the valiant never taste of death but once. —SHAKESPEARE, *Julius Caesar*

A grave injustice or cruelty witnessed firsthand marks you forever, especially if you have been powerless to stop it. Even reading about such a thing can be indelible. But perhaps it's out of such anguish that lasting justice is born.

I was twenty-two or twenty-three years old when I spent a week in the Archives at the University of Wyoming in Laramie, researching women who worked on the land for my first book. Archives are among my favorite places on this earth; it's hard to describe the intimacy of reading real-time accounts of people who lived generations earlier. But such work can be surprisingly painful: more than once I've been reduced to tears at the shock of a sudden loss or calamity recounted in a letter or diary.

During my days in Laramie, I pored over letters, journals, diaries, old newspaper clippings—anything that would give me a sense of the day-to-day lives of women who worked outside in the nineteenth and early twentieth centuries. I was delighted to come across Owen Wister's notebooks from his travels in Wyoming in the 1890s. Wister was a Harvard graduate who originally came west on doctor's orders and became so fascinated by the region and its people that he went on to write *The Virginian*, one of the most popular Westerns of all time. He was an acute observer, and I hoped I might find descriptions of ranch women he met along the way. Instead I found something quite different that affects me to this day.

In 1891, Wister visited the ranch of a man named Tisdale, about sixty-five miles from Casper. He was supposed to meet a friend there, but the friend had not arrived, and Tisdale offered Wister a place to stay. Two days later, the friend still had not shown up, and Tisdale invited Wister to ride with him to the far side of the ranch. They took along two extra horses, which Tisdale tied together.

One of the horses was an outlaw, and several miles into the trip he broke away, towing the other horse behind him. The escape enraged Tisdale, and he pursued the runaways through a series of steep ravines until he exhausted his own mount, which angered him further:

> At length the runaways got far ahead of us and I left Tisdale kicking and cursing his horse, who was now able to walk only. I took the high ground, pretty level and free of holes, to keep the sorrel in sight and Tisdale kept in the trail below in the valley, his horse being too done up to go up the hill. I stopped and he at last came up with me. . . . Tisdale dismounted and kicked his poor quiet beast who stood quite patient. He kicked its ribs, its legs, its jaw, and I saw that red foam was guttering down from the bit. I saw Tisdale was insane with rage.

Then Tisdale gouged out the horse's eye, an act of cruelty that haunted Wister for the rest of his life, especially because he felt powerless at the time to stop it. Tisdale would have easily bested Wister in a fight; it's not clear that Wister even considered accosting him. Instead, Wister wrote in his journal, "I watched him, dazed with disgust and horror. . . . I was utterly stunned and sickened at this atrocious cruelty, and walked back to my own horse and sat down, not knowing very well what I was doing."

The injured horse was eventually able to stand again, and Tisdale mounted him. They headed back to the ranch headquarters, twenty miles distant, Tisdale dismounting and leading the horse across the roughest ground, Wister following at some distance:

> I never spoke to him, nor he to me. . . . I tried to think of other matters, but this damnable thing I had seen done kept burning like a blister through every thought that came to me. Moreover, my own conduct in making no effort to prevent or stop this treatment of the horse has grown more and more discreditable to me. . . . I found myself once or twice hoping the horse would fall and kill him. And I remain the moral craven who did not lift a finger or speak a word.

As Wister tried to make sense of his cowardice, he reasoned that "the situation was a hard one." Even once they got back to the ranch, he was still sixty-five miles from town with no transportation of his own. He had accepted Tisdale's hospitality; the abused horse, after all, was Tisdale's property. But he found his rationalizations weak: "I think this is all a low argument."

Over the next few days, as Wister waited for his friend, he and Tisdale hardly spoke. Wister learned that he had not witnessed an isolated incident; Otto, the cook, told him that "no one in the territory had such a name for cruelty. That the two hundred or so men who had worked for Tisdale at various times, all spoke of it." Several had even witnessed the particular atrocity that shook Wister to his core. Yet the Easterner took no solace from the fact that hardened Westerners had been no more successful at stopping the cruelty than he. Instead, he wrote:

> Nothing disgraceful an acquaintance of mine has ever done has nauseated my soul like this. The man who cheated at

cards; the man who pretended to be my sincere friend and came to my room every day and left it to blacken my character; the man who treated the Cambridge waitress in that way; none of those people's acts have had the sickening effect that the sight of that wretched fainting horse having his eye gouged out has had.

The journal entry is full of despair, and then Wister has a revelation:

Did I believe in the efficacy of prayer I should petition to be the hand that once and for all chronicled and laid bare the virtues and the vices of this extraordinary phase of American social progress. Nobody has done it. Nobody has touched anywhere near it. . . . The fact is, it is quite worthy of Tolstoy or George Elliot, or Dickens.

Owen Wister, the writer, was born that day. He already knew he wanted to write—he was keeping the journal in the first place to record "all the things that are peculiar to this life and country," and he had started a short story he called "Chalkeye." But now, in his disgust and humiliation over his own helplessness and that of the dozens of others who had failed to confront Tisdale's brutality, he had found his subject.

Wister included the incident, with all its gory details, in the short story "Balaam and Pedro," which was published in 1894 in *Harper's Magazine*. In 1902 he included a slightly less violent version of it in *The Virginian*. In both works, the brutal Tisdale was renamed Balaam, and this time his companion on the ride was not an ineffectual dude like Wister himself but a man from Virginia, "in whose brawn and sinew the might of justice was at work." The Virginian beat Balaam to a pulp but did not kill him, and it is clear in both the short story and the novel that Balaam was chastened but not reformed; once the enforcer was out of sight, he would resume his cruel ways.

Balaam is just a side character in the novel; the central drama takes place between the Virginian and Trampas, a cow thief and murderer, and the climax comes when the Virginian reluctantly guns Trampas down. He stands up to the bully when no one else will. It is a role he despises but accepts until, in the words of a cohort, "civilization can reach us." After the villain is vanquished, the Virginian marries his sweetheart and takes his place in society as "an important man, with a strong grip on many various enterprises," one of which, we can assume, is helping to establish a justice system that will take care of thieves and abusers and murderers so that moral men won't have to choose between cowardice and becoming killers themselves. *The Virginian* is an evolutionary tale, the prototype for thousands of Westerns that recount the course from anarchy to frontier justice to the rule of law.

Although the Western genre has fallen out of favor, its essential drama continues to play out in popular culture, recast in drug wars or a post-apocalyptic future. In these action dramas, the costumes and technology have changed, but the essential nature of violence has not.

In the real world, though, something quite different has happened. Although the 24-7 news cycle leaves us with the impression that we are devolving into chaos, the reality is that violence has substantially decreased all over the world.

In his recent book, *The Better Angels of Our Nature: Why Violence Has Declined*, Steven Pinker, a renowned cognitive scientist, reviews a wealth of research that indicates that "violence has declined over long stretches of time." Even today—notwithstanding two world wars, the Holocaust, and the Rwandan genocide in the last century and Darfur, Afghanistan, and Iraq in this one—"we may be living in the most peaceful era in our species' existence."

Pinker cites many examples. In war, for instance, the number of battle deaths has fallen from sixty-five thousand per conflict per year prior to 1945 to less than two thousand per year today.

Or consider the fact that today an execution by lethal injection after a fifteen-year appeal process garners substantial protest; two hundred years ago, "a person could be burned at the stake for criticizing the king after a trial that lasted ten minutes." Even the unspeakable horror of the Holocaust had a more brutal precedent, when the Mongol invaders massacred some forty million people out of a world population one-seventh the size as that during the Nazi era.

Pinker summarizes several theories about why this has occurred. Philosopher Peter Singer, for instance, suggests that our "moral circles" have expanded as networks have grown under the influence of trade, technology, and other interdependencies. At one point, our allegiance was only to the clan, but it gradually expanded to the tribe, then to the nation, then to other races and even to animals. This broadening of concern is enhanced by "the inexorable logic of the Golden Rule: the more one knows and thinks about other living things, the harder it is to privilege one's own interests over theirs." Terrorism challenges this trend but has not reversed it.

I can trace the evolution of compassion toward horses through stories passed down in my own family. I grew up as part of the fourth generation on a ranch in southeast Wyoming fewer than a hundred miles from the Medicine Bow area that was the Virginian's stomping ground. My great-grandfather, J. L. Jordan, was born in 1861, just a year after Owen Wister. J. L's daughter, my great-aunt Marie, told me stories from her childhood about a distant neighbor who was nearly as brutal to horses as Tisdale. By the time I heard these stories, the neighbor had been dead for fifty years, but Marie was still haunted by the fact that no one had stopped him.

In contrast, by the time I came along, a similar violence would have initiated a call to the sheriff, and the perpetrator would have been jailed. Even so, the predominant method of horse breaking was still to "buck 'em out and ride 'em hard"; I was told to "show a horse who's boss." Today, the entire vocabulary has changed:

we talk about "making" a horse rather than "breaking" one, and a respected horseperson will work to the ideal of using no more than two pounds of pressure to signal a command.

Wister would have liked such an evolution. In fact, he anticipated it. "There was a time, not so very long ago," he wrote in his 1894 short story, "when most enlightened potentates extracted secrets and obedience by slowly cracking the bones or twisting off the thumbs of those who had the misfortune to differ from them in matters politic and religious. This is not thought well of to-day; and there are signs that cruelty to anything, even to a horse, will come to be generally discountenanced."

When I was growing up, I don't remember a house that didn't have a copy of *The Virginian* on its shelves, and the book's popularity extended far beyond the ranching community and the West. Over time, as I've discussed the novel with friends, I've come to know that its readers may be hazy about the details of the final shootout, but they usually remember the book's most famous line—"When you call me that, smile"—and the scene where Balaam brutalizes his horse.

As I sat in the archives and read the real-life experience that inspired that scene, I came to understand how anguish can give rise to a work of art. I don't think Wister ever forgave himself for failing to stop Tisdale, but from the distance of years, it's clear that his powerful descriptions wrought a justice of their own. The novel is not responsible for all the improvement in the way horses are treated, but it surely had an effect. The Virginian fought with his fists and his gun; his creator, Owen Wister, fought with the only weapon he handled with skill: his pen.

WRATH

Coming Back to Ourselves

A man is about as big as the things that make him angry.
—WINSTON CHURCHILL

Anger is never without a reason, but seldom a good one.
—BENJAMIN FRANKLIN

"Anger," wrote the stoic philosopher Seneca, who lived at the same time as Christ, "is the most hideous and frenzied of all emotions. The others have something quiet and placid in them, whereas anger is all excitement and impulse. . . . Some of the wise," he continued, "have described anger as 'brief insanity'—it is just as uncontrolled."

I had planned to write this week about moderation, but the comments on last week's post, "For the Horses," have got me thinking about its opposite: wrath. Several readers noted that abuse of horses is still common. One mentioned witnessing a "gentle" trainer brutalize a horse when he thought no one was around. A couple people courageously admitted rageful acts of their own. "Though I can swear on all the holy books I can find that I will never do such a thing again," one wrote, "I know that the other person lives down there inside me."

Of the seven sins, anger is the one that frightens me most, and also the one to which I am most in thrall. My anger is of the controlled and mostly unexpressed sort, though it leaks out in grumpiness and scowls and bouts of sullen resistance. It used to be worse.

Once, when I was in seventh grade, I got into a fistfight with a ninth grader named Ann in the school swimming pool. I have absolutely no memory of what the fight was about; in fact, I can remember nothing of my opponent except her name and the fact that she was dark haired, overweight, and solid—as was I—and that we stood in the shallow end of the pool and pummeled each other for a long time with no intervention from other children or the lifeguard and no decisive victory either way; we just wore each other out. I don't believe we ever punched each other in the face, though afterward, my shoulders and arms were solid with bruise.

I was in my first year of boarding school—in those days, a lot of kids from isolated ranches were sent away after they outgrew the one-room schools close to home—and my parents never knew about the fight. Nor did a school authority respond with either punishment or consolation, something that seems strange to me now. But I must have taken some lesson away from the encounter, for I don't believe that I have hit another living being in anger since.

Which is not to say that I outgrew wrath. I know, as last week's reader put it, "that the other person lives down there inside me." I give vent to frustration when I think no one is about, slamming doors and bashing my fist into my other palm or pounding the kitchen table, and in my private furies, I can let fly the entire vocabulary I learned growing up among working men. I have often turned around after such an outburst to find the dog looking at me in puzzlement and fear, and I grow hot with shame. What beast erupted from deep within? And where has it suddenly gone?

The "brief insanity" of rage is a sort of schizophrenia: we are unrecognizable to ourselves and to others. The author Mary Gordon, in an exquisite meditation on anger, tells the story of her own fury on a hot August afternoon when she was preparing a dinner party with no help: "I was, of course, feeling like a victim, as everyone does in a hot kitchen on an August day. . . . I had been chopping, stirring, bending over a low flame, and all alone, alone!"

Earlier, she had promised to take her children, aged seven and four, and her seventy-eight-year-old mother swimming, but she hadn't done it because she was too busy. Grandma and the kids decided to press the point, loaded themselves into the car, and started honking the horn.

> I lost it. I lost myself. I jumped on the hood of the car. I pounded on the windshield. I told my mother and my children that I was never, ever going to take any of them anywhere and none of them were ever going to have one friend in any house of mine until the hour of their death, which, I said, I hoped was soon. I couldn't stop pounding on the windshield. . . .

> I had to be forced to get off the car. . . . Even then I didn't come back to myself. When I did, I was appalled. I realized I had genuinely frightened my children. Mostly because they could no longer recognize me. My son said to me: "I was scared because I didn't know who you were."

> I know that this is not a sin of a serious nature. I know this to be true because it has its comic aspects. . . .

It could have comic aspects because she had beat on the windshield but not on her children, and because, once she came back to herself, the whole family could talk about it and she could apologize. She could be recognizable once again.

The angry beast can be the stranger inside, or it can be the persona most apparent to the world. I only knew my grandmother as an angry soul. From photographs, I know that she had been beautiful in youth and somewhat vain, but by the time she came into my consciousness, anger had carved a permanent scowl on her face, and her lower lip jutted out to such degree that we joked it could hold a cup and saucer. I can only guess at the sources of her distress. She and my grandfather separated when my father was small, though they never divorced; Dad could not remember a kind word passing between them.

Gran lived in town in an apartment across the hall from her sister, Marj, and their mother, whom I knew as Nana. My brother and I stayed with them from time to time when we were children, and we tried to keep to Marj and Nana's side as much as we were able. Everyone walked on eggshells around Gran, even my father. More than once I remember her railing on him for some service he had failed to provide her, and watching him grow quieter and more clench-jawed until he simply turned and walked out, red in the face, slamming the door.

It was only after she died that I caught a glimpse of something softer inside her, and then in the most peculiar circumstances. I was in my late twenties and trying desperately to get my feet back on the ground after a time of great upheaval. My mother had died a few years earlier, the ranch had been sold, my love life was a mess, and though my first book had come out to good reviews, I seemed incapable of finishing a second. I tried everything I could think of to regain balance: therapy, exercise, and a serious meditation practice.

One day, at the end of a guided meditation, I found that I did not want to come back to waking consciousness. Instead, something pulled me deeper, and I had a vision. I was an infant in a crib, and Gran was standing over me, livid with rage. Her face was contorted into a mask, and she was screaming: "I hate you, I hate you, I hate you! You're ugly, you're ugly, you're ugly!"

I want to tell you: I have no idea if something like this actually happened. Perhaps it was a memory, but as a writer who works with memory all the time, I know it as a highly unreliable source. This could as well have been a dream or a metaphor; whatever it was, it captured the depth of anger that consumed my grandmother. And I have no idea why this vision arose just then, as the particular troubles I was having had no obvious connection to Gran. But memory or metaphor or something else entirely, and wherever it came from, that vision stands as one of the most unexpected and invaluable gifts of my life.

For the moment I saw my grandmother screaming in rage, I burst into tears. These were not tears of fear or sadness or pain; they were tears of incredible, unfathomable relief. "Oh my God," I found myself thinking, "it's not me, it's *you!*" Suddenly, with a purity of insight that seemed almost holy, I saw her unendurable pain, and I knew the voice of rage was not hers alone but went back generations, that the words she screamed at me had been screamed at her. She was giving voice to an existential anguish that was directed at me but had nothing to do with me.

And in that moment of realization, I was flooded with love. The vision shifted, and I found myself holding her in my adult arms, soothing the terrified infant that she had become.

I have always looked at that meditation as a moment of grace, as the purest experience of forgiveness I have yet known. *Forgiveness* is not even the right word for it. Perhaps *understanding* comes closer, or *transformation*.

Aristotle defined *anger* as "a burning desire to pay back pain." We strike out in order to punish the source of our pain, even if what we strike had nothing to do with our injury. We hurtle the book to the floor in frustration that we can't find our keys. Or we vent a lifetime of frustration on an annoyance whose biggest crime is that it is close at hand.

When we slap the bedpost on which we just stubbed our toe, what are we saying except *I hate you I hate you I hate you; you're ugly you're ugly you're ugly?* And who among us hasn't at some time wanted—whether we acted on it or not—to scream at the child who won't stop crying or talking or fighting with the siblings or kicking the back of our seat on an overcrowded airplane? And then, when we come back to our senses and take account of the monster that sprang from within like the beast out of the womb in *Alien*, we realize that our rage was really directed at the universe that failed to organize itself to our avail.

In the movies, the character who experiences a great flash of insight receives the keys to the kingdom. The marriage heals, the business thrives, the children come back with love in their hearts and children of their own. In real life, it's different. After that meditation, my life didn't magically heal. It would be several more years before I found a solid love; even longer before I finished my next book. And though in time I accomplished both, I still have flashes of wrath that bring me to my knees. But something shifted that day. If only for a moment, I saw the source of anger, and I saw an alternative.

LOVE

Traveling at the Speed of Love

There are four questions of value in life . . . What is sacred? Of
what is the spirit made? What is worth living for, and what is
worth dying for? The answer to each is the same. Only love.
—JOHNNY DEPP in *Don Juan de Marco*

You learn to speak by speaking, to study by studying, to run
by running, to work by working; in just the same way, you
learn to love by loving.   —ANATOLE FRANCE

For her ninetieth birthday, Laberta Altermat bought herself
black lingerie. My friend Greer told me this, along with background on other people I was soon to meet, as we drove to a
gathering of a book club in Virgin, Utah, near Zion National
Park. Greer also said that Laberta looked more like seventy than
ninety.

Still, when we arrived, I didn't immediately take the vibrant
woman on the couch to be Laberta. I heard her hearty laugh
before I even entered the room. She had pure-white hair in a chic,
asymmetrical cut and wore a tiger-striped sweater and a large,
Picasso-inspired necklace. Her confidence of style endeared me,
but I was most engaged by her flashing, mischievous eyes. No
nonagenarian could look *that* good.

Sometime during the evening, the conversation turned to love,
and Laberta told a story. Her parents worked well together, she
said, but even as a young child she recognized that they lacked particular affinity for one another. She had a friend, though, whose
parents had something special. In Hurricane, the little Southern

Utah town where she grew up, sleepovers were common—there wasn't much else to do—and she loved to stay at this particular friend's house.

She always slept in the living room, and one time she had awakened early and was sitting quietly in a chair when the mother came in, singing softly to herself. She started making spoon bread over the woodstove, and Laberta watched silently, unbeknownst there in the shadows. Then the father returned from his chores, whistling softly so as not to wake the others. He came up behind his wife as she bent over the stove and embraced her and then gave her a little bump and grind. The mother—she was about seven months pregnant at the time—stood up and gave him a little bump back. He held her tightly, his hands under her round belly, and nuzzled her neck. Laberta was too young to understand everything that was going on, but she knew, nonetheless, that it was rare. "And that became my love map," she said. "That's what I wanted for myself."

Laberta has been married several times. Once was to a man in Hawaii, and soon after they met, she sensed that he was the one with whom she would share this special soul love. She wanted to marry; he wasn't so sure. She told him she wanted a commitment or she would move on, so he married her in spite of his reservations. She soon realized that this had been a mistake. They would live together, and then he'd say he was going to leave, so she would leave instead and come back to Utah. In a little while, he would say he couldn't live without her, and she'd return to Hawaii. About the third time this happened, she said: I'll come back, but it's the last time. Eventually, things went awry, and she returned to Utah. And, true to form, in time he called and wanted her back. But she said no. Much to her surprise, he said: well then, I'm moving to Utah. So he did. But he soon got sick, and she nursed him for three years, and then he died.

Five or six years later, he came back during the night. "I don't know if he was sitting on the bed or standing by it," Laberta told us, "but he was there. And he told me that if he had been able to understand what I meant by love when he was alive, we could have had it. He didn't understand it then, but he did now."

On Laberta's map of love, there are many stops along the way, and it's a journey that takes a lifetime or longer. I think she would suggest that we never complete it. That's not the point. The point is to let our hearts grow stronger and more open as we cover the miles.

Laberta is a guy magnet. I've seen the "Laberta Effect" at a dozen parties. She always finds a couch or easy chair where she can put up her legs—her knees are bad—and in no time at all, half the men in the place are hanging around. Young men, old men, middle-aged men: their attention isn't patronizing, and they aren't looking for a grandmother. Laberta's attraction is erotic, charged with life. Plato believed that Eros helped the soul remember beauty, and Laberta's gift is that she looks into your soul and sees the beauty there, and she is willing to reveal her own. She is generous that way. The love she radiates is as powerful for women as it is for men. Let's just say that there is a lot of competition to get close to the woman we all call The Queen.

Laberta's love map is the work of many cartographers, mentors who have shown her the various ways that love can manifest in the world. She wasn't close to her mother or grandmother. "How do I say this without seeming weary?" she asked once when we talked about her childhood. "They were not the kind of women I wanted to emulate." Her grandfather, on the other hand, was warm and nurturing and full of fun, and she patterned herself after him. She found other models in extended family and the larger community, including the midwife who had delivered her. "She told me I was different than other babies. I came into the world watching."

We know how to measure the speed of light and the speed of sound. It's harder to calculate the speed of love. That night at the book club, after Laberta had related her late husband's visit in the middle of the night, she said, "He told me I would get the love I wanted. I haven't yet."

One of the other women said, "It might happen in another life."

Laberta said, "It might still happen in this one."

GLUTTONY

A Re-enchantment with Food

The only time to eat diet food is while you're waiting for the steak to cook. —Julia Child

When the talk turns to eating, a subject of the greatest importance, only fools and sick men don't give it the attention it deserves.

—Laura Esquivel, *Like Water for Chocolate*

Hal and I, along with our friend Chris, have just returned from six days in Mazatlan, on Mexico's Gulf Coast, where we joined other friends, Randy and Rebecca, in their hilltop casita. Sunshine-filled days on the beach eating fajitas and butterflied shrimp; lazy afternoons on the Malecón, drinking margaritas and *limonada con ron*; long hours at *la casa*, slouched in a variety of couches and easy chairs, reading novels, playing Yahtzee, laughing, and telling stories . . . I know it sounds like an orgy of sloth, but for me it was a working holiday. I needed to conduct experiential research on gluttony, and I did a good job.

Vacation comes from the Latin root *vacare*, to be empty, free, or at leisure, and I took the opportunity to be free from worry about an empty stomach. I packed work gear appropriate for such a task: a breezy sundress that touched me only on the shoulders, shorts and skirts with elastic waistbands, my stretchiest jeans, and a Lands' End, all-over control, Grecian slender swimsuit.

Everyone calls Randy and Rebecca R&R, and the shared nickname comes as much from their generous hospitality as from their initials. Rebecca is a prolific cook, and though she has many other talents, my favorite image of her is at the stove, the rest of us gathered around while she chops and stirs and talks and gestures with the butcher knife or serving spoon or whatever other implement she has in hand. In the midst of this activity, a variety of dishes—never fewer than four or five—somehow magically appear. The first morning she whipped up a breakfast of chorizo and *muchaca* (dried, spiced beef), eggs and potatoes, tortillas, and fresh fruit salad.

To watch such a meal being prepared, and then to sit down together to enjoy it, is to remember that food is a gift, something that nurtures the soul as much as the body. I feel this every time I sit in Rebecca's kitchen, and also every time I come to Mexico, where food is still primarily *hecho por mano*, made by hand, often out in the open. To make food with care, to present it with care, to eat it with care in the company of friends . . . it seems like one of the deepest, truest human communions. But, as we all know, it's seldom that simple. Ever since Eve snagged that apple and offered it to Adam, food has been fraught with complication.

When Pope Gregory I codified gluttony as one of the seven deadly sins in 590 AD, he listed five errors: to eat before one was hungry, to eat expensive food, to eat food that was daintily or elaborately prepared, to overeat, or to eat with delight. Any one of these transgressions was damning. As the Reverend Orby Shipley wrote in his exhaustive 1895 tract, *A Theory About Sin in Relation to Some Facts About Daily Life*, "we may avoid condiments; we may be indifferent to quality; we may be punctual in time . . . we [may not] exceed the amount of food which we consume, . . . [but] we may still offend . . . by partaking necessary food with too much eagerness."

Have you heard the one about the starving man who sought salvation in a Dumpster? The good news is that there was hardly any food and it was rotten; the bad news is that he was so hungry he enjoyed it anyway.

We no longer think of food as a sin against God so much as a sin against the body. If, in the Middle Ages, a properly inhibited appetite was prerequisite to life after death, today we think it will buy us immortality. As Francine Prose phrased it in her book *Gluttony,* "Health consciousness and a culture fixated on death have transformed gluttony from a sin that leads to other sins into an illness that leads to other illnesses."

Even if today's errant food choices are seen as secular transgressions rather than spiritual ones, they nonetheless inspire a puritanical zeal that can cause us to hurt each others' feelings. In a recent article in *Newsweek* titled "Divided We Eat," a young mother tells about offending her in-laws when she bought a bag of organic apples even though there were plenty of non-organic apples on hand. "When we come to your place, we don't complain about your food," her mother-in-law said. "Why do you complain about ours? It's not like our food is poison."

More and more, though, many of us look at food as if it *were* poison. Food has become a generational divide, a cultural divide, and an economic divide. We judge each other by the foods we eat. Try planning a dinner party that caters to the vegan, the carnivore, the macrobiotic, the soy sensitive, the gluten intolerant, the raw foodist, the diabetic, and the adherent to Atkins or South Beach. The only safe offering seems to be a platter of raw kale set out in the middle of the table, though someone will surely get gas from fibrous greens.

Sometimes I long for the world captured in a story that came down through my family. Back in my grandfather's day, the ranch employed a crusty old cook who was sensitive to criticism. When one cowboy complained about the grub, she walked up behind him, pulled a six-gun out of her apron pocket, stuck the barrel in the back of his neck, and said, "Now eat that, and tell me it's good."

America's anxiety about food distinguishes us from other cultures. French sociologists Claude Fischler and Estelle Masson, authors of *Eating: French, European, and American Attitudes Toward Food,* point out that, for Europeans, "food is first and foremost about 'joie de vivre'"—the sensual enjoyment of food, its taste and freshness, its culture and history, and the conviviality that surrounds a shared meal. But in Great Britain and the United States, "food is associated first and foremost with nutrition. In

the United States there are additional elements—the responsibility of the individual towards his or her body and health, and
feelings of guilt if one feels one hasn't made the 'right choices.'"

Fischler and Masson undertook their research to understand
what has come to be known as the French Paradox—the fact that
the French eat as much fat as Americans but suffer only a fraction
of the heart disease and obesity. The reasons are complex, but
they suggest that the American nutritional or scientific approach
to food has led to its "disenchantment." In France and Italy (and
in Mexico), a meal is "reminiscent of communion." In the United
States "it is more a private, intimate, personal act that tends
towards the almost impossible quest for an ideal diet that allows
you to function better, stave off illness, and live longer."

These different attitudes toward food affect the degree to
which eating unites or divides us. "In cultures that load meals
with . . . symbolic weight," the authors note, "expressing prefer-
ences or (particularly) aversions is understandably off limits. To
Americans, on the other hand, one is not to get in the way of
individual choice. The ideal sociable meal, we find in the survey,
is seen more as a contract of sorts between consenting adults and
each is free to choose and manifest his or her likes and dislikes—
even if this sometimes means using the excuse of an 'allergy.'"
In Fischler and Masson's view, the pressure to make the right
choices "reinforces and accelerates a 'disenchantment' of food,"
its use as fuel for the machine rather than manna for the soul.

And so it was a relief to take a vacation from the "right
choices" and fall completely under the spell of Mexico and its
food. Mazatlan can be a noisy city: un-muffled delivery trucks
gear down for the steep hills, teens and seniors alike blare *banda*
music from car stereos at full decibel, and a herd of beat-up pickup
trucks mounted with loudspeakers circle the streets, blasting political ads, *descuentos* (sales), and news of the night's lineup for *lucha
libre*, Mexico's colorful, masked version of pro wrestling. But as
each assault passes, there is a softer sound underneath, almost like
the breath of the city: the quick rhythm of a thousand street chefs

chopping, chopping, chopping—onions and chilies and tomatoes and cilantro; pork and carne asada and grilled chicken; chocolate and cumin, garlic and almonds, coconut and cinnamon.

The magic of food in Mexico is its freshness. On the beach, men and women come around with trays of sugared donuts, hot off the stove; cups of just-sliced pineapple and coconut and cucumber, sprinkled with lime and chili; popcorn balls still warm from the kitchen. Back in El Centro, each day we stopped at the little ice cream shop off the Plazuela Machado to enjoy *paletas*, popsicles made from a dozen different fruits as well as *aguacate* (avocado) and a variety of nuts. (No matter how much we had eaten before, we always found room for at least a *paleta chica*, the bite-sized version that cost only three pesos, or about twenty-five cents.)

Our favorite fancy night out was at Topolo, where we sat in a ruby-walled courtyard under palm trees hung with sparkling lights and watched our waiter prepare us roasted-tomato salsa to enjoy with fresh chips before he served us *pescado al cilantro*, tilapia stuffed with shrimp and celery and garnished with cilantro pesto; *arrechara*, grilled skirt steak on charro beans, guacamole, and grilled onions; and *chamarro de cerdo en salsa de adobo*, pork shank with adobo sauce.

My most memorable meal, though, was on the street. Our last night, following the recommendation of friends, we searched out the street cart that served *papas locas*, crazy potatoes filled with carne asada and *queso fresco*, fresh cheese. Like so many Mexican enterprises, it is a family affair, with Papa and a couple of sons roasting potatoes over an open fire and grilling chicken and carne asada while Mama takes orders and the youngest daughter runs back and forth to a nearby convenience store to fetch cold bottles of *coca light*. The cart is a rolling restaurant with grill and fire pit as well as counters and stools, and the family sets up additional tables along the curb so they can serve twenty or thirty people at a time.

And time is the real enchantment of food in Mexico: time to prepare, time to serve, time to eat slowly and joyfully, and time afterward to sit back and digest and start discussing possibilities for the next meal.

CHASTITY

Although bees pollinate a quarter of the world's food supply, both classical and Christian iconography has more commonly associated them with chastity than with fertility. Worker bees are asexual females; the queen has relations only once in her life, and then in mid-air. The sex life of bees has only recently been observed at all. Monasteries have often kept bees, in part as a nod to purity and immaculate conception.

CHASTITY AND LUST

A Psychology of Sex

Rarely use venery but for health or offspring, never to dullness, weakness, or the injury of your own or another's peace or reputation.   —BENJAMIN FRANKLIN

Honor the body; do not misuse sexuality.
—From the Buddhist TEN GRAVE PRECEPTS

In *This Time Tomorrow*, a novel by Michael Jaime-Becerra, Joyce loses her virginity to the varsity shortstop in a motel room. Two weeks later, after she realizes that he isn't going to call, she is wandering in the mall when she suddenly notices the shoddiness of her purse. "The purse," she thinks, "had helped Freddy draw his conclusions about her."

In a department store, she asks to see a purse in the display case. She caresses its expensive leather and opens the two little pockets in its satin-lined interior. It costs as much as she makes in a week, but she buys it, transfers her belongings, and asks the clerk to throw her old purse away.

She strode through the mall, on the way to the bus stop, taken by her shadowy reflection in the shop windows, conscious of the occasional glint of the purse buckle. If Freddy had happened to catch her then, or if anyone else had been watching, the earlier shame that had marked the afternoon would have seemed to have been dispelled.

The fictional Joyce graduated from high school around the time I did; her creator, Michael Jaime-Becerra, is a generation younger. Her encounter seems almost quaint by the standards of today's permissive hookup culture, and yet we see something timeless in her vulnerability and distress.

I came of age in the 1970s, just a few years after the summer of love. Cheyenne, Wyoming, was a long way from Haight-Ashbury, but sex had been discovered even in such a backwater. (Like all young people, I assumed my generation invented sex; I still underestimate the durability of the institution and am sobered to learn, as historian Richard Godbeer documents in *Sexual Revolution in Early America*, that the Puritans messed around; a third of New England's colonial brides were pregnant when they said their vows.) Several people in my class were sexually active, and when I spent a year as an exchange student in New Zealand before I started college, I found that even Down Under, kids were experimenting. As in the States, I gravitated to the more intellectual set, and one of my closest friends was surprised to find I was still a virgin; she assumed Americans were more advanced.

My parents were rural Republicans, but they had not sent me off into the world unprepared. They were not churchgoers. They read the work of Ayn Rand—*Atlas Shrugged* and *The Fountainhead*—and met with a group of friends in town to study her Objectivist philosophy. Each month, lectures by Rand's colleague, Nathaniel Branden, arrived on vinyl records.

When my folks sat me down to talk about sex, they explained that they hoped I would wait until marriage, but they also hoped I wouldn't marry young, and they knew I would make my own decisions. They trusted me, they said, to make good ones. They gave me information on birth control, and they asked that I listen to Branden's lecture, "The Psychology of Sex."

These lectures have only recently been collected and published as *The Vision of Ayn Rand: The Basic Principles of Objectivism*, by Nathaniel Branden, and I just reread "The Psychology of Sex." The work is long and dense—it runs thirty pages—and I'm surprised I understood it at the age of fifteen or sixteen. Much of it I didn't understand. But I carried enough of it with me to find my sea legs on the turbulent waters of the sexual revolution.

Branden starts out by refuting the traditional dichotomy that sees the soul as sacred but the body as profane. For the Objectivist, mind and body are rationally united, and both are sacred. Sex, then, "is a pleasure, not of the body alone or of the mind alone, but of the person—of the total entity." Romantic love, including the expression of it through sex, is "the greatest emotional tribute that man can offer to himself and to the person he loves. . . . It is an emotion that declares, in effect, 'I, who am of great value, recognize the greatness which is you.'"

Objectivism does not discourage premarital sex. Dagny Taggart, the heroine of *Atlas Shrugged*, has relationships with two men before she ends up with the ultimate hero of the tale, John Galt. But each relationship is deeply committed; both partners gain maturity and depth before they agree to split; and infidelity, a breach of commitment except through mutual consent, would be unthinkable.

So this was the ethical structure I took away from home: that I was a whole person, with both a vigorous mind and a healthy body; that romantic involvement, including sex, must grow out of a deep-seated respect for both the self and the other; and that a relationship didn't have to last forever, but it must not end by deceit. I was slower to get into relationships than many of my friends (and was probably the last of them to lose my virginity), but once in a relationship, physicality seemed wholesome and uncomplicated and downright fun.

None of this protected me from long spates of loneliness when I had no partner, or from having my heart broken when a relationship ended against my will. I know I caused my share of heartbreak as well. Part of learning responsibility is developing the courage to be honest when you can't meet another's needs. I was wounded at times, but I never felt, as did Joyce in *This Time Tomorrow*, like a used purse. I tried to treat my partners with the same respect, and these experiences helped me mature enough to recognize my soul mate when, at the age of thirty-five, I found him.

Recently, I've been reading the winners of the 2008 college essay contest sponsored by *The New York Times* long-running series, "Modern Love." The newspaper asked students "to tell the plain truth about what love is like for them," and then published the top five entries out of twelve hundred. Three of the winners dealt with college hookup culture, where, in the words of Joel Walkowski, "Casual is sexy. Caring is creepy. . . . Planned romance is viewed as nothing more than ambition, so it's important that things be allowed to happen naturally. . . . An encounter is best when unsullied by intentions, leaving lust or boredom to take over." The degree to which all three authors wished for something more old-fashioned stands out to me.

Roger Hobbs, in "Instant Message, Instant Girlfriend," describes how he juggled dozens of girlfriends in high school through an elaborate maze of text messages and face-to-face encounters. Then, when one texted him, "I love you," he realized that real hearts were at stake, but he didn't truly care for any of the girls he toyed with. He broke up with nineteen of them before he went to college. When he met a girl he liked during his freshman year, he told her, "You'll be the only person on my contact list," and he meant it.

Marguerite Fields, in "Want to Be My Boyfriend? Please Define," writes that "despite the fleeting nature of most of my encounters, and despite my own role in their short duration, I think what I have been seeking in some form from all of these men is permanence." But then another brief encounter evaporated into mist. "I tried to remember that I was actively seeking to practice some Zen-like form of nonattachment. I tried to remember that no one is my property and neither am I theirs, and so I should just enjoy the time we spend together. . . . I tried to tell myself that I'm young, that this is the time to be casual, careless, lighthearted, and fun; don't ruin it."

It is Walkowski's essay, "Let's Not Get to Know Each Other

Better," that touches me most deeply. He describes a friend, "a normal girl" who hooks up often and "doesn't regret or over-think it."

> Except for one time when she woke up in some guy's embrace, got out of bed, and noticed his bookshelf.

> I'm not sure what it was about the contents that impressed or moved her; maybe the books suggested a gentle soul. All I know is what she told me: "I only felt bad after seeing his books." The books had made him a real person, I guess, one she liked. Or pitied. Because then it was on to the next.

"I'm not sure any previous generation had our plethora of options and utter lack of protocol," Walkowski continues. "This may reflect how our media obsession has desensitized and hyper-sexualized us, but . . . out of fear, we shrink ourselves. There have been many times I should have cried but stifled the tears. Instances where I should have said, 'I love you' but made a joke instead."

I find myself wanting to call out to these young people: "Don't sleep with each other unless you know what books are on each other's shelves! You are not just bodies; you are minds and bodies and souls! Whole people! Precious people! Protect yourselves!" But I don't think they need my advice. They are giving it to themselves.

Donald Reimold, author of *Sex and the University: Celebrity, Controversy, and a Student Journalism Revolution*, agrees. He reviewed thousands of student newspaper sex columns from over one hundred different student newspapers in the United States and Canada. The columnists can be shockingly explicit, pro-viding endless fodder to conservative talk show hosts and making even those of us who consider ourselves open-minded blanch. But Reimold calls on us to look past salacious headlines and read what the columnists are actually saying:

While documenting the current collegiate sexual chaos, many columnists simultaneously support the return of more defined dating practices—specifically monogamy, emotional intimacy, and love as the means to the happiest end. . . . Not every columnist supports such commitment. . . . Yet overall, the much more common sentiment . . . is one of hope for the reappearance of traditional romance and relationships.

Not all college students, of course, are involved in hookup culture, and religious communities on and off campus have been powerful voices for abstinence. Recently, nondenominational "abstinence clubs" have sprung up, too, beginning in the south in the 1990s and spreading to colleges and universities throughout the country, including elite institutions such as Princeton and Harvard. Rachel L. Wagley, president of Harvard's True Love Revolution, was recently named one of the university's fifteen most interesting seniors.

Several decades ago, my parents gave me the best information they had and trusted me to use it to make good decisions. As I read what today's students are writing, I realize they are trying to do the same for each other. I worry about them. I worry about them a lot. But I'm beginning to trust them, too.

CREATIVITY

Why We Need Art
(and Why We Make It or We Don't)

We work in the dark—we do what we can—we give what we have. Our doubt is our passion and our passion is our task. The rest is the madness of art. —HENRY JAMES

The mediator of the inexpressible is the work of art.
—JOHANN WOLFGANG VON GOETHE

Something inside us knows that art matters, but whenever the economy takes a dip, we view it as something peripheral or dispensable: a luxury. Art, music, and creative writing are among the first courses cut from school curriculums in hard times, and museums, orchestras, libraries, and other cultural institutions suffer whenever the economy stutters. Yet when the chips are down, when we struggle with the deepest challenges of human existence, we turn to art to make sense of our lives.

I remember the aftermath of the tragic events of September 11, when poetry immediately replaced the banal chatter of jokes and trivia on the Internet. Auden's poem "September 1, 1939," Yeats's "The Second Coming," and many other poems circulated among us like life rings thrown out to the drowning. We clung to those words, distilled from previous chapters in the world's book of horrors, and they helped make some small bit of sense out of what was literally insensible. Words from days gone by spoke to us at a moment that we were struck dumb by the present.

It took longer for new words to form that could inform, and

the first new artistic response that really touched me was a visual one, the "Towers of Light" conceived by artists and architects to memorialize the site by recreating the forms of the towers with projections of light reaching toward the heavens, an afterimage, a spiritual echo of the forms and the souls we simply could not grasp departed, vaporized before our eyes.

Art that touches us, that moves us, that gives us hope and meaning in our darkest hours or transports us beyond banality in our moments of comfort and joy, has a quality that John Briggs, a scholar of the creative process at Harvard, calls omnivalence. *Ambivalence* is the sense of neither/nor—something is not quite this but not quite that. But *omnivalence* is the quality of everything at once. Think, Briggs suggests, of the first line to Hemingway's story "In Another Country": "The war was still there, but we did not go to it anymore," a line filled with much more than any single emotion or response: with grief but also relief, with irony and sadness, anger and nostalgia.

Or think of that most universally known icon of art, the *Mona Lisa*. Her smile is simultaneously innocent and knowing, wicked and kind, erotic and virginal. It has stuck with us through the centuries precisely because it carries so many possibilities at once. In this age of mass reproduction, it has become cliché, but imagine standing in front of it a century or two ago, when the only souvenir you would take away would be her image seared in your memory. It is this sort of frisson that keeps our hearts and souls alive. It's why we need art woven through the very fabric of our daily lives.

Joseph Brodsky, a Nobel Prize–winning poet, thinks poetry— and I'm sure he would extend this observation to all the arts—provides "perhaps the only insurance we've got against the vulgarity of the human heart, and it should be available to everyone." He suggests that volumes of poetry should be in motel rooms next to the Bible. "The Bible won't mind this," he says. "It doesn't mind being next to the telephone book."

Art achieves its impact from something Samuel Taylor

Coleridge called its esemplastic power, the ability to make sense out of chaos, to "shape into one" the many truths around us. Art "informs" us: an artist, through his or her work, literally puts into form what has not been clearly understood before. We talk about artists as gifted. Critic and MacArthur Fellow Lewis Hyde, author of *The Gift: Creativity and the Artist in the Modern World*, sees this gift as moving through the artist out into the culture at large. As he explains:

> An artist who wishes to exercise the esemplastic power of the imagination must submit himself to what I have called a "gifted state," one in which he is able to discern the connections inherent in his materials and give the increase, bring the work to life. . . .

> Once an inner gift has been realized, it may be passed along, communicated to the audience. And sometimes this embodied gift—the work—can reproduce the gifted state in the audience that receives it. . . . Sometimes, then, if we are awake, if the artist really was gifted, the work will induce a moment of grace, a communion, a period during which we too know the hidden coherence of our being and feel the fullness of our lives.

To "know the hidden coherence of our being and feel the fullness of our lives . . ." What can be more important than that? What can be more fulfilling? Yet, so many of us who start to make art ultimately quit. The prognosis is not good. Almost all the teachers I know in the arts comment on how few of their talented students still make art a few years after their graduation. They cite various statistics—that only one or two or three in ten recipients of a BFA or MFA engage in artistic endeavor a decade after they complete formal study.

Why, if art is so important, do so many of us turn from its creation? In a word, because it's so damn hard. And what is hard, truly, is not the making of art, those periods in which we are fruitful and working at our limit. What kills us are those times when we are *not* making art, when we have completed a body of work and stand depleted, when we have followed a path of inquiry as far as we are able, and it is still not resolved, or when we are in the middle of some chaos that won't yield to our desire to bring it into form. This is a universal struggle in creation, those fallow periods when the muses have deserted us, when we cannot imagine working fruitfully or with inspiration, when we doubt the value of everything we have ever done, and our newest ideas seem only tiresome clichés.

I know of no artist who hasn't gone through periods like this, some of great length. Theodore Roethke recalled a period of months in which he wrote not a single good poem. But he kept working, and finally, one evening, a poem came to him, and he literally fell down on his knees and wept with joy and gratitude. "What do you suggest for writers' block?" students used to ask another great poet of the Pacific Northwest, William Stafford. He always answered the same way: "Lower your standards, and keep writing."

A few years ago I went back to school to study painting and drawing at the University of Utah, and I asked one of my favorite professors, figurative painter Paul Davis, what he thought distinguished the students who actually became artists from those who went on to other pursuits. He suggested that it related, at least in part, to how well they dealt with boredom.

Boredom. Paul's answer took me by surprise, and I asked him to explain. Genuine artistic growth over time, he suggested, was in large part an ability to embrace your boredom, to struggle with it and remain engaged with it rather than turn away. To learn from your boredom, to let the pain and agony and frustration of it increase until it creates its own energy, until you literally can't stand it anymore and something—call it the esemplastic power—breaks through: that is what distinguishes the real artist from someone who goes on to a line of work with more immediate rewards—in advertising, say, or car sales, or the study of the law.

Boredom, anger, frustration: if we don't turn away from these things, they can push us past our limits. But if we falter, go do the laundry and wait for inspiration to strike, ten years from now we will have a tidy wardrobe, but we won't have a significant body of work.

Paul said something else that has stuck with me and which I've come to think is a corollary of his first observation. "If you don't think you have the talent to be an artist," he said, "you probably don't." Paul believes in native talent—he would be quick to agree that the ability to draw or paint comes more easily to some than to others—but I don't think that was what he was talking about here. Rather, I think he meant that you have to believe that the struggle is worth enough—and, more importantly, that you are worthy of the struggle—or you won't keep working through those dark nights of the soul. You won't wait around for that moment of gratitude that Roethke earned after all those months of nothingness. What history reads as talent, in other words, has as much to do with passion, curiosity, and stubbornness as natural ability.

A favorite cartoon I have taped up on my wall shows the planets falling out of the sky. "Don't look now," one of them says, "but there's nothing holding us up!" The caption below: "If the solar system had human faith." Faith in our own talent is the gravity, the force that keeps us in orbit around the potential of our own passions and ideas, even when we are temporarily marooned on the dark side of the moon.

When we use the term *genius* today, we most often think in terms of celebrity, a term applied to a select group of individuals, but the ancient Romans considered it something nascent in each of us, our own creative or tutelary spirit. The Greeks called this quality our daemon. "This genius," writes Lewis Hyde, "comes to us at birth. It carries with it the fullness of our undeveloped powers. Those it offers to us as we grow, and we choose whether or not to accept, which means we choose whether or not to labor in its service . . . to suffer change."

To suffer change: what an extraordinary term. I've never had much truck with the romantic vision of the tortured artist raving in a garret; I think that for many, even most, artists, the suffering is much more mundane. But the suffering is real, and I believe that artists are born in those moments of greatest doubt.

The Greeks believed that if you were not willing to suffer change in the labor of your genius, then your descendants would be haunted by a lemur, an evil spirit that would cause endless mischief and pain. All these eons later, the metaphor resonates. We only have to look around to recognize its archetypal truth. We know, each of us—just as our parents and their grandparents have known—of the connections among all living things, and yet we have continued to break these connections, to let species become extinct and our waters and air grow cloudy with debris. And our children will in fact be visited by lemurs; lemurs skulk among us right now.

William S. Burroughs wrote that "all serious artists attempt the miraculous, the creation of life. They dream for those who have no dreams of their own to keep them alive." All of us who dream must constantly gird our loins. God give us courage to keep dreaming through the dark nights of the soul.

ENVY

Envy and Its Discontents

Envy is the great leveler: if it cannot level things up, it will level them down.　　　　　　　　　　　　　　—Dorothy Sayers

Envy is the art of counting the other fellow's blessings instead of your own.　　　　　　　　　　　—Harold Coffin

M y first recollection of envy comes from when I was six or seven years old. Friends of the family had taken me swimming in town, and I remember watching the father play with his three kids in the water, helping them climb up onto the side of the pool and then inviting them to jump into his arms. They were all splashing and laughing and leaping about, and I felt a longing so keen it makes me catch my breath to think of it now.

My own father didn't swim, nor did he play. He was a giant of a man, and fierce. He had a sense of humor with adults, but children baffled him, and he didn't have a playful bone in his body. He had other strengths: he was patient teaching us to ride or rope or double-clutch the truck, and from as far back as I can remember, he told me I could do anything that, in his words, I had balls enough to tackle, a permission not widely granted to girls in the 1960s. But he was not a cuddly papa, and in that moment at the pool, I realized how much I wanted one.

Many philosophers divide envy into two types. Benign envy is admiring or emulative; that's what I experienced by the pool.

But invidious envy involves a rival and, in the view of Immanuel Kant, aims, "at least in terms of one's wishes, at destroying others' good fortune." Some philosophers don't consider the benign type to be envy at all—perhaps *yearning* is a more accurate term—and it can even lead to something good if it inspires us to action. But invidious envy begrudges another's happiness, success, or wealth, and it is often ugly. The 1994 attack on figure skater Nancy Kerrigan at the U.S. Figure Skating Championships comes immediately to mind, a crime that earned a felony conviction for her teammate, Tonya Harding, and sent both Harding's husband and her bodyguard to prison.

Envy can be so intent on destroying another's happiness that one's own welfare becomes irrelevant. *The Ways of the Righteous (Orchot Tzaddikim)*, a fifteenth-century Hebrew text of moral instruction, captures this masochism in a parable. A greedy man and an envious man come before the king to ask his favor. He tells them that he will give one of them whatever he desires, but whatever one asks for, the other will receive twice as much. Each waits for the other to go first, the greedy man because he wants the most he can possibly receive, and the envious man because he can't stand the thought of someone having more than he. Finally, the greedy man convinces the envious one to make his request. "Pluck out one of my eyes," the envious fellow says, willing not only to forgo a fortune but also to endure a great deal of suffering as long as his rival fares worse.

When misfortune strikes us, the tendency is to say, "Why me?" When good fortune strikes others, the tendency is to say, "Why them?" Envy brings out the worst in us. As is true for its cousin, jealousy, its color is green, the shade, I have always imagined, of bronchial phlegm. It is the "hidden emotion," the one we least want to cop to. It hides behind the flatterer's tongue and lashes out in the backhanded compliment. It eats us up: classical literature and mythology portray it as hissing snakes, burning coals, and a poison that invades the body. "Of the seven sins, only envy is no fun at all," notes Joseph Epstein, who addressed the issue for the New York Public Library and Oxford University Press. Lust, greed, sloth and gluttony have their delights, pride can feel good, and anger at least scratches an itch. Only envy offers no reward. It doesn't even have to focus on a rival to ruin our day.

The seven sins are not equal-opportunity tormentors. As Epstein asks, "Why is it given to some people to feel envy glancingly if at all, others to use envy toward emulation and hence self-improvement, and to still others to let it build a great bubbling caldron of poisoning bile in them?" I'm not tortured much by envy. Anger has me in a hammerlock several times a week, and sloth and gluttony are always lurking in the shadows, calling my name, but my husband tells me I'm the least envious person he knows. I can't take credit for it; I just feel lucky and give much of the credit to my upbringing. My father's clan could be prickly, but they did not begrudge others' good fortune. I could say the same about our larger ranch community, which was remarkably free of the feuds and rancor that I have seen tear other rural neighborhoods apart. I don't know why this was so, but when I try to remember examples of envy, I come up short.

With one exception. Almost all of a ranch's income comes once a year when the calves are sold. We could sell on contract, at a price decided several months in advance, or we could take our chances with market conditions when we weaned in the fall. If we made a good deal, we felt competent and wise. We had assured the ranch's solvency for the foreseeable future and won a modicum of comfort, perhaps even of luxury. But if we learned that our neighbor had gotten five cents more a pound, a cloud came into the sky. Nothing had diminished our family's good fortune, but suddenly we did not feel as smart as we thought we were just moments before; we didn't shine as brightly in God's favor. We didn't have to resent our neighbor's success in order to feel, nonetheless, that ours had gone sour. I suspect everyone in the neighborhood experienced something similar more than once; and perhaps no one is entirely free of the dark, transformative hand of envy that in a moment can turn gratitude into grief.

Homer said that anger is a short emotion. He might have added that envy is a long one. Its discontents make us turn not only on our peers but also on ourselves. Invidious envy has no upside. But like all the sins, it exists on a spectrum and has the possibility of being not only benign but also beneficial. For as I think back to the day I watched my friends play with their father in the water, I see something I could not have been aware of at the time, a sense of myself as an observer looking in on an unknown country and recognizing possibilities not found at home. My ninety-two-year-old friend Laberta talks about how, as a child, she witnessed a moment of sweet affection between the parents of a friend that would become her "love map." I recognize now that I must have started to chart my "family map" that day by the pool, a circuitous path that led eventually to Hal, my husband of more than twenty years, and his daughter Anneliese, two of the most playful people I know. I might never have known to look for them if envy hadn't worked its way inside my heart.

RESOLUTION (AND VANITY)

Becoming Helenka

Resolve to perform what you ought; perform without fail what you resolve. —BENJAMIN FRANKLIN

I give vanity fair quarter wherever I meet with it, being persuaded that it is often productive of good to the possessor, and to others that are within his sphere of action.
—BENJAMIN FRANKLIN

Helen Szarlip, the daughter of Polish immigrants, was only seven or eight years old and living in an orphanage in Toledo, Ohio, when she found her way into the Toledo Museum of Art for the first time. She stumbled upon the Egyptian collection and stood enchanted, lingering at the coffin of Ta-Mit, a priestess whose name meant "she-cat." I imagine her gazing at the green face on the sarcophagus that symbolized new life. Or maybe she focused on the winged sky goddess Nut, incised on the figure's chest, who gave birth to the sun each day, or the hieroglyphs that spelled out magical prayers to protect Ta-Mit as she passed from one realm to another. Everything spoke of rebirth, and it must have been heady stuff for an abandoned girl with dreams of a better life.

Two weeks ago, Helenka Szarlip Bimstein passed away at the age of ninety-six while taking a bath and listening to a recording of Vladimir Horowitz playing the *Moonlight Sonata*. Her whimsical paintings of Egyptian figures filled every room in her house. She had created most of them in the last three years, since moving to Salt Lake City to be close to her son. On the kitchen table, a half-completed painting waited for her to finish her ablutions and get back to work. She was preparing for a show, her third in a year.

I met Helenka soon after she moved to Salt Lake from Santa Fe, and I became one of the dozens of friends she made here. She met many of us through her son—Phillip Bimstein is a musician and composer with a wide network of friends—but she quickly forged her own independent relationships. She loved parties and she loved to talk, especially about art or music or writing or gardening or anything else that brought something new and colorful into the world. Almost all her friends were at least a generation younger than she was, and she didn't like old people. "Old people over decorate," she told a reporter a few months ago. "They have clutter, and they wear old-people clothes." Helenka did not wear old-people clothes. She dyed her hair carrot red and spiked it, and if you asked her age, she would tell you seventy-two. She didn't care if you chose not to believe it; after all, she chose not to believe she was ninety-six.

Resolve can take many forms. It can flourish within a daily routine, a list prepared each night and answered each day. Or it can take a more organic form, a desire formed and kept in view, something to move toward as time and circumstance allow.

Helenka traced her resolve to live creatively to that first visit to an art museum. As she walked from gallery to gallery, she sensed a way of life that glittered somewhere in the distance, and she spent the rest of her life moving toward it. She had few other models to inspire her. Her father disappeared when she was five or six—the family figured that he returned to Poland, but no one knew for sure—leaving five children behind. Her mother, overwhelmed by the responsibility, often left the children alone; some evenings she entertained men at home. In time, she resigned the children to an orphanage, and though she later reclaimed them, she was not the nurturing type. Helenka left for good when she was fourteen to live at the YWCA and work as a waitress. Eventually she met LeRoy Bimstein, a young traveling salesman with a warm and quirky sense of humor.

They married, and LeRoy rose to become sales manager for a large encyclopedia publisher and then president of his own company. They raised their four children in Chicago, Glencoe, and Winnetka, Illinois, leading what appeared, on the surface, as a typical middle-class suburban life, with Helenka the stay-at-home mom who made tacos and played games with the kids, drove her husband to the train every morning, and picked him up at night. They had a large circle of friends with whom they played bridge, threw cocktail parties, and vacationed at the beach.

But Helenka continued to move closer to the glitter that attracted her. She was always taking lessons—sculpture, painting, piano, public speaking, singing, and interior design. She became an accomplished figure skater, an activity she shared with the kids, just as she took them along to art classes. LeRoy had his own enthusiasms—among other things, he was an amateur magician—and though he wasn't particularly conversant with art, he liked the whirlwind of activity that swirled around his pixie wife.

After the kids left home, Helenka pursued painting more seriously, though she left it for long periods to devote herself to other interests. At times, she practiced piano several hours a day. In her seventies, following the example of her daughter Barbara, she mastered windsurfing. She and LeRoy moved to Venice Beach, California. When he passed away in 1992, she moved to Aspen, Colorado, and then to Santa Fe. In her final home in Salt Lake, she enjoyed her most fertile period ever, painting dozens of canvasses, many of them large.

I think Helenka drew strength from the attention she garnered. None of us had ever met anyone like her. She was a parakeet, colorful and perpetually in motion. Even her walker—which she hated to use—was metallic fuchsia. She dressed for effect, and she liked being the center of things. We liked placing her there, though at times, her self-involvement could be startling. I remember a concert where Phillip premiered a new piece to a standing ovation. Helenka greeted him afterward, I assumed to congratulate him. Instead, she asked, a little peevishly, "Why didn't you introduce me?" A few minutes later, she pulled a chair up to the table where Phillip and the other performers were signing CDs to add her own signature to the disks.

Phillip always seemed more amused by such behavior than annoyed, perhaps because it had emerged late in life. Helenka had been a playful and attentive mother when he was a child, and more recently she had cared for his father with tender patience through the ravages of Alzheimer's. Through it all she kept some inner flame alive, and whatever vanity emerged was balanced by a generosity of spirit. I think Phillip understood that his mother would not have pursued her interests with such passion and persistence if she hadn't had some taste for the spotlight. Because he was charmed by her unabashed love of attention, we were, too. Helenka was Helenka, one of a kind.

With no familial models to draw on, Helenka had invented herself out of her own unconventional resolve. Like the painting left unfinished on the kitchen table, she saw herself as a work in progress. She once told friends that she wanted to become the Egyptian Goddess of Love when she left this earth. But that was for later. Her "Code of Living," recently revised and scribbled on the back of an envelope, hung on the refrigerator. The opposite side revealed a shorter list, titled simply, "Be Young."

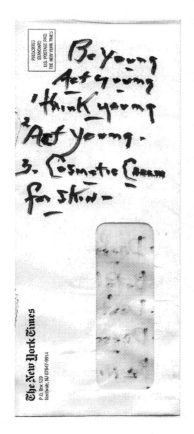

"We need to find God," wrote Mother Theresa of Calcutta, "and he cannot be found in noise and restlessness. God is the friend of silence. See how nature–trees, flowers, grass–grows in silence; see the stars, the moon and the sun, how they move in silence... We need silence to be able to touch souls."

HUMILITY

The Listener

Humility is attentive patience.
—Simone Weil

Listening creates us. It makes us unfold and expand. When we listen, ideas actually begin to grow within us and come to life.
—Brenda Euland

My poor husband. Our poor friends. These days, I'm always quizzing them about virtue and vice. A couple of nights ago we joined Peter and Amy for dinner, and I asked about humility—what did they think it was? How had it played in their lives? Peter, an inspired architect and teacher, said that from as far back as he could remember, he had been taught not to boast. We all nodded, thinking of our own parents' warnings against arrogance and braggadocio. But then Peter told a story that cast things in a more subtle light.

In 1980, when Peter was ten, his family moved to Germany so his father could take a position with the car company Adam Opel. While his father learned the ropes and his mother set up house-keeping, company drivers often took care of Peter, and he grew particularly close to one of them, whose name was Gunther. At that point, Peter loved anything mechanical, and he spent much of his time building model warplanes and battleships. One day, after talking at length about his latest project, he asked Gunther about German battleships. Gunther grew quiet and then said, "Since the war, I don't think much about battleships."

"What *do* you think about?" Peter asked. "Jazz," Gunther replied. He said his interest had begun during the war when he sneaked a radio into his home—he would have been about Peter's age at the time—and listened to American broadcasts. He especially loved swing and the big bands, Glenn Miller in particular. Hitler had banned jazz as a degenerate art form, so Gunther's act represented a real danger for his family. Peter remembers how Gunther's face lit up whenever he talked about music, and how he taught Peter to really listen to it. Looking back, Peter realizes that Gunther taught him how to listen to more than just music; he began to hear the deep chords of what was both said and unsaid. "I began to understand that jazz represented more than simply an enthusiasm for Gunther, and it was more than youthful rebellion. It was freedom."

Peter began to understand as well the conflicted emotions at play among his new neighbors. West Germans held good feelings toward the United States for the food drops immediately after the war and the mass reconstruction made possible through the Marshall Plan. Mainz, the industrial city on the Rhine where Peter's father worked, had been virtually obliterated during World War II but was largely rebuilt by the time Peter arrived. Once, when he was marveling at the new buildings—everything was so shiny, so new!—a woman took him gently by the arm, and he realized, though he didn't have language for it at the time, that "the veneer of optimism represented by all that concrete masked a deep sadness."

I had never thought before how listening—deep listening, with the ears but also with the body, the mind, and the heart—is an act of humility. Benjamin Franklin loved conversation, but he struggled with humility. When, at the age of twenty, he developed a list of virtues he wished to cultivate in himself, he added humility only after a Quaker friend suggested it.

[He] kindly informed me that I was generally thought proud; that my pride show'd itself frequently in conversation; that I was not content with being in the right when discussing any point, but was overbearing, and rather insolent, of which he convinc'd me by mentioning several instances; I determined endeavouring to cure myself, if I could, of this vice or folly among the rest, and I added Humility to my list, giving an extensive meaning to the word.

The "extensive meaning" Franklin referred to was his charge to himself to "imitate Jesus and Socrates." He drew on Christ's model for how he wanted to interact with the world. "Help me, O Father," he petitioned in a prayer he wrote shortly after he drafted his list of virtues, "That I may have Tenderness for the Weak, and a reverent Respect for the Ancient; That I may be kind to my Neighbours, good-natured to my Companions, and hospitable to Strangers . . . That I may be honest and Openhearted, gentle, merciful and Good, chearful in Spirit, [and] rejoicing in the Good of Others."

I suspect he chose Socrates because the philosopher was a good listener.

Legend holds that Socrates found his calling after a friend asked the oracle at Delphi if anyone was wiser than Socrates. When the priestess answered that there was not, Socrates set out to disprove her, searching out people of high reputation in order to learn from them. But as he questioned them, he realized they were blinded by what they thought they knew and in fact possessed little real understanding. He came to understand the oracle's proclamation as paradox: he was wiser than others because he alone realized he knew nothing.

Socrates set out to explore the great moral concerns—goodness, justice, virtue—by breaking each concept into a series of questions that would probe assumptions and lead toward truth. This has come down to us as the Socratic method, and we can

imagine Socrates as a humble questioner, at least in the beginning, interested not only in leading others to greater insight but
using their answers to increase his own understanding.

But Socrates himself struggled with arrogance. He never
wavered from his pursuit of truth and his exploration of ethics,
and his devoted students revered him for it, but it caused him
trouble. In the end, he believed he was indicted and ultimately
sentenced to death not only because his accusers believed that
he had corrupted the young, offended the gods, and challenged
the state, but also because he had shamed them by showing them
the shoddiness of their thinking. In the words of scholar Richard
Kraut, "No one will say, 'I hate Socrates because I cannot answer
his questions, and he makes me look foolish in front of the
young.' Instead, people hide their shame and the real source of
their anger by seizing on the general impression that he is the
sort of philosopher who casts doubt on traditional religion and
teaches people rhetorical tricks that can be used to make bad
arguments look good."

Young Franklin had not studied Socrates in depth when he
chose him as a model, or he might have foreseen his own fate
when he tried to put the Socratic method into practice:

> I was charm'd with it, adopted it, dropt my abrupt contra-
> diction and positive argumentation, and put on the humble
> inquirer and doubter. . . . I found this method safest for
> myself and very embarrassing to those against whom I used
> it; therefore I took a delight in it, practis'd it continually, and
> grew very artful and expert in drawing people, even of supe-
> rior knowledge, into concessions, the consequences of which
> they did not foresee, entangling them in difficulties out of
> which they could not extricate themselves, and so obtaining
> victories that neither myself nor my cause always deserved.

When he realized that his "humble" approach had instead
turned him into something of a bully, he retreated, understanding

that when you "express yourself as firmly fix'd in your present opinions," you not only fail to convince others, but you also prevent yourself from learning what they know. He believed that "the chief ends of conversation are to inform or be informed," and it must have occurred to him more than once that he needed to tone down his own certainty and listen more fully. Franklin worked for the rest of his life to be less aggressive in his opinions and to open to those of others. In his old age, he wrote, "For these fifty years past no one has ever heard a dogmatical expression escape me," and if that assessment seems lacking in humility, his reputation among both friends and diplomats as a good listener suggests it held at least a modicum of truth.

What touches me about my friend Peter's story of his boyhood in Germany is that he began to learn the art of listening at such an early age. A passionate child in a strange land, he wanted to know what created a passion of equal intensity in his new, much older friend. "I wondered what he heard in the music that meant so much to him," Peter told me. As he listened to find out, he learned not only about music, but also about how the world opens to us when we allow our own enthusiasms to quiet long enough to understand those of another.

———◦———

Postscript: Throughout his life, Benjamin Franklin affirmed the importance of Jesus as a model, but he was not himself a Christian. Rather, like many enlightenment thinkers, he was a deist. He believed in one God, the immortality of the soul, and that "the most acceptable service we render to [God] is doing good to his other children." He was less certain about the divinity of Christ. "As to Jesus of Nazareth," he wrote near the end of his life in a famous letter to the theologian Ezra Stiles, "I think his system of morals and his religion, as he left them to us, the best the world ever saw or is likely to see; but . . . I have . . . some doubts as to his divinity."

Of all his opinions, Franklin was most humble about his own religious beliefs and never pressed them on others. He asked Stiles to hold in confidence the views he had shared in the letter: "I have ever let others enjoy their religious Sentiments, without reflecting on them for those that appeared to me insupportable and even absurd. All Sects here, and we have a great Variety, have experienced my Good will in assisting them with Subscriptions for building their new Places of Worship, and as I have never opposed any of their Doctrines I hope to go out of the World in Peace with them all."

JEALOUSY (AND OTHER TRIALS OF LOVE)

Cupid: The Soap Opera

Life has taught us that love does not consist in gazing at each other, but in looking outward together in the same direction. —Antoine de Saint-Exupéry

Love comes when manipulation stops; when you think more about the other person than about his or her reactions to you. When you dare to reveal yourself fully. When you dare to be vulnerable. —Dr. Joyce Brothers

Valentine's Day is just around the corner, the sweetest holiday for those newly in love and a comfort to those who have grown old together with a degree of harmony. For a great many others, though, the holiday, like Christmas, is complicated.

No matter how content singles are with their lives during the rest of the year, Valentine's Day conspires to make them feel judged and lonely. Even seemingly happy couples can experience turmoil. As syndicated radio host and clinical psychologist Dr. Joy Browne points out, "Valentine's Day can be a sort of Armageddon. . . . No matter what, it's probably not going to be enough. You know, 'I got the candy and the flowers, but what about the card?' And if you are in an evolving relationship and have dodged the Christmas–New Year's 'should we get engaged?' thing, it's now Valentine's Day."

Cupid, that cute little winged cherub, looks innocent enough, flitting about with his magic arrows and setting hearts aflutter. So why is it all so complicated? It's easy to assume that our angst grows out of contemporary life, but it has deep mythological roots. The gods and goddesses on Mount Olympus often made a mess of things. The story of Cupid goes back a couple thousand years, and it makes our own lives seem calm by comparison.

For those of you whose grasp on classical mythology has dimmed through the years, I'd like to offer a reprise of the tale of Cupid and Psyche as a gift to the season. My version is based on *The Golden Ass*, written by Lucius Apuleius in the second century AD. The only novel written in Latin that has survived in its entirety, it's a tale worthy of the tabloids or at least a miniseries on HBO.

———◦———

Once upon a time, a king and queen had three beautiful daughters, the fairest in all the realm. The two older ones married kings of their own and moved away. Then Psyche, the youngest daughter, came of age, blossoming into a beauty so far beyond anything seen before on earth that people came from all over the kingdom to set eyes on her. In time, the streets outside the castle filled with thousands of admirers, and even the King and Queen knelt at her feet.

Venus, the Goddess of Beauty, enjoyed her reputation as the most beautiful being in all of heaven and earth until she caught wind of Psyche's allure. Venus looked down to find her temples deserted and left in disarray as people flocked to see a mere mortal. She grew blind with rage and jealousy and called on her son Cupid, the God of Love, to avenge her.

By this time, Cupid had a reputation for mischief and even for malice. He'd lost his baby fat, his wings were strong, he was brash and hardy, and he spent his nights flying from house to house, inciting infidelity and marital discord. Venus told him of Psyche's great affront, and Cupid agreed to pierce the young girl's breast and cause her to fall in love with someone so vile and wretched that no one would ever see her as a rival to Venus again. This was just the sort of errand Cupid enjoyed, but then, when Venus pointed out the target of his attack, Psyche's beauty took his breath away. He tripped over one of his own arrows and fell helplessly in love, a fact he hid from his vengeful mother.

In the meantime, things weren't going all that well for Psyche, whose beauty had proven to be a curse. Men couldn't take their eyes off her, but no one had nerve enough to ask her for a date. At first her sisters had envied her, but now they gloated—*they* weren't alone on a Saturday night—and her parents worried that she would end up an old maid. Her father sought counsel from the Oracle of Apollo, who told him to dress his daughter in mourning black; she would be wed to a dark, winged serpent, evil and fierce.

Psyche's parents wept as they escorted her to the rock on top of a high hill where she would meet her fate, but she braced herself. "Why are you crying now?" she asked them. "Why didn't you cry for me earlier when you saw that my beauty brought only envy and loneliness?" At least now, she would have company. She sent them away, but no winged monster came for her. Instead, Zephyr, the West Wind, picked her up and gently carried her down into a lush valley, where she fell asleep in a bed of flowers.

She woke on the edge of a clear stream and made her way to a mansion built on pillars of gold, whose silver walls glowed like a lantern in the sun. She ventured inside to find floors of precious stones, rooms of treasure and art, and comforting voices that she could hear but not see that invited her to dine, to bathe, to sleep, and to enjoy every imaginable comfort. She fell asleep to a chorus of angels, accompanied by a harp.

In the center of the night, Cupid came to her with such tenderness and affection that she knew he could not be evil. She wanted to gaze upon him, but he warned her: if she ever looked at him, he would leave her forever. He departed before first light but returned the next night, and each night after, and she fell deeply in love with his gentle and ardent attentions.

In time, she grew lonely for company during the day, and she begged to see her dear sisters who grieved for her as if she were dead. Cupid warned against it—he knew they would bring her nothing but grief—but she cried so piteously he gave in with a dire warning: "Do not let them convince you to look at me. If you do, you will lose me for all time."

Zephyr delivered the sisters, and they fell into each other's arms weeping with joy. The sisters rejoiced to find Psyche well and in such great estate, but as she showed them through the luxurious rooms of the castle, and seated them at a table laden with rare delicacies, envy began to grip their hearts. They peppered her with questions about her husband, and when she began to fear she might divulge too much, she filled their arms with treasure and sent them away.

Before their visit, the sisters had felt favored above all others, but now, seeing the far grander circumstances that Psyche enjoyed, they recoiled with disgust. One realized her own husband was old and weak, as bald as a coot; the other complained that her husband had gout and bad skin. And as for that sister of theirs— how dare Psyche treat them so arrogantly, sending them packing with a few trifling pence? They plotted against her.

Cupid sensed the sisters' treachery. Again, he warned his wife. But by then she was swelling with child and was more beautiful than ever. She missed her sisters dearly; now, of all times, she needed them. Once more, Cupid acquiesced with warnings, and Zephyr ushered the women down. This time, seeing Psyche's radiance, they told her that everyone knew her husband was a vile serpent, that he treated her kindly to put her off guard, and that he would devour her and the baby the minute it was born. She needed to hide a razor in her gown, they told her, light a lamp while he was sleeping, and slice off his serpent head before he could wake.

Psyche loved her gentle husband, but the sisters' words hit

their mark. She remembered Apollo's prophesy. The question nagged her: why couldn't she see her love unless he had something horrible to hide? And now, of course, she must protect the baby at all costs. Still, her husband was so kind to her, so true. Such thoughts tossed her back and forth between the shores of faith and doubt. At last she resolved to take up razor and lamp, as her sisters counseled, but she would move with caution. She had to know if he was god or demon.

He came to her as always in the night, tender and passionate, and after he fell asleep, she lit the lamp and gazed upon the most perfect creature she had ever seen: his golden hair, his strong, white neck, the rise and fall of his muscled chest, the beautiful plume of his wings. She dropped her razor and picked up one of his arrows, so beautifully crafted. She accidently pricked her finger, and love washed over her like a tidal wave. She embraced him, kissing him a thousand times, jostling the lantern so that a drop of hot oil burned into his shoulder. He awoke with a start, enraged. How dare she betray him? Didn't she sense he was Cupid? Love cannot live without trust. She would never see him again, he vowed, and he flew away.

Devastated by her own actions and with no will to live, Psyche threw herself in the river, but when she washed up on shore, she realized she must find Cupid and plead with him to take her back. She petitioned the gods for help, and though they looked on her with pity, no one dared risk the wrath of Venus. And so began the lonely odyssey familiar to all who have been discarded in love. She obsessed about him constantly, aching to catch a glimpse of him and devising ways to try to win him back.

She visited her first sister, who offered comfort before sending her on her way. As soon as Psyche was out the door, the sister ran to the mountain and called out to Cupid to take her as a more worthy bride. Zephyr heard her, and since he'd never liked her in the first place, he picked her up and dashed her on the rocks. Psyche visited her second sister, and she too, after giving false comfort, offered herself to Cupid but met the same fate.

In the meantime, Cupid had repaired to his mother's home in anguish. When Venus saw her dear son wounded and in pain, she started to minister to him. Then she learned he had betrayed her to Psyche. Insane with rage, she lashed out: She would clip his wings! Cut his hair! Quench his fire! Break his arrows! And he would never, ever escape the prison of his room. She locked the door and stormed off to design a proper torment for her rival.

Alas, poor Psyche; she wandered aimlessly, deserted by men and gods, her every waking moment and even her dreams tormented by thoughts of Cupid. Deranged with desperation, she decided to offer herself up to Venus as a servant. Perhaps she could convince the goddess of her sincerity, or maybe catch a glimpse of Cupid in his mother's home.

When Venus learned that Psyche was nigh, she unleashed her handmaidens, Sorrow and Sadness, to whip and torture the girl before Venus herself set upon her, bashing her head against a rock. Then Venus took Psyche by the hair, taunting her: "Look at you now. No one will have you except as a maid. Prove your worth." She threw the girl onto a great heap of poppy seeds, wheat, barley, and beans, and commanded her to sort them by nightfall. Then she swept off to a banquet held in her honor.

Psyche lay paralyzed with pain and despair, but the ants took pity on her and sorted the seeds into neat piles, which Venus found upon her return. Needless to say, she was not pleased. She set another impossible task: the girl must find the sheep with the golden fleece and bring back an armful of their wool. Psyche knew the sheep were vicious and would kill any mortal who came near, but she set off, intending to throw herself into the water and end her misery once and for all. At the water's edge, a green reed took pity on her and told her to wait until the sheep came in to drink and then left again for the day; Psyche could gather the wool that caught on the thorny briars.

Now Venus devised an even more impossible task. Psyche must fill a flask with water from the raging waterfall that fed the River Styx. Psyche arrived at the jagged cliffs that banked the falls and once more yearned to throw herself to her death, but this time an eagle, the great bird of Jupiter, came to assist. He took the flask and filled it, and then sent her back to Venus.

Venus told Psyche, quite literally, to go to Hell. She gave her a box and sent her to find Proserpina, queen of the underworld, and petition a measure of beauty. Venus needed this supplement, she explained, because her tender ministrations to her poor, wounded son had taxed her. At mention of Cupid, Venus saw pain carve deeply in Psyche's face, and this gave her cruel delight.

Of all the tasks, this last one was truly beyond human endeavor. Psyche would have to cross the River Styx and pass by Cerberus, the three-headed dog who guarded the gates to Hades. At least, Psyche thought, the River Styx will drown me and end my woes. This time, a watchtower came to life to help her: "Take these two sops of bread," it said, "and carry two halfpence in your mouth. Give one coin to the ferryman to cross the river, and a sop to Cerberus to win his calm. On your way back, give Cerberus the second sop, and pay the ferryman your remaining coin. But mind, dear child, this single caution: Proserpina will fill your casket with beauty, but do not, do not, prize open the lid."

As the tower foretold, the ferryman granted her safe passage, Cerberus licked her hand, Proserpina was generous, and soon Psyche headed back to Venus. Finally, Psyche hoped, Venus would find her worthy of Cupid. But as Psyche thought of meeting her love once again, she took stock of the ravages she had endured. What if Cupid found her ugly? Perhaps she could borrow just a smidgeon of beauty. She cracked the lid on the box only to find nothing inside, and then she fell into an impenetrable sleep.

For all the torments that Psyche had endured, Cupid was in his own world of pain. No matter his earlier rage, he had to find a way to return to his one true love. At length he discovered an unlocked window and escaped. He flew to Psyche's side, wiped the sleep from her eyes and returned it to the casket, then pricked her finger with an arrow to revive her. He chided her for her curiosity that once again had wrought havoc, but then he told her to make haste to his mother. Give her the box, he said, and all will be well. He flapped his wings and flew away.

Psyche thrilled at her lover's touch but lost heart as she watched him disappear. This time, though, she would do as he bid her. With trepidation, she made her way toward Venus.

Cupid, in the meantime, sought the aid of Jupiter, his mother's father and king of all the gods. Jupiter knew he should be peeved at his grandson—he was such an uncontrollable lad and in his youth had even made Jupiter a fool for love by turning him into a bull. But now Cupid was charming and manly, and Jupiter couldn't hold a grudge. He agreed to speak to his daughter, and he called together a meeting of all the gods and goddesses to celebrate the marriage of the young couple, a bond, Jupiter hoped, that would put an end to Cupid's high jinks and give them all some rest.

At the wedding feast, Jupiter invited Psyche to drink from the cup of immortality, and Venus decided that she could accept a goddess as a daughter-in-law. The story ends with Venus dancing to great admiration while Cupid and Psyche rest happily in each other's arms, soon to give birth to a child named Pleasure and live happily ever after. Or at least until the sequel of one of antiquity's greatest soap operas.

———◦———

"The religions of ancient Greece and Rome are extinct," wrote Thomas Bulfinch in his introduction to *Bulfinch's Mythology*, the classic work he began in the 1850s. "The so-called divinities of Olympus have not a single worshipper among living men." Yet, he continued, "they still hold their place, and will continue to hold it, for they are too closely connected with the finest productions of poetry and art, both ancient and modern, to pass into oblivion."

He might have mentioned that myths continue to speak to us about our own confusions, often more instructive for the foibles they illustrate than for the strengths they model. Cupid, or Eros, is the god of love, and Psyche is the soul. Many of us spend our lives reconciling the two, wrestling with jealousy, anger, and betrayal; striving to see each other as we really are; and hoping to learn how to trust others and to be trustworthy in return.

Just some thoughts as Valentine's Day draws near. . . .

TRANQUILITY

Introduction

Some years ago, I heard a National Public Radio interview with a pediatric oncologist. "Isn't it difficult," the host asked, "to work with young children who are desperately ill?"

"Yes," the doctor answered. "It is hard to see children in pain. But they deal with it differently than adults. When they hurt, they cry. When they don't hurt, they play. They don't spend time asking, 'Why me?'"

I don't remember the oncologist's name or what program I was listening to, but I've never forgotten the exchange. As the doctor spoke about the resilience of children, he touched my greatest fear: not of cancer itself, but of my ability to endure it—or any long-term challenge that involves a great deal of pain and powerlessness—with strength and dignity. It's not only that I fear self-pity (which I do); I also wonder if I have what it takes to find something meaningful, even joyful, in the experience.

In January 1987, Terry Waite, an envoy for the Church of England who had successfully negotiated the release of hostages in Iran, Libya, and Lebanon, was himself taken hostage in Beirut.

In November 2008, Brooke Hopkins, four weeks after his retirement as a professor of literature at the University of Utah, suffered a bicycle accident that left him paralyzed from the neck down. Two decades and half the circumference of the globe separate their experiences. One was chained in a cell for almost five years, mostly in solitary confinement; the other has been surrounded by loving friends and excellent medical care since the day of his accident but is chained forever in the cell of a non-responsive body. They both are citizens of another country, a terrain of unfathomable pain and unrelenting challenge that most of us inhabit only in nightmare.

This week, as I contemplate tranquility, I turn to their stories to learn something of serenity under seemingly impossible conditions. To suggest that Waite and Hopkins, like the children the oncologist referred to, cried when they hurt and played when they did not would be to trivialize their experiences. But both decided almost from the moment that the tectonic plates shifted beneath their feet that they would find meaning in the ordeals that faced them, and the strength of that commitment led them to realize moments of transcendence, tranquility, and joy.

TRANQUILITY

The Long Road: Terry Waite's Story

The spirit is not indestructible, but in hell one can get a sight of heaven.
—Arthur Koestler

Everything can be taken from a man but one thing: the last of the human freedoms—to choose one's attitude in any given set of circumstances.
—Victor Frankl, *Man's Search for Meaning*

As a special envoy for the Archbishop of Canterbury, Terry Waite was negotiating for the release of Associated Press journalist Terry Anderson and several other hostages when he himself was seized. During his first night in an underground cell in the Lebanese gulag, he resolved that he would have "no regrets, no sentimentality, no self-pity." The first few days he fasted to strengthen his resolve and walked the circuit of his tiny, tiled cell, counting his paces to figure the distance, up to fourteen miles a day.

He feared torture, and it struck him that the cell was tiled to make it easier to clean. He realized that his captors wanted him to be afraid. He thought of people he knew through the course of his work who had endured jail and torture but survived as "wholesome, lovely people." He told himself, "Today you have entered a new community of the imprisoned. Become one with them. Hold on to light and hope, hope, hope." But hope was difficult. Almost in the same breath he found himself thinking, "I am so alone. Only a few days, and I feel so alone."

After a short while his captors moved him to another building, and from then on they kept him in chains, usually for all but the ten minutes a day they gave him to use the bathroom. Always, before they entered his cell, they ordered him to put on his blindfold; he wouldn't look another person in the eye for four years. To hold onto his sanity, he started writing his autobiography in his head, peopling it with everyone he knew.

Early in his imprisonment his captors interrogated him, and when he had nothing of value to tell them, they battered the soles of his feet. The experience was horrifying but also strangely empowering.

> For a moment I am arrogant enough to link myself with some of the people I most respect: Solzhenitsyn, Arthur Koestler, my friend Desmond Tutu. . . . I need the support of others who have suffered. I need their understanding, their courage, their dignity, their fellowship. This room is part of the university of the world. . . . The guard stirs and mutters in his sleep, while I try to get comfortable. My chains have bound me in a fetal position. I am a baby totally dependent on others, totally at the mercy of others, totally vulnerable.

Waite was not beaten again, but there are many types of torture. The guards tormented him with rumors of release. They forbade him news. In windowless rooms, he had no way to tell night from day. He endured months with nothing to read. One day a new voice told him he had five hours to live and ordered him to write a letter. Soon, the man returned and stuck a gun to Waite's head, only to snarl, "Later," and walk out. Sometimes, when they moved him to a new location, he would take off his blindfold to find himself in a room with a window and no chains. But soon someone would order him to put on his blindfold and he would hear the sound of drills fastening bolts in the floor and a steel plate over the window. He broke a tooth. He got an eye infection and then an ear infection. In one gulag, a generator ran constantly, and fumes damaged his lungs, leaving him with serious asthma.

"I need a structure," he realized early on:

> Wake, pray, eat, wash, exercise, pray, think, eat, and so the day passes. By creating a pattern in the vacuum in which I live, I exercise my choice, affirm my identity. Even when the guard tells me that I am to be chained again, I have a schedule for the remaining hours of the day.

He prayed the communion service. He worked out complicated mathematical problems in his head. He started writing a book in his imagination, something he found sustaining if also peculiar. "I sit chained to an iron radiator with nothing but my thoughts. Some memories stream back like great pools of light. I see people I have known and feel the warmth of their company. Other days are lost to recall, waiting for the magic touch which will bring them to life again."

His moods cycled: anger, despair, boredom, but also—and increasingly over time—tranquility. "I am learning to be quiet and still within; perhaps calm is a better word. I don't want too much stillness as I need a certain inner tension to keep my mind alive."

Finally he received a Bible, and then other books. After he had been completely caught up in Freya Stark's memoir of travel in the Middle East, *Beyond Euphrates*, he wrote:

> Reading in captivity is sheer delight. . . . Modern life is fragmented, full of distractions. . . . Here I can discover how to convert my loneliness into creative solitude.

Waite had sought solitude throughout his life, but only now did he recognize its real beauty, a gift he vowed to take with him if he were ever freed.

The experience deepened Waite's spiritual understanding as well. He had considered monastic life as a young man and had spent his career in high-level advisory capacities to both the Catholic Church and the Church of England. At the time of his capture, he had been special envoy for the Archbishop of Canterbury for seven years. But the Bible brought him little solace. After a particularly bleak period in which he wanted to die, he thought:

> An individual with greater faith than I would remind me that a Bible is at my elbow and contains all the help I need. It's too easy . . . I cannot take faith, contentment, peace, or love cheaply. I desire them so much, have so often in the past sought them outside myself. Now I have no option. It's as if I am passing through a very narrow gateway, completely naked, totally alone.

Once, in the depths of depression, he told himself, "Your prayers are the prayers of a child. Your faith is nothing more than superstition. Your love is self-love. You had better grow up." Over time, his faith entered new territory. Though he knew he might die in captivity, he also knew that he had not been destroyed. He had always appreciated the Orthodox liturgy and the profound mystery that could never be explained. Late in his captivity he realized that his prayers "have been puny but once or twice I have touched the awesome mystery which lies at the heart of the universe, which I call God."

After more than four years of solitary confinement, Waite found himself in a cell next to three other hostages, Terry Anderson, John McCarthy, and Tom Sutherland. By that time, asthma tormented him, and the other hostages could hear his agonized fight for breath through the wall. They pleaded with their captors to let Waite join them. Finally, he did.

By that time, Waite was living from so deep within, he feared he had lost the power of speech. He had often wondered in his years of solitude if he would ever be able to communicate normally again. In with the others, he found himself "disturbed and confused," but Terry Anderson in particular was patient and compassionate; he petitioned the guards to get Waite medical care and sat with him in the night, helping him calm his breathing. Finally, Waite received an inhaler, which literally saved his life. In a few more months, all four men were set free. Waite had spent 1,763 days in captivity.

After his release, he lived with his family in London on weekends but spent the weeks in a windowed office in Trinity Hall at Cambridge, deep in the solitude he craved and needed in order to commit the book he carried inside his head to paper. As he looked back over his years in captivity, he found his experience distilled in the words inscribed on a cellar wall where one of Hitler's victims hid and died:

I believe in the sun even when it is not shining.
I believe in love where feeling is not.
I believe in God even if he is silent.

TRANQUILITY

The Long Road: Brooke Hopkins's Story

He who has a why to live can bear with almost any how.
—FRIEDRICH NIETZSCHE

How do you want this to change your life?
—PEGGY BATTIN

In the fall of 2008, at the age of sixty-six, Brooke Hopkins retired as a professor of English literature at the University of Utah. Much beloved by his students and the recipient of every teaching award the University had to offer, he was also an avid outdoorsman and traveler. He and his wife, Peggy Battin, a renowned medical ethicist, had plans.

But first, as a retirement gift to himself, he bought a new bike. Less than a month later, he was sailing down City Creek Canyon above Salt Lake City when he came around a curve and collided with another rider. The other man was unhurt, though the impact snapped his bike in two. Brooke, however, landed facedown, unable to breathe. He had broken his neck and was paralyzed from the neck down.

Before the accident, Brooke was always in motion. Tall and exuberant, his vitality was the first thing people remarked about him. Now he could hardly move his head. On a ventilator, he couldn't speak. His secretions had to be suctioned every four hours and sometimes as often as every few minutes. Helpless as a baby, he needed to be fed by others, picked up and moved by others, bathed by others, his bodily functions managed by others. At first he experienced little pain, but as the "spinal storm" of the initial trauma receded, spasms often wracked his body, and nerve pain left him feeling like he was being stabbed with a million needles, set on fire, and crushed by a whole-body vice.

Peggy's career had focused on end-of-life issues, especially physician-assisted suicide and euthanasia. She and Brooke had spent years discussing the right of mentally competent adults to decide for themselves whether or not life was worth living. But advocating the right to make a decision is not the same as knowing what decision you, yourself, would make. A few days after the accident, crying together in the ICU, Brooke mouthed to Peggy, "We can still have a wonderful life together," and Peggy answered, "Yes, we can."

Their daughter Sara started a blog a few days after the accident to keep friends and family informed. As Brooke's condition stabilized, Peggy started writing, and in time, as a speaking valve on the trach tube allowed Brooke to speak for increasing amounts of time, he added his voice. At this point, Brooke and Peggy have written the blog together for nearly two and a half years, creating a portrait of an almost unfathomable experience that, as Brooke's rehabilitation doctor, Jeffrey Rosenbluth, points out, is "as close as you can get to understanding [paralysis] without being paralyzed." But the blog is more than an odyssey of physical endurance and adaptation; it takes us deep into the essential meaning of life.

From the first days after the accident, Brooke never thought he wanted to die. He had always sought out extreme experience: monthlong treks in the Himalayas and Peru, ten-day Vipassana meditation retreats. He chose to view this new experience as a combination Buddhist retreat and marathon training. In addition, he and Peggy welcomed sustenance from their broad network of close friends, some of whom came almost every night with food and laughter, buoyed themselves by Brooke's amazing spirit.

Even in the ICU, he mouthed that he was beginning to understand who he really was, and that he found the love showered on him "transformative."

At that point, he and Peggy had no idea of the brutal road that lay ahead. Initially the doctors said that he would go home in February, less than three months after the accident. In fact, it took more than two years, every step forward followed by yet another life-threatening setback: cardiac arrest, repeated returns to the ICU for pneumonia, urinary tract infections, a scrotal abscess.

Small reversals could be just as frustrating. Moved to a rehabilitation facility, Brooke had been able to get outside on occasion in the "Cadillac," a motorized wheelchair. But when a small sore on his rump prevented him from sitting, he became prisoner to his bed again for months.

Weaning off the ventilator proved a Sisyphean task. Normally, thousands of muscles and nerves interact to facilitate breathing, but the accident left Brooke with only a handful of them working. Each breath took incredible effort. At first, even a few minutes off the vent proved terrifying; he felt like he was drowning. Gradually, he built strength and endurance. During one thirty-minute session, he fell into a meditative state, which he described to Peggy and she later described in the blog:

> For the first time in his life, he says, he experienced what he had always been looking for in Buddhist meditation, but had never actually found: the full life of breath. By the time the thirty minutes were over . . . he had attained a serenity beyond anything he ever expected to experience in his life.

Later, as his breathing strengthened and these transcendent experiences became more common, Brooke wrote about the "paradox of prison" that can hold the body in confinement—"in my case, not just confinement but paralysis—and yet liberate the spirit. My monastic cell—when it's not serving as a hospital room or a living room for receiving friends and family and guests—is like that kind of prison, confining and yet sometimes strangely liberating when I breathe. . . . I like it. I love it."

These ecstatic moments seldom lasted. He would work up to several hours off the vent, and then an infection or simple fatigue would set in, and even twenty minutes became unbearable.

Less than an hour ago Brooke was howling I can't do this anymore, this is too hard, I'd put a knife through my heart if I could, and Peggy was saying it would be like putting a knife through her heart too—hyperbolic talk, perhaps, but expressing real pain. . . .

Then a gentle gesture from an aid would fill Brooke with gratitude, a friend would stop by with food or music, or Brooke and Peggy, as they wrote together, would reach a deeper understanding and measure of grace. "Maybe this isn't the saddest night after all," they wrote after one particularly brutal day. "If there's a lesson we've been learning . . . it's about not assuming that good will stay good or, more important, that bad will stay bad."

Writing the blog together became an essential activity, what they *did* together in the way they used to hike and ski and dance and travel. Sometimes the voice was Peggy's, sometimes Brooke's, more often the two voices merged into one. "It's like having an intimate conversation with one another. . . . It's male and female combined . . . [there is] something androgynous about it but also something somehow erotic." It was a way "to make something truthful, even sometimes beautiful, out of the suffering of the past year." In addition, as they struggled to be honest, they confronted difficulties they might otherwise have skirted.

One night, their friends Roger and Jane came for dinner in the rehabilitation center. Roger had been diagnosed with ALS about the time Brooke had his accident. Now, while Brooke slowly improved, Roger gradually declined. When they were younger, the two men had mountaineered together, and sometime during the evening, Roger said, "We're brothers in adventure again."

More accurately, they were brothers in adversity, and the two couples discussed their reasons for framing something as an adventure rather than a disaster, even when "it means death for one and permanent disability for the other." By the end of the evening, Peggy wrote in the blog post, "Brooke and Roger had reaffirmed: 'We're brothers in adventure again.'"

Although Peggy and Brooke usually write together, Peggy wrote this post alone, and when Brooke read it the next day, he objected to the ending. "I don't think you were aware of Roger watching . . . the kind of pain I was in while you and Jane were talking," Brooke said. "Roger was just watching, watching, his eyes bugging out as if to say, 'I can't believe all the crap you have to go through with all that suctioning and cathing and stuff.'" Brooke worried that the ending trivialized what Roger had ahead of him; in fact, Brooke looked back on many of his own posts as ending too easily with a "rhetorical bow."

> I used to say . . . "this is going to be such a journey" and "I look at this as an opportunity," stuff like that—but I don't think I knew what I was talking about. . . . This is a hundred treks. This is a hundred marathons. . . . The reason we come together, you and me and Jane and Roger, is because we're fortifying each other, not just adventuring out in the wilderness when we choose.

Shortly after the accident, Lama Thupten Dorje Gyaltsen, the head of a Tibetan Buddhist temple in Salt Lake City, came to see Brooke in intensive care and told him three things. First, he said, "the body is nothing; it is ephemeral; the mind is everything." Next, he instructed Brooke to not ask why the accident had occurred, and to just accept the fact that it had. His third instruction had seemed perplexing, even esoteric, at the time but has perhaps proved most helpful of all. "Your suffering," he told Brooke and Peggy, "has and will produce compassion, even deep happiness, in many, many people who know you and even those who do not."

Brooke and Peggy are teachers. They have devoted their lives to forging a deep understanding of their respective academic disciplines in order to pass on the gift of that knowledge. In this new discipline of a changed life, they have continued that generosity through the blog.

Brooke also wanted to teach students directly, and last fall, he arranged to teach a class on Thoreau's *Walden* for the University of Utah's Osher Lifelong Learning Institute. Though he had taught the book many times, he had friends read it to him and he listened to tapes. He practically memorized the text since he wouldn't be able to page back and forth in class.

Although he still lived at the rehab center, he had almost weaned off the ventilator, and he hoped to teach once a week at home, initially during short trial visits that would allow him and Peggy to troubleshoot his permanent return, scheduled for halfway through the semester.

He was ecstatic to get back to two things he loved, home and students. He taught four classes and was about to move home permanently. Then he woke up with ice-cold skin and plummeting blood pressure. Soon he was incoherent. Rushed to the ICU in septic shock with aspiration pneumonia, once more he found himself on the vent and heavy antibiotics.

As soon as he stabilized, he started thinking about Thoreau again, preparing his aide to teach the chapter "The Pond in Winter" if he could not. A couple of classes were postponed while Brooke recovered, and then he taught "Where I Lived and What I Lived For." Afterward, Peggy asked Brooke point-blank: "What *do* you live for?"

When Brooke addressed the question in their next post, he cited two reasons. The first was existential, the basic will to live, to keep going. The second was to bring some sort of gift into other people's lives. He wrote about the extraordinary depth of giving and receiving love that he had experienced since the accident, of the pleasure of collaborative writing, and of the importance of "trying to bring to whoever is out there reading this some sense of what it's like to live with nearly continuous suffering and still have some sense of joy."

"This may seem outrageous to you," he told Peggy after they had worked on the post for a while, "but I think I'm happier than I've ever been." Then he hastened to add, "It isn't always that way; sometimes it's really, really hard."

At the end of November, two years and two weeks after his accident, Brooke finally made it home. The challenges continue; in some ways, as Brooke and Peggy wrote recently, "the hard part is just beginning." They considered discontinuing the blog but realized how vital it had become to both of them, "our joint project, our mutual work, the thing we can do together, really *together*. Dropping it, even for a couple of weeks, has made us lonely and isolated in ourselves. It's as if we couldn't talk anymore." In truth, the blog provides not only a way to talk to each other, but to delve deeper than talking allows.

Last fall, invited to speak to an English honors class, Peggy told the students about Brooke's accident and the role that writing plays as they struggle to thrive in spite of their vastly changed lives. She suggested that students meet their own experiences of adversity with the question, "How do you want this to change your life?" Afterward, a student wrote her, "I can't stop thinking about this question . . . I don't have an answer yet, but I'm looking forward to figuring it out."

———◇———

Brooke lived for nearly five years after the accident, and in the end, he chose to die with as much intention and vigor as he had lived. When he recognized that his mental acuity was declining and with it his ability to continue teaching and engaging in deep conversation—the factors that had given his life meaning—he submitted a formal request to disconnect all life support. After it was granted, his hospice doctor asked when he would like to have the ventilator removed. Brooke said, "Today." When the doctor replied that it could be arranged, Brooke broke into a huge smile, which Sara caught on film. A few hours later, on the afternoon of July 27, 2013, with Peggy lying beside him, surrounded by family and friends, and with the help of morphine to prevent the pain of "air hunger," Brooke enjoyed the "generous death" he had told those closest to him he desired.

SELF-RELIANCE

Benjamin Franklin, Ayn Rand, and the American Spirit

The worst thing you can do for anyone you care about is anything that they can do on their own. —ABRAHAM LINCOLN

As for the men in power, they are so anxious to establish the myth of infallibility that they do their utmost to ignore truth.
—BORIS PASTERNAK

To grow up on a ranch fifty miles from town is to have an inbred respect for self-reliance. In a bad winter, we might be snowed in for three weeks at a time; a summer flash flood could wash out the crossing over Chugwater Creek and maroon us for days. We didn't have a phone until I was halfway through grade school, and even with phone service and a clear road, when someone got injured, it could take hours to load them up and transport them to town. So we had a storeroom stocked with medical supplies—sutures and needles and inflatable splints, oxygen, morphine, blood stopper, and antibiotics—and enough food to feed everyone who lived on the ranch for a month. Roundups, brandings, and fighting fire were neighborhood affairs.

With such habits, we considered ourselves among the last of the rugged individualists. My parents were great readers, and their shelves held inspiration for anyone interested in the stoic, the resourceful, and the self-sufficient: *The Adventures of Daniel*

Boone, Andy Adams's *The Log of a Cowboy,* Emerson's essays, *Atlas Shrugged* by Ayn Rand, and, of course, *The Autobiography of Benjamin Franklin,* to name just a few.

Lately, I have found myself thinking about self-reliance on a national scale. We are five years into recession, Washington has gridlocked so severely that the country's credit rating has been downgraded, and Congress is unable to pass a budget or conduct the nation's business. No country can thrive if it can't govern itself, and as I've been pondering the relationship among individualism, self-reliance, and governance, I find myself thinking about two names that figured prominently in that family library, and who did much, each in their own time, to shape the American spirit.

Benjamin Franklin and Ayn Rand were born almost exactly two centuries apart (Franklin in 1706 and Rand in 1905), but they nonetheless had much in common. From childhood, both were precocious readers and prolific writers. Rand had written four novels by the time she was eleven; Franklin published more than a dozen articles under the name of Silence Dogood when he was just sixteen. A year later, Franklin ran away from his family home in Boston to seek better prospects in Philadelphia; Rand was twenty when her family helped her escape the horror that was post-revolutionary Russia in order to try her hand in Hollywood.

Both grew up to write books of lasting impact. *The Autobiography of Benjamin Franklin* stands as one of the most influential memoirs of all time; Rand's bestselling novel *Atlas Shrugged* ranked second only to the Bible in 1999 when the Library of Congress and the Book-of-the-Month Club polled readers about which book had made the most difference in their lives. Both continue to shape the political reality of our time. Franklin is the only one of the Founding Fathers to have signed all four documents that created our nation: the Declaration of Independence, the alliance with France, the treaty with Britain, and the Constitution. Rand's Objectivist philosophy has influenced libertarian thought for well over half a century, and placards with slogans such as "Ayn Rand was Right" and "Who is John Galt?" (the first line of *Atlas Shrugged)* are common at Tea Party rallies.

Both figures devoted their lives to the inalienable right of the individual to life, liberty, and the pursuit of happiness. In personality and philosophy, however, the two couldn't be further apart in their perceptions of how these rights should be secured.

Franklin was an extrovert by nature and replaced his parent's Puritan fatalism with optimism while retaining the Puritan commitment to community spirit and public improvement. He loved politics and building consensus. Rand was an introvert whose family lost everything in the Bolshevik Revolution. To her, calls for the "common good" were inherently corrupt and manipulative, and the only true hero was one who stood immovable and entirely alone.

———◄○►———

One of Franklin's earliest memories was of the time he organized playmates to steal stones from a building site in order to construct a wharf. In his autobiography he regretted the theft but reveled in his ability to bring people together to construct something useful. Later, in Philadelphia, he founded the first subscription library in America, a fire brigade, an insurance company, a hospital, a militia, a university, and, over time, dozens of other institutions at home and abroad, a commitment to the social contract that did not diminish with age. Just three years before he died, he accepted the presidency of the Pennsylvania Society for Promoting the Abolition of Slavery. "The good men may do separately," he wrote, "is small compared with what they may do collectively."

If Franklin excelled at organizing people in order to make things happen, he was also a born conciliator. He understood human nature, in part because he so frequently put himself in other peoples' shoes, having started to assume the viewpoints of different characters from the time he first started writing. Later, during a stint in London as an agent of the colonies, he published some ninety articles under forty-two pseudonyms, some of whom were American and others of whom were Brits.

Perhaps because he understood the English so well, he resisted the conclusion that a break with the mother country was inevitable. As the biographer Gordon Wood pointed out, "just as 'every Affront is not worth a Duel,' and 'every Injury not worth a War,' so too, [Franklin] was fond of saying, 'every Mistake in Government, every Incroachment on Rights is not worth a Rebellion.'" In London, he tried to represent the colonists' interests in a way that could keep them within the Empire. But when he became convinced that compromise was impossible, he returned to America more revolutionary than his compatriots who had stayed at home. "He does not hesitate at our boldest Measures," wrote John Adams to his wife Abigail, "but rather seems to think us too irresolute and backward."

Franklin joined Adams, Thomas Jefferson, and two others to write a formal Declaration of Independence. Then the patriots set upon the task of winning it. When it became clear that the Revolution needed foreign assistance in order to succeed, Franklin joined a delegation to France. John Adams eventually replaced the other delegates, but Franklin alone had the diplomatic skill to win the French military alliance and then keep them on board throughout our escalating needs for arms and money, something that in the end totaled what would amount to thirteen billion dollars today.

In his bid for assistance, Franklin touted America's value as a future trading partner, but more importantly, he won allegiance to the American idea. He distributed copies of the Declaration of Independence and other colonial writings, arguing that "tyranny is so generally established in the rest of the world that the prospect of an asylum in America for those who love liberty gives general joy, and our cause is esteemed the cause of all mankind. . . .

We are fighting for the dignity and happiness of human nature." Many historians of the Revolutionary period believe that without Franklin's unique personality, the colonists could not have gained French support, and without French support, they could not have won the war.

Franklin had an ability to unite people around the power of an idea, and his crowning diplomatic success came during the Constitutional Convention in 1787. By then he was eighty-one years old, twice the average age of the rest of the delegates. In the end, few of his specific proposals made it into the final document: not the unicameral legislature that he favored, nor leadership by an executive council rather than a president, nor the requirement that Federal officials serve without pay. What he did win, however, was a climate in which an inspired document could take form.

Repeatedly, when dispute threatened to disband the effort, he turned down the heat. Sometimes he invited individual delegates to enjoy tea under the mulberry tree in his yard nearby, other times he appealed to the full congress during debate. "Both sides must part with some of their demands," he said at one point. "We are sent hither to consult, not to contend, with each other," he said at another. And in a verity we would do well to remember today, "Declarations of a fixed opinion, and of determined resolution never to change it, neither enlighten nor convince us. . . . Positiveness and warmth on one side, naturally beget their like on the other."

The most contentious issue, and one that threatened to scuttle the convention several times, was the issue of representation. Although Franklin did not originate the idea that would eventually evolve into the Connecticut Compromise—providing equal representation for each state in the Senate and representation proportioned by population in the House—he repeatedly cooled tempers to a degree where it could be discussed, and he eventually reprised that debate into a specific motion that won approval.

On the closing day of the convention, in a speech that the historian Clinton Rossiter deemed "the most remarkable performance of a remarkable life," Franklin called for unanimous consent to the document they had crafted. He admitted it wasn't perfect—how could it be, "for, when you assemble a number of men, to have the advantage of their joint wisdom, you inevitably assemble with those men all their prejudices, their passions, their errors of opinion, their local interests, and their selfish views. From such an assembly can a perfect production be expected? It therefore astonishes me," he continued:

> to find this system approaching so near to perfection as it does; and I think it will astonish our enemies, who are waiting with confidence to hear that our counsels are confounded like those of the builders of Babel, and that our states are on the point of separation, only to meet hereafter for the purpose of cutting one another's throats. Thus I consent, sir, to this Constitution, because I expect no better, and because I am not sure that it is not the best.

Like other delegates, he had his doubts. But, he said, he had never "whispered a syllable of [his objections] abroad," and he enjoined the others to similar restraint. If each were "to report the objections he has had to it, and endeavor to gain partisans in support," they would "lose all the salutary effects and great advantages resulting naturally in our favor among foreign nations, as well as among ourselves, from our real or apparent unanimity." He asked that everyone "on this occasion, doubt a little of his own infallibility" and, "act heartily and unanimously in recommending this Constitution wherever our influence may extend, and turn our future thoughts and endeavors to the means of having it well administered."

Franklin did not get his wish for unanimity. In the end, only thirty-nine of the original fifty-five delegates signed, but it was enough to make the United States Constitution a reality and set our nation on the task that absorbs it to this day, "endeavor[ing] to the means of having it well administered."

———◄O►———

Franklin spent his life working for the common good, a value he first absorbed at home from his parents' Puritan beliefs. Ayn Rand's sense of civic duty was diametrically opposed, though it, too, was shaped by values she learned as a child.

Rand grew up in St. Petersburg during the years surrounding the 1917 Russian Revolution. She was not close to her mother, Anna Rosenbaum, whom she later described as a social climber and petty tyrant. Anna told her daughter she had never wanted children but had sacrificed herself to the duty of motherhood.

Ayn remembered a time when she was five and her mother, annoyed by the number of toys scattered about the playroom, told Ayn and her younger sister to give up half of them for a year. Rand handed over her favorites, thinking how much she would enjoy recovering them later. But when she tried to reclaim them, her mother seemed amused. She had given them to an orphanage, she told her daughter. If Ayn had valued the toys, she wouldn't have given them up in the first place. "This may have been Rand's first encounter with injustice masquerading as what she would later acidly call 'altruism,'" wrote Anne C. Heller in a recent biography.

But it was not her last. As much as she disliked her mother, she admired her father, a fierce individualist and successful pharmacist. She was twelve and visiting his shop when Bolshevik soldiers arrived to sack it and bar its doors, "looting the looters" in Lenin's phrase. She never forgot the look of anger and helplessness on her father's face. Later the family also lost control of their home, as did almost every family Rand knew. The Rosenbaums fled to the Crimea, only to return to St. Petersburg, now renamed Petrograd, after the communists succeeded in subduing the entire country.

Rand experienced firsthand the violence and injustice perpetrated in the name of the Marxist creed, "From each according to his ability, to each according to his need." She witnessed the ways in which the "humanitarian" urge and its concomitant call to sacrifice could mask brutality and a will to power, and later, in both her philosophy and her fiction, she divided people into two categories: hardworking and individualistic producers like her father, and the looters, moochers, and parasites that made up the rest of the world.

As these experiences shaped the philosophy of enlightened self-interest that she later called "the virtue of selfishness," her introversion also played a role. She was a desperately shy child, socially awkward with a "painful intensity" that took people aback. She had few friends but convinced herself this was because others envied her great intelligence and sought to "punish her for her virtues." Later she would write an open letter to her readers stating that "I have no hobbies. I have few friends. I do not like to 'go out.' . . . Nothing [besides writing] has ever mattered to me too much."

Solitude became a defining virtue in her philosophy. In her 1941 "Manifesto of Individualism," she wrote that "independence of man from men is the Life Principle. Dependence of man upon men is the Death Principle." When Howard Roark, the hero of *The Fountainhead,* stands trial for his ideals, he tells the jury that, "The only good which men can do to one another and the only statement of their proper relationship is—Hands off!"

In Rand's black-and-white world, one was either heroic in the ability to stand entirely alone or completely dependent and morally bankrupt. On this, Franklin and Rand couldn't be further apart. When Franklin returned from his first trip to London, he happily proclaimed, "Man is a sociable being," exactly the sort of sentiment Rand placed in the mouths of her worst villains to prove that they were emotional parasites or "second-handers." *Inter*-dependence was not in her vocabulary.

Nor, to large extent, was compromise. She allowed that compromise was honorable in trade, as two parties negotiated a mutually agreeable price. But in moral values, there could be no accommodation. "What would you regard as a 'compromise' between life and death?" she asked. "Or between truth and falsehood? Or between reason and irrationality?" For Rand, truth was absolute; every question had a single answer, arrived at by rational thought. "Just as there are no contradictions in my values and no conflicts among my desires—so there are no victims and no conflicts of interest among rational men," says John Galt in *Atlas Shrugged*.

Rand's greatest appeal has always been to adolescents and young adults. Objectivism offers a "round universe," where the meaning of life is clearly stated and an explicit moral code extends to every aspect of human existence. Because truth is rational and absolute, even matters of the heart have right and wrong answers. Rachmaninoff's compositions are noble because they are Romantic; Beethoven's are "malevolent" because of their tragic themes.

In Objectivism, the most introverted or socially awkward can become heroes through the strength of their convictions. The philosophy appeals to more than those who disdain the crowd. Anyone who has ever felt pressured into something he or she doesn't want to do can take solace in John Galt's oath, a single-sentence summary of Objectivist philosophy: "I swear by my life and my love of it that I will never live for the sake of another man, nor ask another man to live for mine."

People tend to drift away from Objectivism as they mature. Since in Rand's universe all rational people will come to the same conclusion and all irrational people are evil, the logical application of her philosophy makes it immoral to maintain relationships with those who hold views even slightly different than one's own. This tends to cause problems for anyone with a spouse, a child, or a job. It makes politics—which derives from *polis*, the Greek word for "city" or "body of citizens," both of which are, by definition, diverse—completely impossible.

Those who originally turned to Objectivism in part because it released them from others' expectations found that it replaced one orthodoxy with another. Asked in her famous *Playboy* interview in 1964 if she thought it was immoral to value friendship, Rand answered, "Friendship, family life, and human relationships are not primary in a man's life. A man who places others first, above his own creative work, is an emotional parasite; whereas, if he places his work first, there is no conflict between his work and his enjoyment of human relationships."

Inevitably, the philosophy caused problems for Ayn and her closest associates. In 1968, her tightly knit discussion group—who ironically called themselves "The Collective"—imploded when in a highly publicized move, Rand broke with Nathaniel and Barbara Branden, the couple who had been second only to Rand herself in developing and popularizing Objectivism. Only after Rand died did the reason for the break become widely known. Ayn and Nathaniel had conducted a fourteen-year affair. During its last several years, Branden wanted out but couldn't bring himself to confront his much older paramour; he entered into another affair, which he kept secret from both Rand and his wife.

Other, equally shocking accounts of what actually went on in the discussion group came out from dozens of Rand's onetime followers. Anyone who challenged Rand's ideas was subjected to grueling interrogation in kangaroo-style courts and reeducated through invasive psychotherapy conducted by Nathaniel and Ayn. In the end, if the errant did not do "everything possible to remedy [his or her] thinking and adjust [his or her] attitudes," he or she would be expelled. Ayn Rand, the rabid anticommunist and champion of individualism, resorted to Stalinist tactics to protect the hegemony of her ideas.

The Collective consisted of people who wanted to study with Rand, most at least a generation younger than she, but virtually all her friendships eventually broke over irreconcilable differences that Rand interpreted as errors of thought. In the end, her only close associate was Leonard Peikoff, a much younger acolyte who had survived several pogroms to be the last one standing as her intellectual heir. She died in her apartment in 1982, attended only by a nurse.

As a child in Russia, Rand had seen how Marxism invoked the

common good in order to rise to power, something she watched happen again in Nazi Germany. In her absolutist thinking, she could not imagine communitarian sentiments leading to anything else, and in a speech titled "Fascism and the New Frontier," she mined John F. Kennedy's speeches in order to liken him to Hitler. If her lens had been different, she might have likened him instead to the Founding Fathers, almost all of whom made at least occasional reference to such ideas, and who chose *E pluribus unum*—out of many, one—as the motto for the Great Seal of the United States.

Individualism in the political sense means that government exists to serve the people rather than the other way around. Kennedy's suggestion that Americans "ask not what your country can do for you but what you can do for your country" enraged Rand. But Franklin would have been comfortable with Kennedy's words; in fact, they are not unlike what he might have coined himself and included among Poor Richard's aphorisms. He did not confuse country with government. Country was America, made up of Americans. It was a noun. Government, on the other hand, was the embodiment of a verb, something in its American form that Abraham Lincoln later phrased as "of the people, by the people, and for the people," a blend of commitment and action that made independence—which is to say self-reliance—possible.

Franklin understood that someone who believed his own opinion inviolate and saw compromise as a moral flaw could dictate but never govern. In his view, community and self-reliance were intricately intertwined. His commitment to public service and his life-long belief in tolerance, compromise, and mutual respect made it possible not only to draft the Declaration of Independence, win the Revolutionary War, and ratify the American Constitution, but also to build the only country in which Ayn Rand wanted to live. "Compromisers may not make great heroes," wrote Walter Isaacson in *Benjamin Franklin: An American Life*, "but they do make democracies."

CURIOSITY

Curiosity may have killed the cat, but it saved the raccoon. Early in the 20th century, research psychologists used raccoons as test subjects because of their intelligence and curiosity, but the creatures proved hard to handle. As indomitable as they were inquisitive, they would chew through their cages and hide out in unexpected places. In time, researchers turned to rats, which proved to be more tractable.

CURIOSITY

Growing Pains

I have no special talents. I am only passionately curious.
—ALBERT EINSTEIN

The best thing for being sad . . . is to learn something. That is
the only thing that never fails.
—TERENCE H. WHITE, *The Once and Future King*

When we were little, my brother and I often sat in front of
the record player in our living room for hours at a time.
We lived too far from town to pick up TV, but we enjoyed a
generous collection of children's albums: Boris Karloff reciting
Mother Goose and Danny Kaye reading the Brothers Grimm;
narrated versions of *Peter and the Wolf*, *The Nutcracker Suite*,
Sleeping Beauty, and *the Peer Gynt Suites*; a boxed set of 45s
on crimson vinyl that introduced us to each instrument in the
orchestra.

Unlike our grandmother's big cabinet stereo in town, our
record player was nothing fancy. It had a single speaker that
fronted a box only slightly larger than an orange crate but polished with a deep mahogany stain. It sat on a metal stand. We
could stack several records at a time on the turntable's spindle,
and I loved the whir as the stabilizing arm rotated back, a record
dropped, and the needle swung over, placing itself magically at
the edge of the first track.

Of all the albums, my favorite was the story of Peer Gynt. My heart raced as he fled the trolls in the Hall of the Mountain King, and I fell into peaceful bliss as morning dawned on the Moroccan desert. As I absorbed the music, I studied the record player itself, running my fingers over the raised gold letters that spelled out *Zenith* with the *Z* extended in a jag of lightning, moving on to caress the nubby cloth that covered the speaker. I remember the way a shaft of sun through the window glinted on the dark wood, and I would lean closer and closer to study it.

One day, I started to gnaw on the corner of the cabinet. I can still remember the perfumy taste of the varnish and its granular texture, the give of the wood as I scraped away at it with my teeth, and how the sound of my gnawing channeled through my jaws directly into my brain, a sensation different but somehow complementary to the swirl of music. I remember a sense of perfect reverie. And then my mother came in, instantly horrified. What, oh what, had I done?

Years later, when I was in my thirties and lived in a cottage perched on a hill above the industrial district in Portland, Oregon, I came down the steps to the sidewalk as three young boys approached, absorbed in play and completely unaware of me. Just as I reached the street, one of them leapt in the air and karate-kicked at a young tree my neighbor had planted in the parking strip, breaking one of its supports. "Why did you *do* that?" I said with shocked harshness. The boy, startled to find me there, looked up with bewilderment. "I don't know," he said, and it was true. He had no idea. He wasn't a vandal, or at least he didn't mean to be. He was just lost in the world he shared with his friends, testing its limits and his own.

Curiosity gets us into all sorts of trouble. Think of Eve. And Pandora. Poor Psyche not only looked at Cupid after he expressly forbade it, but also peeked into a box she had procured at great travail to win back his love, though by this time, Cupid had come to appreciate her spirit and responded to the transgression with fondness if not outright approval. Curiosity may kill the cat, but it also keeps him highly entertained and makes him interesting to others. With luck, before he runs through all nine lives, he may learn to harness the trait to good effect.

Benjamin Franklin was famously curious. We can hardly conjure his name without seeing in our mind's eye a kite in a stormy sky, and kites intrigued him long before his electrical experiments. As a boy, he loved swimming as much as he loved flying kites, and one day at the lake, torn between the two, he realized he could indulge both at the same time. He raised his kite into a steady breeze and entered the water. "I found that, lying on my back and holding the stick in my hands . . . I began to cross the pond with my kite, which carried me quite over without the least fatigue, and with the greatest pleasure imaginable."

Young Ben read voraciously and devoured every book he could get his hands on in his older brother's print shop, where he apprenticed from the age of twelve. To make time for reading, he ate at his desk while his brother and the other employees went out to lunch, and he ditched church on Sundays.

He taught himself to write by studying *The Spectator,* a British periodical, jotting down the main points of its articles and then recreating them from memory days later. Sometimes he rewrote the pieces in verse in order to develop a better sense of variety and rhythm. When he compared his versions to the originals, he noted that "I discovered many faults and amended them; but I sometimes had the pleasure of fancying that . . . I had been lucky enough to improve the method or the language, and this encouraged me to think I might possibly in time come to be a tolerable English writer, of which I was extremely ambitious."

Such ambition is unusual, even worrisome, in one so young. "So far as any record shows," wrote Carl Van Doren in his Pulitzer Prize–winning biography, Franklin's "work and his studies were his whole life from twelve to sixteen." Yet we never have a sense of Franklin driven by grim determination so much as drawn by a boundless love of inquiry. He devised his exercises in rhetoric, for instance, not primarily with an eye to later success—though he knew writing well would help him—but rather to keep up with a friend in their lively debates. Throughout his long life, curiosity energized Franklin, and I can imagine that near the end, as conflicts and setbacks receded into the past, he might have viewed his unparalleled accomplishments as statesman, publisher, humorist, inventor, and diplomat as having been as effortless and filled with delight as that youthful glide across the lake behind a kite.

Franklin combined curiosity with a love of community and communication, and those elements seem essential to a sense of enjoyment. In 2000, a Gallup poll of more than 130,000 people in 130 nations revealed that the two factors that most influenced a person's satisfaction on any given day were "being able to count on someone for help" and whether or not they "learned something yesterday."

Curiosity can be addictive, most especially that aspect of it known as *seeking*. Cognitive scientists divide the physiology of curiosity into two parts, seeking and liking. Seeking stimulates the dopamine system and excites us. It gets us out of bed in the morning, energizes us when we are on the steep part of the learning curve, and keeps us coming back for more. Liking, on the other hand, interacts with the opioid system and gives us a sense of pleasure and fulfillment, providing time to organize and integrate what we have found. Of the two systems, seeking is the more powerful—our brains light up more when we are anticipating a reward than when we actually get it. As the science writer Emily Yoffe explains, "Wanting and liking are complementary. The former catalyzes us to action; the latter brings us to a satisfied pause. Seeking needs to be turned off, if even for a little while, so that the system does not run in an endless loop."

Cocaine and amphetamine overstimulate the dopamine system, and addicts crave increasing stimulation even as the pleasure they derive from each hit decreases. Google can have the same effect, and I suspect I'm not the only one who has looked up from my computer at the end of the day with a glazed look on my face, wondering what happened to the hours. Checking email and text messages can be even more compulsive, each new arrival signaled with a ding or vibration, the contemporary versions of Pavlov's bell. As Yoffee points out, there's a reason we call it "CrackBerry."

Yet a life without inquiry is hardly worth living. A lack of curiosity leads to sloth and even despair. Igniting curiosity, on the other hand, can pull us out of the doldrums and even turn the tide on serious depression. It is an itch yearning to be scratched, a magnetic attraction. As clinical psychologist Todd Kashdan notes in his book *Curious? Discover the Missing Ingredient to a Fulfilling Life,* "Curiosity is hard-wired in the brain, and its specific function is to urge us to explore, discover, and grow. It is the engine of our evolving self. Without curiosity, we are unable to sustain our attention, we avoid risks, we abort challenging tasks, we compromise our intellectual development, we fail to achieve competencies and strengths, we limit our ability to form relationships with other people, and essentially, stagnate."

Kashdan cites five aspects of curiosity: intensity, frequency, durability, breadth, and depth. Any one of these in excess can short-circuit us. The autistic with an encyclopedic knowledge of train schedules or vacuum cleaners is obsessed with depth; the Google addict hits "search" with intoxicated frequency. Benjamin Franklin, on the other hand, won his singular place in American history—and in our hearts—with a curiosity that was not only exceptionally robust but well rounded: intense, constant, durable, broad, and deep.

The curious person is in love with the world. One of my favorite stories about my husband, Hal, comes from his childhood. He was always restless, endlessly exploring, and he found the four hours each Sunday that his family spent at the Mormon ward a trial. He escaped Sunday school and other duties whenever he could. One Mother's Day, he poked around the recreation room. It had a stage at one end, and when he went behind the curtain, he found a row of flowering plants lined up for presentation to the mothers. The blossoms seemed to glow in the diffused light, and they were so beautiful that he ate them. All of them. When he was done, the pots held only empty stems. "The plants were just beginning to flower," Hal remembers, "and there was only a bud or two on each one. They were pretty, I was hungry, and I loved my mother. The combination of those things—I didn't have any sense of it being wrong until later, when they opened the curtain and everyone gasped."

I told this story to Hal's large family one time when we had gathered for dinner and conversation turned to what endeared us to our spouses. They all remembered the mangled plants, but none of them knew that Hal had been the culprit. Luckily, the statute of limitations had expired, and no one sent him to his room. For my part, his enduring curiosity keeps me endlessly intrigued. I get mad at him sometimes, but I never get bored. I do, however, keep a close watch on the houseplants.

PROCRASTINATION

Do It . . . Next

Nothing is so fatiguing as the eternal hanging-on of an uncompleted task.

—WILLIAM JAMES

Only Robinson Crusoe had everything done by Friday.

—AUTHOR UNKNOWN

When I was writing my first book, I came down with a brutal case of procrastination. I had all the research done, but I couldn't seem to sit down to the actual writing. I missed one deadline and then another, and right about the time that suicide seemed the only honorable course, I bought a little book titled something like *Overcoming Procrastination* in which the author suggested writing the affirmation "Do it now" on a slip of paper, taping it to the bathroom mirror, and repeating it a thousand times each morning and a thousand times again each night before bed.

I was desperate, willing not only to try such a prescription, but determined to improve upon the technique. I wouldn't simply scribble "Do it now" on a piece of paper like a lazy piker; I would needlepoint it onto a plaque.

I had done needlepoint before, but I had never designed my own canvas, so that took some research. I struggled over a design, discarding several before I came up with the right one. Then there was the trip to the craft store for supplies, time spent transferring the pattern onto the canvas and working the needlepoint, and finally the trip to the framer's. Since they didn't have a frame in the exact shade of green I wanted, I painted it myself. The whole project took at least a week, maybe two, during which I didn't have to worry about the book because I was doing something else so obviously worthwhile.

I suspect that Joseph Ferrari, a psychology professor at Duke University who has studied procrastination for twenty years, would find my little project downright pathological. His last name suggests a certain lack of sympathy for anyone in the slow lane, and he has come to view people like me as impulsive quitters who lack willpower. Our fault is, in his view, a "nasty, unattractive" quality of human behavior that "merits extirpation."

"We sound like those FBI psychological portraits of serial killers or pederasts," Emily Yoffe wrote after her interview with Ferrari for a *Slate* special issue on procrastination. "Fortunately, our malady prevents us from carrying out any nefarious plans that we might have." (The special issue, by the way, came out two weeks late.)

In contrast to Ferrari, many others who study procrastination see it not as an aberration but rather as a defining human characteristic. Economist George Ainslie, a leader in the field, argues that putting things off is "as fundamental as the shape of time and could well be called the basic impulse." At any rate, few people, even the most renowned, are entirely free of it. St. Augustine said, "Give me chastity and continence—but not yet." Leonardo da Vinci's inability to finish many of his projects caused him great duress. Ralph Ellison and Harper Lee were brilliant writers who never quite got around to nailing that second book.

Economists like Ainslie are particularly interested in understanding procrastination because it costs us so much money. Americans waste hundreds of millions of dollars each year when they don't get their taxes in on time and forgo millions more in employer contributions to their retirement security because they fail to sign up for 401(k)s. Businesses implode and whole economies suffer when important decisions are put on hold, as our current budget crisis—and in fact most budget crises—so painfully illustrates.

The recent anthology *The Thief of Time: Philosophical Essays on Procrastination*, edited by Chrisoula Andreou, draws together the work of Ainslie and other experts from a breadth of disciplines to explain (and even offer some excuses) for this trait that causes so many of us so much grief. They consider the matter a philosophical concern because it revolves around both the fluid nature of identity and our relationship with time.

The economists in the group talk about what they call "hyperbolic discounting," the tendency to make the best choice in the future but not in the present. In one experiment, subjects are offered $100 today but $110 if they wait until tomorrow. Then they are offered $100 in a month or $110 in a month and a day. In each case, waiting 24 hours increases the reward, but many subjects who readily agree to wait an extra day in the future choose not to wait when the lower reward dangles right in front of them. Hyperbolic discounting explains why we stuff our Netflix queues with important documentaries and subtitled films, but when we plop down in front of the TV tonight, we click on *Desperate Housewives*.

Several of the authors draw on the theory of multiple selves, the idea that each of us contains multitudes. The procrastinating self is not the same as the self who gets things done, and the responsible self might not even be the same as the aesthete who thinks we should watch *Battleship Potemkin*. The idea of multiple selves is not new. As Otto Von Bismarck wrote, "Faust complained about having two souls in his breast, but I harbor a whole crowd of them and they quarrel. It is like being in a republic." When it comes to procrastination, then, as James Surowiecki, who reviewed *The Thief of Time* for *The New Yorker,* notes, "the first step to dealing with procrastination isn't admitting that you have a problem. It's admitting that your 'yous' have a problem."

Overcoming procrastination is sometimes a matter of negotiating among the selves. Philosopher Don Ross, for instance, suggests that "although the television-watching self is interested only in watching TV, it's interested in watching TV not just now but also in the future. This means that it can be bargained with: working now will let you watch more television down the road." Procrastination is "the result of a bargaining process gone wrong."

Other times, the more responsible self can bring outside forces to bear on the inner slacker through a process called self-binding: think of Odysseus lashed to the mast so he could listen to the sirens without steering his ship onto the shoals. Victor Hugo ordered his valet to hide his clothes and then sat at his desk naked so he wouldn't be tempted to stroll the avenue when he should have been writing. In an age when few of us have access to either masts or valets, technology steps into the void. On the website StickK, you secure your intent with a sum of money that goes to charity if you fail to come through. If you want to put real pressure on yourself, designate a cause you loathe.

We procrastinate for a host of reasons. Dr. Ferrari divides us into arousal procrastinators and avoidance procrastinators. The first thrive on the adrenalin rush of working under pressure; the latter measure their self worth by their accomplishments and put things off to avoid having to confront whether or not they are actually any good. Then there are those who simply avoid distasteful tasks. One of the earliest scholars to focus on the subject, the Nobel Prize–winning economist George Akerlof, identified procrastination as a field that could shed light on the human condition after he had delayed sending a package to a friend for months.

Bill Wilson, founder of Alcoholics Anonymous, thought procrastination was no more than a five-syllable word for sloth, but indolence suggests a degree of pleasure, and few of us are more miserable than when we avoid something our better self really wants to get done. Besides, avoidance itself can take a lot of effort: it's not easy to design and needlepoint a plaque. Stanford philosophy professor John Perry notes that many procrastinators work very hard, just not at the right things. In an essay titled "Structured Procrastination," he suggests, only slightly tongue in cheek, that we design a hierarchy of importance (or unpleasantness) and always have something looming more odious than the thing we really need to accomplish. He also suggests having a lot of tasks on board:

> Procrastinators often follow exactly the wrong tack. They try to minimize their commitments, assuming that if they have only a few things to do, they will quit procrastinating and get them done. But this goes contrary to the basic nature of the procrastinator and destroys his most important source of motivation. The few tasks on his list will be by definition the most important, and the only way to avoid doing them will be to do nothing. This is a way to become a couch potato, not an effective human being.

Perhaps this explains the cliché "If you want something done, ask a busy person." She may jump at the chance to take on your task in order to avoid what she really should be doing.

DEFENSE

We often think of a venomous person as "a snake in the grass," but the snake has not always connoted evil. In 1754, Benjamin Franklin featured the reptile in the first political cartoon published in the colonies, a wood-cut of a snake chopped into eight pieces–representing the number of colonies at that time–with the caption "Join, or Die." During the American Revolution, he suggested that the rattlesnake stood for the best in American character. "She never begins an attack," he wrote, "nor, when once engaged, ever surrenders: She is therefore an emblem of magnanimity and true courage . . . [S]he never wounds till she has generously given notice, even to her enemy, and cautioned him against the danger of stepping on her."

GRUMPINESS

The Grouch Settles In

I'm only grouchy and moody on days that end with Y.
—SOURCE UNKNOWN

Grouches are a separate species.
—Muppet Wiki entry on OSCAR THE GROUCH

I've been grumpy all week. It's sort of like having the flu without the aches and pains and fever. The flu, though, has a sense of inevitability; it's something you catch. Not your fault. But grumpiness—shouldn't I be able to simply shake my head and disperse it? Yet it has settled over me like a catarrh, for no good reason that I can discern, and only now, after several days, does it seem to be lifting of its own accord.

It has been a week full of endless but necessary chores like bookkeeping and filing and appointments, and I suppose I can blame my bad mood on the burden of minutia. We coin terms for such things: pecked to death by ducks, a pomegranate of impossible tasks.

Or I could blame it on genetics. Once, when I was in high school, a friend drove out to the ranch. He took a curve too fast on the gravel road and flipped his car. Luckily, he was unhurt, and later, as we viewed the wreckage, he joked, "I'll sue! I'll sue! I come from a long line of sewers!"

I come from a long line of grumps. My father was often volatile, his father cranky, and my paternal grandmother downright impossible. My first awareness of resolve came in the thought: I don't want to be like that; when I grow up, I *won't* be like that. This grouchiness challenges my very sense of self, so I'm not just grumpy but also grumpy about being grumpy. Deep down, I'm a much nicer person, really. We all live in denial. As the Chilean autocrat Augusto Pinochet said, "I'm not a dictator. It's just that I have a grumpy face."

Grouchiness is an argument with reality, a tantrum against the way things are. I can't necessarily control my circumstances, but I can control my *response* to them. I know this, or at least I think I do, and generally that belief helps me dispel my self-indulgent moods. But this foul temper seems to have a life of its own. My inner Buddhist is in a fistfight with my inner bitch, and it's not a pretty sight.

The sense of being at war with myself is real and, like procrastination, can be explained to some degree by the emerging theory of multiple selves, which affirms what Walt Whitman suggested so many years ago, that we do contain multitudes.

Advances in cognitive studies present all sorts of questions and quandaries about what makes up a self, and even if such a thing exists. We know that our thoughts influence our state of mind, and that we can often change our sense of wellbeing by changing the way we perceive things. But another emerging field, personality neuroscience, studies the degree to which heredity and external factors such as brain damage, hormones, and changes in the level of neurotransmitters like serotonin, dopamine, and endorphins affect what we think of as identity.

A recent episode of WNYC's brilliant science show, *Radiolab*, told the story of Anna, a churchgoing pillar of her community who turned into a gambling addict after she started taking a pseudo-dopamine to treat her Parkinson's disease. Parkinson's results from the death of dopamine molecules in a part of the brain that controls motion; dopamine is also the "sex, drugs, and rock & roll neurotransmitter" that responds to pleasure and underlies addiction. The pseudo-dopamine completely reversed the symptoms of Parkinson's, but Anna needed ever-larger doses as time went on. One day, she stepped into a casino and was immediately and almost fatally addicted. Before her doctor made the connection between the drug and her changed behavior, she had lost her husband and her life's savings and resorted to stealing quarters from her grandchildren. Once off the drug, her gambling compulsion evaporated as quickly as it had appeared, though the Parkinson's symptoms returned with a vengeance.

The theory of multiple selves suggests strategies for negotiating between competing parts of ourselves. The more responsible self, for instance, can devise a system of "self-binding" that makes it difficult for the reprobate to act out. My diligent self can disable the Internet to keep the slacker from surfing the Web; my inner athlete can foil the glutton by sending extra cheesecake home with a guest (leaving her competing selves to fend for themselves). But little short of physical shackles could have kept Anna from the slot machines during the time her dopamine system was on overdrive.

This week, my gracious self has failed to bind the grump. The more I tell Her Nastiness to behave, the more petulant she becomes. I'd like to think she is a malignant visitor rather than an inherent part of me, and I blame her for riding in on a surge of hormones or a deficit of serotonin. I like this view of her as a guest, who even uninvited I will treat with a degree of courtesy, accepting her foibles without allowing them to enrage or panic me, and minimizing her effect on my family by trying to keep her—which means me—out of their way as much as possible. I draw strength from the thought that however much she overstays her welcome, she will leave in time, at least for a while. One part of me is still grumpy, but at least the rest of me is less irritated about it.

DISTEMPER

Grumpiness has been called the weakest form of anger, a watered-down version of rage, but most of us know it as something with a life of its own. On *Sesame Street*, Oscar the Grouch declared himself a member of a separate species. An angry person often wants to act out against someone else. A grump, on the other hand, is more likely to growl, like Oscar: "Leave me alone and get lost!

STUBBORNNESS

Holding On for Dear Life

I have always liked the phrase "nursing a grudge," because many people are tender of their resentments, as the things nearest their hearts.
—MARILYNNE ROBINSON, *Gilead*

We do not grow absolutely, chronologically. We grow sometimes in one dimension, and not in another; unevenly. . . . We are mature in one realm, childish in another. . . . We are made up of layers, cells, constellations.
—ANAÏS NIN

It was mid-August in the third year of drought, a day so hot and dry it made my skin ache. The drought had brought a plague of grasshoppers, and dozens leapt ahead of me when I stepped out of the pickup to open the gate so my father could drive through. We were headed up to summer pasture to scatter salt and mineral for the cattle, a job I would normally have done alone. Today there was a problem at the reservoir that I couldn't fix on my own, and I had asked Dad for help. It was the first time we had worked together in a week.

As I struggled with the barbed-wire gate, the grasshoppers electrified the air with their relentless buzzing and threw themselves at my legs. Finally the gate gave way, and my father drove through. I closed it and climbed back into the un-air-conditioned cab. The temperature was over a hundred degrees, but what I remember most is the chill.

Dad hadn't spoken to me in days. Seething with anger, he sat so stony and quiet he frightened me. We had been stepping around each other all week, his only communication when he laid out the day's work each morning in short, clipped phrases. He had never shut me out so completely before, and I didn't know what I had done wrong.

I assumed it had something to do with his new wife, Mary. My mother had died suddenly a year and a half earlier, a loss that had devastated us both. I withdrew from my junior year of college so Dad wouldn't be alone on the ranch, though I needed him at least as much as he needed me. We gave each other whatever solace we could muster over the winter, and then I returned to summer term in order to finish my degree on time the next spring.

Dad came back East for my graduation and surprised me with the announcement that he was going to marry again. I had hoped he would find someone else, but I hadn't expected it to happen so soon. Still, when I returned to Wyoming to work on the ranch for the summer, I found Mary substantial—a bit stiff, but also intelligent with a good sense of humor. She doted on my father as much as he doted on her. I liked her, and when she and my father returned to the ranch after their honeymoon, our relationship felt comfortable.

One day, things changed abruptly. If I came into a room where Mary read, she stood up and walked right past me. If she entered a room and found me in it, she turned and left without a word. Dad stopped talking to me as well.

I didn't know what had gone wrong. I knew that step relationships could be fraught, but as much scrutiny as I turned on myself, I couldn't find any unacknowledged hostility. I didn't feel that Dad had betrayed either my mother or me. My folks had talked openly about what might happen if one of them were to die, and I knew Mom never wanted Dad to be alone. Nor did I feel that Mary usurped my role. I had no illusions about taking care of my father, and he certainly would not have allowed it. I must have offended her, but I pored over everything I could remember of our conversations and other interactions, and I didn't know how.

I had just begun to regain my balance after the loss of my mother and the knowledge that the ranch would pass out of our family at the end of the summer. Now it seemed as if I had lost my father as well. I couldn't let that happen. I hoped that finally, that day in the pickup, we could sort things out.

"Dad," I said after I got back into the truck, "what's wrong? What's going on? You are furious with me, but I don't know why."

He glared at me, his eyes as hard as granite, his hands gripping the steering wheel as if he wanted to rip it off its column. "Please, Dad, talk to me. Tell me what's wrong." Still, he didn't speak. "Don't be like this," I said, but his teeth were clenched, and he stared at me without blinking.

I started to cry, big slow tears that I batted away self-consciously. I'd only cried in his presence once as an adult, when he met my plane after my mother's aneurism. We were not a family that wore emotion on its sleeve.

But neither were we a family that used silence as a weapon. Now, he glared at me a moment longer and then turned away, slamming the pickup into gear to lurch forward on the rough dirt road. I devolved into gut-wrenching sobs.

It was a long time before I had myself under control, but neither of us said another word. We fixed the head gate at the reservoir, we distributed salt, we returned home. Somehow, over the next few days, we patched things up to where we could work together in reasonable comfort and share the dinner table with politeness if not ease. At the end of the summer, I moved to Casper, Wyoming, and then to Denver, Colorado, to work on my first book.

My father and I stayed in touch, devoted to each other in our way. But we never really trusted each other after that. I didn't ask again what had happened. I suppose I was afraid to see that look in his eyes. Still, I never stopped wondering. At one point, I wrote Mary. I realized I had done something that hurt her, I told her. I didn't know what it was, but I wanted to make amends. I supported her marriage with my father; I didn't want us to be estranged. Please, couldn't we talk?

"Maybe someday that will happen," she wrote back. "As ever, Mary."

It would be over twenty-five years and after my father and Mary had long been divorced before I learned what had gone wrong. It turned out it had nothing to do with my stepmother. She was just taking Dad's side after an offense I knew nothing about. "Dad told me about that boyfriend of yours who called him a fascist," my brother told me one time when we were reminiscing about the last year on the ranch. "I don't think Dad ever forgave you."

Blade said it casually; to him, it was just an event from long ago. But I sat in stunned silence. All those years, and I'd never had a clue. Even as I tried to reconstruct the summer and figure out who might have said such a thing, I felt a deep anger. Dad never forgave me for something someone else had said when I wasn't even in the room?

I'd always had a lot of male friends, and several came to visit that summer. We had plenty of housing on the ranch and an open-door hospitality. Many of my classmates set out on a summer of adventure before they settled into graduate school or serious jobs, and outback Wyoming had cachet. My boyfriend drove west with me after graduation and stayed a couple of weeks, but he hadn't been around when the troubles began. Was it Larry from New Hampshire, I wondered? Or the two Phils from Oregon?

I could easily imagine a conversation that might have provoked such an epithet. The Vietnam War had ended two years earlier, and maybe they argued about the pardons President Carter had just granted draft evaders. Or it might have been the legalization of marijuana and other drugs, a debate much in the news. My father was never shy with his opinions. A massive man with an Irish temper, he gave way to belligerent certainty when angry. I could imagine him swelling in size and growing red in the face as he spat out: *Every single draft evader should be tried as a traitor and imprisoned or shot.* Or: *Legalize anything you want so long as not one red cent of taxpayer money goes to help some addicted punk.*

And I can imagine any number of my friends fighting back. We were young and full of ourselves, middle-class kids from small towns and suburbs who had just graduated from an elite institution. Even without such bona fides, it was a moment in history when the generations were at odds. *Dad,* I wanted to scream back through the years, *we've been estranged all this time because someone called you a name?*

I understood why the word *fascist* had wounded him. A veteran of both the post–World War II occupation of Germany and the Korean War, the only thing he hated more than the Communists was the Nazis. But it was a name, hurtled in anger. Wasn't he supposed to be the adult?

———◆———

In my early years, my father and I had been inseparable. I was gutsy and indomitable, and I embraced the hard and dangerous work of the ranch with a passion my brother lacked. I suspect my father saw himself in me. I know he hoped I would become a military commander or corporate CEO, aspirations that slipped out of his own grasp when he lost his hearing as a young tank commander. But as I developed a mind of my own, he saw that I would not fulfill his dreams. He was a warrior who liked rules and rigidity; I liked questions more than answers and leaned toward an artistic life. My mother bridged the gap between us and kept us more amused by each other than annoyed, but in her absence, a chasm had opened that neither one of us could bridge.

Although tensions between my father and me had been building almost from the minute I reached puberty, I was fiercely proud of him. He had grown up hard. His parents split when he was a child, and though his mother moved to town, they never divorced. They loathed each other and used their only child as a conduit through which to keep fighting. His childhood took place in a war zone of angry outbursts and manipulation. Family pictures show an overweight little boy with the look in his eyes of someone who wanted only to please. Sent away to military school in seventh grade, he felt secure for the first time in his life. "At last," he told me, "my world was quiet and consistent. There was no more bickering over my head."

He vowed that he would create a different kind of family of his own. Neighbors still remark on the devotion my parents felt for each other and the way one of them lit up whenever the other came into the room. For my brother and me, he wanted to create a world that was predictable and safe. He was strict but just, and patient as he taught us about the ranch. I can't remember a time when he responded with anger if one of us made an honest mistake. "Here's something to think about next time," he would say if we headed a cow the wrong way or mired a piece of equipment in a bog. Sometimes his temper would explode over some trivial matter—I remember once I used the word *cement* when I should have said *concrete*—and my brother and I sensed an underlying rage that kept us tiptoeing around him even as we also knew that he was trying as hard as he could to be the sort of parent he had wanted for himself.

I recognized early that my parents sought to make an intentional life. When I was in junior high and high school, they joined a study group based on Objectivism, the philosophy of Ayn Rand, and they came back from each meeting on fire with ideas.

My father first encountered Rand when he read *The Fountainhead* in high school. He introduced my mother to the book in college, and they both devoured *Atlas Shrugged*, Rand's next novel, when it appeared during the early years of their marriage. These books celebrated extreme individualism and unfettered laissez faire capitalism and had wide appeal to conservatives. It is easy to understand why Rand's protagonists, who rose above injustice to become utterly self-reliant and were able to interact with the world through pure reason alone, had especial appeal to my father as he tried to define himself in opposition to the erratic and emotionally charged world in which he was raised.

I wrote earlier about the particular appeal that Rand's books, with their moral certainly and clear definition of the meaning of life, hold for the young, but how many devotees start to distance themselves from Rand's absolutism over time. I believe Rand's work holds special resonance for those who grew up in unloving families. This figured in Rand's own biography. Born in Russia before the revolution, she actively disliked her mother, an "extremely social" woman who was "not really interested in ideas." Her father, on the other hand, stood as an avid individualist of "severe integrity" who was "a rarity in Russia: a self-made man." She adored him, but he largely ignored her until she was in her teens.

Some think Rand never stopped trying to earn her father's love. For Rand, love, like money, was something to be earned, and the concept of unconditional love was corrupt. "You love only those who deserve it," she told the journalist Mike Wallace in a 1959 interview. "You love people . . . for their values, their virtues, which they have achieved in their own character."

Wallace asked if that meant that there were people who were "beyond love."

"If a man wants love, he should correct his weaknesses," Rand responded. "He cannot expect the unearned, neither in love, nor in money. . . ."

Wallace protested that very few of us would qualify by Rand's standards, and she agreed.

"Unfortunately . . . yes . . . very few. But [love] is open to everybody, to make themselves worthy of it and that is all that my morality offers them. A way to make themselves worthy of love although that's not the primary motive."

For the unloved, such a philosophy can be liberating. You only need to hold the right views. Since a rational person will love anyone who is virtuous, someone who doesn't love you is morally corrupt. On the other hand, if love is something that must be constantly earned, a single moment of weakness can catapult you back into the abyss. For this reason, one should never reveal authentic feelings. In *Atlas Shrugged,* the heroes resolve that "suffering must not be granted recognition in [a loved one's] presence, that no form of claim between them should ever be motivated by pain and aimed at pity." The book's hero, John Galt, is revered as the man whose face "bore no mark of pain or fear or guilt."

Randian heroes have no messy families to deal with. Their parents are dead; they don't have children together. Nor do they engage in real conversation. Rather, one character lectures another until the junior member comes around, after which they commune in the silence of complete understanding. They never hurt one another because such action would be contrary to their values. Nor do they help each other through grief or other emotional upheaval. They don't need to. As Rand wrote of Howard Roark in *The Fountainhead,* "His emotions are entirely controlled by his logic . . . he does not suffer, because he does not believe in suffering."

Rand created her characters to carry her ideas, and as such, she cut them out of cardboard. As might be said of Rand herself, they lacked what is now called emotional intelligence, the ability to integrate emotions with critical thinking and problem solving, to empathize, and to tolerate, though not necessarily agree with, conflicting ideas.

Although I didn't realize it at the time, my mother provided most of the emotional intelligence that held my family together. She could balance our various personalities and beliefs without condemnation. She knew the ache of rejection. My grandmother had been in her late forties when she gave birth to my mother. Soon after, she suffered sudden and severe osteoporosis. Crippled and in pain for the rest of her life, she blamed my mother: "If it weren't for you, I wouldn't be sick."

But Mom also knew how it felt to be loved. The osteoporosis so debilitated her mother that much of Mom's care fell to her much-older brother and his wife, who adored her, and a family friend called Aunt Zoey, a jolly, roly-poly woman who made Mom feel cherished right down to her bones. Perhaps that's why she could love my father unreservedly. No matter how deeply Dad fell into one of his black moods or how difficult he became, she would say, "I know who he *is.*" And however corrupt a devoted Objectivist finds the *idea* of unconditional love, the reality of it is wonderful to receive. Mom was the only person Dad fully trusted. She could lead him in family negotiations and even help him tolerate the unorthodox views of his daughter and her friends.

Mom had begun distancing herself from Objectivism at the time of her death, and I suspect that, with her support, Dad might have moved away as well. All I can know for certain is that in her absence, he fell back on Rand's philosophy as his one pole of true support. An agnostic who found religion hypocritical and steered clear of other organized communities such as Rotary or Kiwanis, he called *Atlas Shrugged* his Bible and read it at least once a year until he died more than three decades later. Although the book is massive, over 1,100 pages, neither it nor any of Rand's eleven other books of fiction and essays contain a single scene or piece of advice that would have helped my father and me bridge the gulf that had opened between us.

———◄○►———

When my brother first told me what had infuriated my father so many years earlier, my first reaction was anger: He was the head of the family; he was supposed to keep us intact. How could he be so stubborn, so silent, and not just at the time but through all the intervening years?

Still brewing about such things, I had a dream. Its imagery grew out of my father's love of fast cars. He was a serious driver. When I was little, he bought a used Austin Healey; later, he had an old Corvette. When he could finally afford it, he bought a new

Mercedes, a car that could accelerate up to 160 miles an hour, and I loved to ride with him. The fifty-mile road to town was almost always deserted, and it had challenging twists and turns. Dad particularly loved to accelerate into the S curves at the old McPhee place.

In my dream, he was entering the S curves much too fast. I wanted to tell him to slow down, but I knew better than to correct him. I gripped the seat in fear, but he continued to accelerate until I knew I had to protest. I looked toward him, but the driver's seat was empty. I turned to find him standing outside my passenger window on the running board, his eyes wide with fear, holding on for dear life.

----◄○►----

In his book *Crossing the Unknown Sea: Work as a Pilgrimage of Identity*, the English poet David Whyte tells the story of a barely averted shipwreck when he worked as a deck hand as a young man. The captain had fallen asleep, and Whyte woke just as the boat was about to crash into a cliff.

> My first reaction was the easy one. I could see only his neglect—his almost criminal neglect, to our seagoing minds— as captain. . . . But there was rising disquiet beginning to beat in my own chest. I and my fellow crewmember Carlos really knew our boat better than this new captain. . . . We should have persisted in our shared opinion the previous night about our need to put out a second anchor line. . . . We should have woken too. . . . The edge is no place for apportioning blame.

When a leader is in over his head, Whyte says,

> We look and look and finally realize they are not available, they are deep inside some insulation which cannot be engaged and therefore cannot be trusted. Not because they

are bad people but because they are not awake people. . . . At that moment we are orphaned from a familiar parent-child relationship but we are also, if we can rise to the occasion, thankfully emancipated. We are ushered into an adult-adult conversation with our own powers. Something must be done: We must speak out, take the wheel, call the rest of the crew ourselves, or, if all of these avenues are blocked, abandon ship, resign, and go elsewhere.

I don't blame myself for not taking the wheel that summer; both Dad and I were reeling from my mother's death, far more than we realized. But in the years that followed, I was the one who was best positioned to steer us back on course. The very stability and security that my father worked so hard to provide for his children gave me a platform from which to gain greater emotional resilience than he himself enjoyed.

I realize now that I abandoned ship. In Whyte's terms, I resigned and went elsewhere. In some ways, I was emancipated. I entered into an adult conversation with my own powers. I sought professional help. I read, I ran, I meditated, I did everything I could think of in the search for resilience. After many failed attempts and dark nights of the soul, I learned enough to be able to find Hal and forge a good marriage, and to build a strong bond with his daughter.

When I joined forces with Hal and Anneliese, I entered a family culture entirely different than the one in which I was raised. Anneliese was fourteen at the time of our wedding. A few nights afterward, we all shared a hotel room. In the wee hours, she woke crying. She had dreamed she had died and Hal and I wouldn't bury her body. Hal and I crawled into bed with her and held her as we talked long into the night. We were able to reassure her that we would never leave her behind; in fact we talked about all of our fears for the uncharted voyage that lay ahead.

Anneliese and I have been close for nearly a quarter of a century now, and I've often thought about that night and how much harder things might have been if she had not been able to articulate her fears, or if I had been too scared to respond. I'm grateful to her parents for the emotional intelligence they nurtured in her, which gave her the ability to recognize her doubts and the courage to speak openly. And I'm grateful, too, for the maturity I had gained that allowed me to hear.

But if I could act with more emotional intelligence in my new family, I failed in my old one. I have a drawer full of letters I wrote my father over the years and never sent; the transcripts of my interior conversations with him, filled with understanding and conciliation, would fill a book. But each time I was on the verge of reaching out, the old fears paralyzed me. We were kind to each other, and thoughtful in material ways. But neither one of us had the courage to talk authentically.

Several years ago, I had a horse named Badger who came in from winter pasture with a terrible infection in his ears. He was in excruciating pain, so head-shy he was impossible to bridle. I worked with a vet to diagnose and treat him, but even after he had healed completely, he still panicked when I needed to touch his ears.

Badger was a rare and gifted horse, but this affliction made him dangerous. I took him to a workshop with Tom Dorrance, a legendary horse trainer. Tom explained that I was continuing to signal anxiety. The horse figured that if I was worried, he should be too. Tom asked his assistant to demonstrate, and the man walked up to Badger and began rubbing his ears and all around his head. He had approached as if he assumed Badger was healed, and the horse trusted him. Badger not only didn't explode; he leaned into the touch. The workshop showed me how much we can lock each other into predictable behavior. It let Badger and me regain trust in each other. If only my father and I could have learned the same thing.

TRUST

Will Rogers, Where Are You Now?

Jesters do oft prove prophets.
—KING LEAR

Rumor travels faster, but it don't stay put as long as truth.
—WILL ROGERS

In 1992, just months after the Soviet Union had dissolved, Hal and I took part in a sister-city exchange between Salt Lake City and Chernivtsi in western Ukraine, on the edge of the Carpathian Mountains. We arrived in spring to find the countryside green and in flower; the citizens, too, glowed with a sense of rebirth and promise, filled with hope as they shrugged off the Soviet yoke and looked forward to taking their place in the free world. Our hosts, unfailingly kind, offered us hospitality beyond their means.

As we got to know people, we noticed that one theme turned up repeatedly in conversation. How, many of our new friends wondered, could they rebuild the trust necessary for a free society to flourish? The Soviets had cultivated distrust between citizens as a matter of state policy; people who don't trust each other are easy to control. Americans seemed able to cooperate with each other and get things done. How could Ukrainians learn to do the same?

Of all the things that impressed us during that trip, our hosts' concern about distrust has remained the most vivid. Even back then, Hal and I worried about the decline of trust in our own country. We both knew enough about history to recognize that the national unity born of the Great Depression and World War II had been challenged in each succeeding decade, first by the McCarthy years, then the turbulent Sixties, Vietnam, Watergate, and Iran-Contra. But we also knew that, by and large, Americans still saw the good in each other, and our time in Ukraine drove home what a valuable and irreplaceable resource the United States enjoyed in the mutual goodwill of its people.

Twenty years later, things look different. You can hardly turn on the radio or TV without hearing an angry voice, and politics are more divisive now than they have been since the end of the Civil War. So I read with particular interest a new biography of a man credited with helping unite the nation during earlier years of war and economic crisis, *Will Rogers: A Political Life*, by Richard D. White, Jr.

When Rogers died in a plane crash in Alaska in 1935, he was the biggest celebrity in America and arguably the most trusted public figure. Only Shirley Temple beat him at the box office, he was one of the country's most-read columnists, and his radio program reached sixty million people each week, which meant, in a country with a total population of under 130 million, that nearly half the country tuned in. (For contrast, the most listened-to contemporary radio personality, Rush Limbaugh, enjoys an audience of fewer than twenty million out of the current population of almost 310 million.) Rogers's funeral attracted a bigger crowd than any since the death of Abraham Lincoln, and Carl Sandburg, Lincoln's biographer, noted a "curious connection" between the two men: "They were rare figures whom we could call beloved with ease and without embarrassment."

Three-quarters of a century after his death, Rogers has come down to us as the folksy, part-Cherokee cowboy comedian who first garnered attention as a rope twirler in the Ziegfeld Follies and who famously said, "I never met a man I didn't like." We recognize him as the godfather of contemporary political humor, and much of his material sounds fresh today:

"A fool and his money are soon elected."

"Everything is changing. People are taking their comedians seriously and the politicians as a joke."

"The more you observe politics, the more you've got to admit that each party is worse than the other."

"The country has come to feel the same when Congress is in session as when the baby gets hold of a hammer."

"I belong to no organized political party. I am a Democrat."

But Rogers left a legacy larger than his innumerable one-liners. White suggests that the contemporary view of him as a hayseed savant underestimates his genuine political acumen and nuanced understanding of world affairs. "Scholars and biographers rarely recognize his impact upon the political scene," White writes, "discounting his influence because of his humorous routine, bucolic and innocent demeanor, lack of formal education, and Native American heritage. . . . [He was] a savvy commentator, well-read, and the possessor of a keen knowledge of human nature [who had] a streak of genius behind his beguiling grin."

Rogers often started his routine with the words "All I know is what I read in the papers," and in fact he was an assiduous student of the news, reading several papers a day. He also studied people and sincerely wanted to know how they thought. In 1925 during his first lecture tour, a sweep of the country that brought him to seventy-five audiences in ten weeks, he wrote, "All I used to know was just what I read in the papers . . . But NOW all I know is just what I see myself. . . . I am out to see how America is living. . . . I am meeting the regular Bird." Reporters met him at each stop, but before he answered their questions, he plied them with questions of his own, displaying a curiosity that never waned through dozens of treks across the United States and three trips around the world. (He was on his fourth when his plane crashed in 1935.)

Rogers was the first comedian to poke fun at a sitting president. In a 1916 performance in Baltimore that Woodrow Wilson attended, Rogers joked about the Army's inability to catch Pancho Villa and moved into humorous but nevertheless serious concerns about the nation's lack of military preparedness during a time much of the world was at war. He joked that the country had only a single machine gun. "If we go to war we will just about have to go to the trouble of getting another." Wilson was sensitive about this issue—the press had ruthlessly criticized what it saw as his naive pacifism—but Rogers, by refraining from personal attack, found a way to address the issue in a way Wilson could hear and even laugh at. After the performance, the president invited Rogers to his box and later said he would travel a long way "to listen to a man as wise as Will Rogers." He heard Rogers in performance at least four more times.

Rogers befriended every president from Teddy Roosevelt to FDR and served serious, if informal, diplomatic functions for several of them. During the Coolidge administration, for instance, he helped repair embittered relations with Mexico when the U.S. ambassador invited him on a six-day tour of the country with the Mexican president. In 1931, after Japan invaded Manchuria, the Hoover administration sent him to China to assess Japanese intentions, the ability of the Chinese to defend themselves, and how Russia was reacting.

He was even more successful as a diplomat among his own people, as his humorous but wise observations brought a note of balance into even the most divisive affairs. The Scopes trial in 1925, when a young high school science teacher in Tennessee was charged with violating the law by teaching evolution, provides a good example. William Jennings Bryan, three-time Democratic presidential candidate and a Christian fundamentalist, argued for the prosecution; Clarence Darrow, a renowned atheist and the most successful defense lawyer in the country, argued in Scopes's favor. Rogers chided both sides as he reminded folks that the more important issues were religious freedom and basic human decency:

> If I was in either one of those men's places I wouldn't spend the best years of my Chautauqua life trying to prove or disprove my ancestry. With the condition the Democratic Party is in at present, instead of trying to prove he didn't come from a monkey, Bryan had better be spending his time trying to prove he didn't descend from a Democrat.

> And as for Clarence Darrow, he just don't naturally believe in anything. If the sun is shining, Darrow will put you up an argument, assisted by expert testimony, to show you that it is raining and that you are cockeyed and just can't see it. . . . What Darrow should be doing and trying to disprove is that he didn't come from Chicago. . . .

> The Lord put all these millions of people over the earth. They don't all agree on how they got here, and 90 percent don't care. But he was pretty wise when he did see to it that they do agree on one thing (whether Christian, Heathen, or Mohammedan), and that is the better lives you live the better you will finish.

Rogers's politics aligned more easily with Democrats than Republicans—as he put it during the Depression, "Ten men in our country could buy the whole world and ten million can't buy enough to eat"—and he called out corporate greed, corruption, and Republican policies for their roles in creating economic disaster. But he also sought to defuse scapegoating, noting in a radio broadcast that Hoover "just happened to be the man that was left watching the dam when the dam busted and we expected [him] to put the water back."

In 1931, Hoover asked Rogers to join him during a broadcast to raise support for the President's Organization on

Unemployment Relief, the ironically named effort designed to generate private funds for those without jobs. Never before had a president invited a private citizen to be part of a national address; by doing so, Hoover acknowledged that Rogers "was probably the most influential and trusted man in the country."

Hoover stressed that Federal monies not be used for direct relief, a position he knew that Rogers opposed. When Rogers spoke afterward, he cited the seven million people out of work as "our only problem. There is no other one before us at all." He criticized the administration for its stance against Federal relief, but he did not resort to personal attack. As White sees it,

> It would have been easy for Rogers to attack Hoover and Republican policy makers personally and hold their policies up to public ridicule. But Rogers knew he would not have been acting in the best interests of the country. He knew his duty was to lift public morale, to try to explain to a confused people exactly what was happening to their country. . . . Rogers did not have many answers, but he suggested reforms in ways that did not increase the disillusionment the public had developed in their elected government and in the democratic process.

It's an almost-unthinkable moment today: by standing with the president—and by Hoover choosing to stand with Rogers, knowing his stance—they modeled a world in which people could differ in their approach and still acknowledge the other side's sincere concern. Hoover twice more asked Rogers to stand with him in public addresses, and Rogers agreed. Even as he became increasingly disenchanted with the president's policies, he never lost sight of the fact that he wanted him to have a workable relationship with the American public. He wanted Hoover to succeed because he wanted *us* to succeed—not only individual Americans, but the United States as a whole.

Rogers was much more closely aligned with Franklin

Roosevelt's view of the world than with Hoover's, and White suggests that, with the exception of FDR himself, Rogers "probably did more than any other American to convince the public to accept the New Deal." Immediately after the inauguration, Rogers wrote:

America hasn't been as happy in three years as they are today. No money, no banks, no work, no nothing, but they know they got a man in there who is wise to Congress, wise to our bankers, and wise to our so-called big men.

The whole country is with him. Even if what he does is wrong they are with him. Just so he does something. If he burned down the Capitol we would cheer and say, "Well, we at least got a fire started anyhow."

Shortly after FDR took office, Gulf Oil hired Rogers for a series of Sunday-evening broadcasts that soon reached an audience of thirty million, something that led clergy to complain that attendance at Sunday evening services had dropped 50 percent. Several times, Roosevelt scheduled his fireside chats immediately after these broadcasts, and the two men were so aligned in their views that a rumor circulated that Rogers wrote the president's speeches (he did not).

When Rogers disagreed with parts of the New Deal, he made his own positions clear. He opposed welfare, criticizing New Deal programs that let people receive "more for not working than . . . working and more for not raising a hog than raising it." He worried about inflationary policies and supported a balanced budget. As he had been with Hoover, he stood true to his own views, but his overriding concern was with helping to create an environment in which the president—and thereby the people he served—could succeed.

And therein lies the difference between Rogers and so many politicians and political commentators today. Even though he enjoyed a celebrity unparalleled in the world in his time, he always put the success of the American people ahead of his own. He was averse to cheap shots, he largely avoided personal attacks, and he never hit someone when they were down. He would have been disgusted by the ad hominem attacks that are the currency of our day.

According to research compiled by political scientist Keith T. Poole for the Carl Albert Congressional Research and Studies Center at the University of Oklahoma, we are more divided now than we have been at any other time during the last 130 years, but we have recovered from periods of great polarity before. Polarity plummeted during the years Will Rogers spoke to the nation, and it stayed low throughout World War II. Rogers can take only a small amount of credit. Those years saw a sense of shared sacrifice—a phrase not much in use these days, as our current engagements in Iraq and Afghanistan are the only wars from the War of 1812 to the present that have not been supported by an increase in taxes. Also, income disparity, so closely aligned with political division, declined drastically during WWI and again during the Great Depression. Economic inequality today, on the other hand, has continued to rise during the past decade of war and economic crisis.

But if Rogers can't take all the credit, he was a major unifying force during desperate times. "For there to be another Will Rogers today," wrote an earlier biographer, Ben Yagoda, in 1993, "he (or she) would have to combine the separate attributes of Johnny Carson, Roy Rogers, Clark Clifford, Walter Cronkite, Bill Cosby, Bob Hope, Russell Baker, H. Ross Perot, and James Reston." If Yagoda compiled such a list today, he would add other names to the list such as Oprah Winfrey, Jon Stewart, Baxter Black, and an earlier incarnation of Rush Limbaugh when, at least at times, Limbaugh could be funny and not just hyperbolic and mean. "It just can't happen," Yagoda wrote, "which is all the more reason to take a look back to how it once did."

Yagoda is probably right. Even if someone came along with Rogers's blend of political astuteness, gracious humor, generosity, and genuine goodwill, media is fragmented with hundreds of news channels on radio and TV and an incalculable number of voices on the Internet, the majority of them competing to gain attention in the 24/7 news cycle through ever-increasing volume and manipulation of alarm. We become ever-more ghettoized within our own persuasions, hearing only voices that confirm our worst fears, and it is hard to imagine, yet alone act upon, the idea that we might, after all, be in this together.

Jon Meacham—whose article in the *Washington Monthly* almost twenty years ago, "What Will Rogers Could Teach the Age of Limbaugh," is still relevant today—noted that "as polarization increases, so does the audience for polarizers." We must remember that we make up that audience. If we can't summon a new Will Rogers out of the ether, we can at least choose what we listen to.

As I make my own decisions, I think about an aid for critical thinking offered by the Western-history scholar and MacArthur Fellow Patricia Nelson Limerick. Several years ago, only partly in jest, she put forth the 10 percent Jerk Rule. Some small portion of every group, she suggested, consists of jerks. Depending on your own faith in humanity, you can tweak the percentage up or down, but you should question any portrayal that falls hugely outside this range. In the movie *Dances with Wolves*, for instance, all the white guys except for Kevin Costner are jerks, and none of the Native Americans are. The movie might be highly entertaining, but it's not believable.

I call this rule to mind every time I hear a voice screaming on the airwaves. What is he or she asking me to believe about particular individuals or some segment of the American people? If the speaker renders them all as jerks, I turn the dial. Every now and then, I tune into a voice that inspires more confidence. In the meantime, I remember the advice of one of our earliest political savants, Benjamin Franklin, who said in 1776, just before signing the Declaration of Independence: "We must, indeed, all hang together, or most assuredly we shall all hang separately."

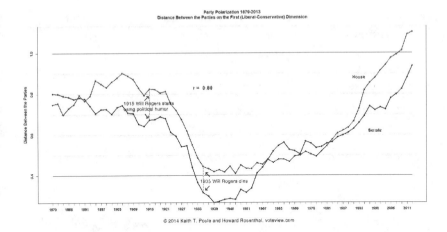

c. 2005 Carl Albert Congressional Research and Studies Center, University of Oklahoma.
Will Rogers data added.

DEFENSIVENESS AND FAITH

Choosing Our Battles

Only those are fit to live who do not fear to die; and none are fit to die who have shrunk from the joy of life and the duty of life. Both life and death are parts of the same great adventure.
—THEODORE ROOSEVELT

Defense is the first act of war.
—BYRON KATIE

A couple of years ago, a few months after my father's death, I attended a retreat with Byron Katie, whose work had been recommended to me by a psychologist friend as being particularly effective when dealing with both anxiety and grief. The retreat took place in a large hotel near the Miami airport, and we began each day with a walking meditation around the lushly landscaped grounds, silently naming whatever our eyes landed upon as simply as possible: leaf, tree, curb, flower, cloud. The idea was to remain grounded entirely in the present moment, something that is harder to do than it sounds.

During the third or fourth morning's walk, an argument inside my head consumed me. Earlier in the week, Katie had suggested something that was, to me, a radical notion: defense is the first act of war. At first I recoiled. I come from a warrior clan, raised to believe that we have not only the right to defend ourselves but also the duty. Defense is the first act of war? This was just the sort of thing that made my father ridicule anything that came under the rubric of the human-potential movement, and I could imagine him stomping out in disgust, finding Katie not only naive but dangerous.

But as the week progressed, I began to understand her words on a different level. "Defense is the first act of war" is not a prescription but rather a statement of fact. It doesn't tell us not to fight; it simply points out that it takes two to do so. It asks the question: is this a situation in which you want to be at war? I began to think about how estranged my father and I had become in the last many years of his life and to imagine how the dynamics might have changed if either one of us had let down our defenses, even for a moment.

So in this argument that was raging in my head, I was defending Byron Katie's ideas to my father—trying, really, to justify the fact that I was listening to her at all—when suddenly I came back to the present moment and realized that an immense jet had just taken off from the airport nearby and was roaring overhead. The sound was so intense that my whole body vibrated, and when I looked up, the plane seemed close enough to touch. Yet I had been unaware of it until that second, so wrapped up in an argument with a dead person that a jumbo jet had been able to tiptoe up behind me, tap me on the shoulder, and say, "boo."

Defense is the first act of war. I gained a great many insights during that weeklong retreat, but this is the one that continues to resonate. At first, I understood it primarily in terms of personal relationships. I began to see that a level of defensiveness played a role almost every time my husband and I had words. If one of us refrained from retort, the argument dissipated as effortlessly as it had arisen. As the idea has matured, however, I grow increasingly aware of how it plays out on a larger stage.

Recently, in an episode of *On Being*, the public radio show about faith, I heard a Wisconsin police captain, Cheri Maples, describe her experience during a domestic violence call. Something had gone wrong during a custody exchange, and she arrived to find a man holding his daughter hostage while his estranged wife quivered with fear. "Ordinarily," Maples told host Krista Tippett,

"I would have said, 'That's it,' slapped the handcuffs on him, taken him to jail." But that night, the officer responded differently. She talked him into releasing the girl, and after she ushered the child and her mother to safety, she returned. She gently asked the man to tell her what had gone wrong, and then she listened with her heart. He started to cry. "I mean, I've got this big gun belt on. I'm about five foot three, right? And this guy's like six foot six. And he's bawling. . . . And that's when I started realizing that what we deal with is misplaced anger, because people are in incredible pain." Three days later, he ran into her when she was off duty, and he picked her up in a bear hug. "You saved my life that night," he told her. "Thank you."

Maples had just returned from a mindfulness retreat with the Buddhist monk Thich Nhat Hanh. Central to his teaching are the Five Mindfulness Trainings, the first of which is the vow not to kill. When Maples first encountered the idea, she resisted it. "I'm a cop. I might be in a position where I have to kill somebody." A senior monk recognized her struggle and talked with her at length. "Who else would we want to carry a gun except somebody who will do it mindfully?" the monk asked. "Of course, you can take these trainings."

In Buddhist teaching, a bodhisattva is an enlightened person who chooses to stay on earth to serve others. The monk explained that there was such a thing as a fierce bodhisattva. Later, after Maples expressed her concern to Thich Nhat Hahn, he spoke for two hours "on the different faces of love and why it's possible to be a bodhisattva and carry a gun."

Halfway across the world, Army Lieutenant Colonel Chris Hughes relied on keen instincts and an ingrained sense of respect rather than mindfulness training when, during the early weeks of the Iraq war, he led a small troop of American soldiers through the streets of Najaf. Under orders to make contact with Grand Ayatollah Ali al-Sistani, something the U.S. Army felt was politically crucial, the soldiers neared a mosque when a huge mob of enraged Iraqis surged into the street from all sides. In "Battle

Lessons," an article in *The New Yorker*, Dan Baum described the event. He was not on the scene that day. Rather, he watched it unfold live on CNN:

> The Iraqis were shrieking, frantic with rage. . . . This is it, I thought. A shot will come from somewhere, the Americans will open fire, and the world will witness the My Lai Massacre of the Iraq war. At that moment, an American officer stepped through the crowd holding his rifle high over his head with the barrel pointed to the ground. Against the backdrop of the seething crowd, it was a striking gesture— almost Biblical. "Take a knee," the officer said, impassive behind surfer sunglasses. The soldiers looked at him as if he were crazy. Then, one after another, swaying in their bulky body armor and gear, they knelt before the boiling crowd and pointed their guns at the ground. The Iraqis fell silent, and their anger subsided. The officer ordered his men to withdraw.

Baum interviewed Hughes two months later. He asked the officer how he had learned to tame a crowd. Was the gesture of pointing his rifle at the ground particular to Iraq? To Islam? "My questions barely made sense to Hughes," Baum wrote. Hughes explained that he had been trained to use a helicopter's rotor wash to disperse a crowd, or to use warning shots, but too often "the next thing you have to do is shoot them in the chest." Making contact with the Ayatollah was both vital and delicate. Hughes immediately understood that the crowd was enraged by what they saw as American disregard of their mosque. The obvious response, in Hughes's assessment, was a gesture of respect.

We can't know what might have happened if Hughes had ordered gunfire. Instead, the event has become a textbook example of the army's attempts to encourage new and more flexible ways of thinking among its officers.

Neither Maples nor Hughes laid down their guns, but they

became more effective protectors as they grew more mindful of their use. Some callings reject violence altogether. The French film *Of Gods and Men* tells the story of seven Trappist monks who were kidnapped from their monastery in the mountains of Algeria and killed by Islamic extremists in 1996. The monks were greatly loved within the Islamic community they had served for many years, but in the mid-1990s, a radical Islamism erupted that terrorized not only foreigners but also Muslims who did not agree with its particular interpretation of the Koran.

After extremists slaughtered a group of Croatian workers, the Algerian army offered the monastery protection, and the French government ordered the monks to leave for their own safety. They refused both armed guard and refuge, though they knew their lives were at stake. As the film explores the reasons that each monk chooses to stay, it presents an extraordinary portrait of courage and faith.

At first, several monastics want to leave. "I became a monk to serve, not to have my throat slit," says Father Christophe. Later, as he walks with the prior, Dom Christian, he says, "Dying for my faith shouldn't keep me up nights. Dying here and now: does it serve a purpose?"

"Staying here is as mad as being a monk," the prior agrees. "Remember, you already gave your life when you agreed to follow Christ."

"I pray," Christophe says. "I hear nothing. I don't get it. Why be martyrs? To prove we're the best?"

"No," Dom Christian says, "out of love and fidelity. Our mission here is to be brothers to all."

As conditions worsen, the community threatened not only by the extremists but also by the corrupt Algerian army, the monks unite around their commitment to stay. They cannot abandon their community, nor can they abandon their vows of nonviolence. In what was to be one of their last dinners at the monastery, Dom Christian remembers Christmas Eve when the extremists broke through the door and demanded that the doctor, Brother

Luc, come away with them to treat their injured fighters. The monks refused: Brother Luc would treat anyone who came to the clinic, but he would not abandon the villagers who depended on his care. The extremists left empty-handed, but the monks knew they would be back.

"All we had left to do was live," Dom Christian recalls. "The first thing we did was celebrate the mass of the Virgin and Child. It was what we had to do. It was what we did. Afterward we found salvation in our daily tasks. We had to resist the violence."

Of Gods and Men captures a distinction between doctrine—codified belief—and a deeper faith in what, at the most profound level, one stands for. The former nun Jan Phillips recently articulated this difference in a post for the *On Being* blog. She speaks in Catholic terms, but the quality of the realization she refers to is equally appropriate to Maples's awakening through Buddhist teaching and Hughes's insight as a military leader.

Phillips had been a young postulant in her first theology class when a Jesuit priest asked the students what they believed about God. One by one, the young women quoted lines from the catechism:

"God made me to show His goodness and to share His everlasting life with me in heaven."

"In God there are three divine persons, really distinct, and equal in all things—the Father, the Son, and the Holy Ghost."

"God can do all things, and nothing is hard or impossible to Him."

With each contribution, the priest grew more impatient until finally he burst out, "You should be ashamed for having nothing more than catechism answers to this question. Are you just a bunch of parrots, repeating everything you've been taught?"

His words devastated Phillips. "He asked for our ideas about God and yet, when we said them, it felt like he took a sledge hammer and smashed our beliefs into a thousand pieces." But what he said next planted the seed that allowed Phillips to take responsibility for the maturation of her calling.

"If you are to be a nun worth your salt," the priest continued, "you have to arrive at a faith that is deeper than your learning, one that is rooted in your ultimate concerns and rises up from the nature of who you are.

"What you believe, that is religion," he said. "Who you are, what you live for—that is faith."

The patrol leader, the police captain, the monks: all had moved beyond rote belief into an understanding, on the deepest level, of what they lived for. As Lieutenant Colonel Hughes searched for the gesture of respect that would diffuse the crowd, as police captain Maples tried to not only prevent an act of domestic violence but relieve the anger that had provoked it, as the Trappists lived and died for their commitment to the community they served, they all acted from an understanding of what mattered to them most. The soldier and the policewoman served their missions with weapons at their call; the monks chose not to. In the spaciousness of mindfulness, they all had more options than were apparent at first glance.

Each of us carries a gun. For most of us, it is not made of metal but rather of emotion, forged from the many ways we have to shoot down the spirit of those we love as we defend against our own fear, frustration, and vulnerability. We choose whether or not to go to war a dozen times a day. Sometimes we must choose to enter battle. But knowing we have a choice can change the world.

The word *glad* derives from Old English *glæd*, meaning bright, shining or joyous. Merriam Webster tells us that in contemporary usage glad refers to a state, something temporary or changeable: "experiencing pleasure, joy or delight: made happy." Although Western science tends to view emotions as independent and transitory, Buddhist tradition suggests that meditation and spiritual practice can train the mind toward positive emotions such as gladness and compassion and away from destructive emotions such as rage and envy.

GLADNESS

The Mysterious Lightness of Being

Gladly accept the gifts of the present hour.
—Horace

We must have / the stubbornness to accept our gladness in the ruthless / furnace of this world.
—Jack Gilbert

I woke up the other morning with a single word on my mind: *glad*. A word in isolation always sounds strange and improbable. *Glad*: just the thought of it made me smile. Yet, to say it to myself, to "see" it spelled out in my mind: how could that short, stumpy word capture the lightness of spirit I woke to?

Moods blow in like weather and move out as another "front" displaces them. After the long spate of grumpiness I wrote about a couple of weeks ago, I was relieved to wake in a buoyant mood, with a humor that stayed with me through the day, even in the face of improbable circumstance. We've been having an unseasonably rainy spring here in Salt Lake City, as dark and gloomy as winter on the Oregon coast, and this was yet another cold, wet day. But when the heart gladdens, storms don't matter. After a cup of coffee, I grabbed my raincoat, whistled to Abby, the dog, and headed out.

On a bad day, everything seems to conspire to make things worse. I often forget that on a good day, events equally conspire for delight. We live in a historic section of Salt Lake, and Abby and I often pass through the old City Cemetery on our way to the foothills. A graveyard on a stormy day may not strike you as a particularly cheerful environment, but when we came to a plot I hadn't noticed before where the Glad family lay next to the Gay family, I laughed out loud. I found myself thinking of other names that make me happy, like the staff at the medical clinic I used for years, Doctors Joy, Gay, and Paisley, and my childhood dentist, the amazingly painless Dr. Devine. I've always loved names that play with vocation: my sixth-grade bandleader, Mr. Sharpe, and the art teacher in junior high, Mrs. Musick. In my present mood, even in the midst of a steady drizzle, these whimsical musings rose like bubbles in champagne.

In high school, I was chosen to be a Rotary exchange student to New Zealand. In preparation, my mother and I attended an orientation session in Denver where we met students from all over the world as well as Americans who had just returned from their year abroad. I still remember a young man from Germany, blond and of medium build, attractive but not unusually so. What distinguished him was the sense he radiated of complete and authentic joy, a gladness of heart that made each one of us feel better just to be in the room with him. I was smitten, as was my mother and, as far as I could tell, everyone else at the gathering.

Perhaps I can be forgiven for wanting to adopt his affect. I was sixteen at the time, about to spend a year seven thousand miles from everyone I'd ever known. For all the advice we received that day on local protocol and etiquette, ways to smooth over difficulties with host families, and what sort of gifts to pack, it struck me that all I really needed to get along was an inner glow. So for the next few days, I smiled and beamed, or tried to. I'm sure the effect was as convincing as a grin plastered on a mannequin. What had seemed so effortless for the German student was exhausting for me. His gladness of heart emanated from his very essence, and I reverted inevitably to my own inheritance, a tangled Irish temperament that was not without its charms: a certain heartiness coupled with an affinity for laughter, music, and storytelling, tempered nonetheless by spates of anxiety and a tendency to brood.

The word *glad* derives from Old English *glæd*, meaning "bright, shining, or joyous," and from Old Norse *glaðr*, meaning "smooth or bright." Merriam Webster tells us that in contemporary usage, *glad* refers to a state, something temporary or changeable: "experiencing pleasure, joy, or delight: made happy." The archaic sense of the word, though, carries an inflection of something innate: "having a cheerful or happy disposition by nature." What my mother and I sensed in the young German was a native lightness of spirit. Maybe deep down he was just as moody as the rest of us acne-prone, hormonally challenged teens, but his joy seemed so deeply rooted and authentic that it remains vivid after all these years.

In fact, I didn't encounter a similar effervescence until 2003, when I attended a conference in Boston led by the fourteenth Dalai Lama. His gladness of heart is one of the most consistently reported details about him, something that beamed out to the furthest corners of the 1,200-seat auditorium where I spent two days in his presence during a symposium titled "Investigating the Mind: Exchanges between Buddhism & Biobehavioral Science."

For over twenty years now, the Dalai Lama has convened meetings between Buddhist scholars and leading cognitive scientists to explore what the two traditions can teach each other. The meeting I attended was the first one open to the public. The different ways in which the two disciplines view emotion is a topic woven through many of the gatherings. In part because of collaborations and research inspired by these meetings, meditation has become increasingly integrated into Western psychology and medical practice, proving effective in relieving depression, anxiety, stress, pain, and anger.

Many of the participants knew each other and had worked together before, and they shared a general sense of ease and good humor, but the two groups differed noticeably in their affect. All the participants were focused, knowledgeable, and extremely articulate, and the scientists appeared genial. But only the Buddhists emanated a sense of joy.

Western thought tends to view emotions as outside conscious control, "exactly that part of human mental life most apt to degrade or 'swamp' normal systems of cognitive reasoning and control." Buddhist tradition, on the other hand, suggests that meditation and spiritual practice can train the mind toward positive emotions such as gladness and compassion and away from destructive emotions such as worry, rage, and envy. Western science tends to view emotions as related to specific conditions and of short duration, while the Buddhist scholars speak of emotional states as enduring, a distinction that caused UC Berkeley psychology professor Dacher Keltner to ask at one point, "What is it like to reside in well-being?" The wistfulness in his tone reminded me of my own yearning, at the age of sixteen, to experience the gladness I saw in another.

However naive my thought so many years ago that I could simply assume such a state, the urge behind my yearning—and the scientist's—has the potential to be profound. The same question transformed Ashoka the Great, an emperor in the third century BC who expanded the Mauryan Empire across what is now India, Pakistan, Afghanistan, Nepal, Bangladesh, and part of Iran. In his early years, Ashoka was notoriously cruel and ambitious, but after he conquered the kingdom of Kalinga on the northeast corner of India, killing over one hundred thousand people, he suffered remorse. As Sharon Salzberg tells the story in *Lovingkindness: The Revolutionary Art of Happiness,*

> One day, after a particularly terrible battle . . . he walked on the battlefield amid the appalling spectacle of corpses of men and animals strewn everywhere, already rotting in the sun and being devoured by carrion-eating birds. Ashoka was aghast at the carnage he had caused.

Just then a Buddhist monk came walking across the battlefield. The monk did not say a word, but his being was radiant with peace and happiness. Seeing that monk, Ashoka thought, "Why is it that I, having everything in the world, feel so miserable? Whereas this monk has nothing in the world apart from the robes he wears and the bowl he carries, yet he looks so serene and happy in this terrible place."

Although Ashoka had been nominally a Buddhist before, he now devoted himself to serious practice. He embraced non-violence, outlawed torture and capital punishment, instituted a policy of broad religious tolerance, and devoted his reign to fairness and accessibility, earning himself an enduring reputation for justice and good governance in what was at the time one of the world's largest, wealthiest, and most ethnically diverse empires.

The recognition that equanimity and even happiness could exist in the midst of chaos planted the seeds of Ashoka's transformation. He did not, of course, just assume these traits but rather developed them through extended study and meditation and a devoted practice of compassion, the monastic traditions that still serve the Dalai Lama and the other monks at the conference.

Westerners tend to think of joy as a momentary experience; more accurately, it is the experience of the moment, a time free of regrets about the past or worries about the future. To us, gladness often seems beyond conscious control, something that arises when nothing else is in the way. Our ability to reprise the past and plan for the future is fundamental to our sense of responsibility; to give up such vigilance, even for a moment, can feel dangerous. Yet the Dalai Lama, as head of a nation in exile, and the Buddhist scholars, as serious practitioners, teachers, and prolific writers, function effectively in a world as complicated and urgent as that of their Western colleagues. They neither forget the past nor ignore the future, but they have trained themselves to attend to these concerns without the obscuring and afflictive distractions of negative emotions. In the space this creates, joy has room to arise.

Most of us will never make the commitment to extended practice that underlies the Dalia Lama's joyful presence or made possible Ashoka's transformation. But studies show that even a few minutes of mindfulness practice a day can diminish the hold of destructive emotions and promote more rational and compassionate response.

That day in the cemetery felt like a gift that fell out of the sky, bestowed by rare and unknowable factors—a surge of beneficent hormones, perhaps, coupled with a good night's sleep. Buddhist practice suggests that gladness is available in every moment, a thought that not only leads me to the meditation cushion, but also makes me glad to go there.

PUNCTUALITY

The Gift of Time

As if you could kill time without injuring eternity.
—HENRY DAVID THOREAU

To live is so startling it leaves little time for anything else.
—EMILY DICKINSON

When I was a kid, I often spent the afternoons playing black-jack with my grandfather. By this time, he was so beat up from horse wrecks and a series of small strokes that he could no longer work outside. A rancher of the old school, he was gruff and not prone to frivolity. He disliked cats and kids, or said he did, but if the big Siamese or I failed to turn up for our afternoon game, he'd scowl around the house: "Where's that damn kid?" he'd ask my mother. "Where's that cat?"

On the afternoons I joined him, he dealt out the cards on his red leather ottoman while the cat slept in his lap. Not one for small talk, he seldom responded to my chatter. One afternoon, though, when I complained about how long it took Christmas to arrive, he looked up from his cards. "Every year, you get older," he told me, "time goes faster. Seems to me like Christmas rolls around every couple of weeks."

I respected my grandfather and seldom questioned anything he said, but in this case I remember thinking: He's just an old man. He doesn't know a thing. Now, of course, I realize that he nailed it. Our sense of time changes radically as we age, but even early on, we attend it with a measure of fear. I was afraid of time passing too slowly; my grandfather, even as he struggled to fill the hours, worried about how little time he had left. During the years of raising a family and building a career, many of us feel that we will never catch up. "Oh dear! Oh dear! I shall be too late!" the White Rabbit fretted as he scurried past Alice in his first appearance 150 years ago, and he would only need to replace his pocket watch with a smartphone to be entirely up-to-date with the contemporary panic that leaves us feeling like we need to pick up the pace or someone, somewhere, will cut off our heads.

Time pressure is nothing new. From the moment humans moved out of the temporal zones into winter country, the need to gather sufficient food and fuel before the first storm started a race against time that was literally a matter of life and death. We have complained about time for at least as long as we have been able to measure it with any accuracy. "The gods confound the man who first found out how to distinguish hours!" cursed the Roman playwright Titus Maccius Plautus two hundred years before the birth of Christ. "Confound him, too, who in this place set up a sundial to cut and hack my days so wretchedly into small portions!"

But however old our battle with time, the contemporary world really is picking up speed. As James Gleick notes in *Faster: The Acceleration of Just About Everything*, a fascinating romp through technology, psychology, philosophy, and physics, when we can do something faster, we almost always choose to. Presidential sound bites, for instance, decreased from over forty seconds in 1968 to less than ten in 1988, and they now tweet out in fewer than 140 characters. "We humans have chosen speed and we thrive on it—more than we generally admit," Gleick notes. "Our ability to work fast and play fast gives us power. It thrills us. If we have learned the name of just one hormone, it is adrenaline. No wonder we call sudden exhilaration a *rush*."

Time has its ironies. We love the "rush" of time, but we don't love to rush. The more time-saving devices we enlist, the less time we seem to have. We only feel entirely at ease with time when we are so absorbed that we lose track of it entirely. And while Gleick is right that we choose to go fast, the faster we go, the less able we are to make good choices.

This last point ties into what might be called the ethics of time. In 1973, in what came to be known as the Good Samaritan experiment, psychologists John Darley and Daniel Batson set out to better understand compassion. They asked what mix of personality, cultural conditioning, and momentary circumstance would lead a person to help a stranger in distress.

They decided to design an experiment around a group of people preselected to value compassion and conversant with the Biblical parable of the Good Samaritan, where a band of thieves beats up a man on the road from Jerusalem to Jericho and leaves him for dead. A priest comes along but ignores the wounded man. Then a Levite passes by, but he, too, looks the other way. Finally, a Samaritan stops, comforts the man and dresses his wounds, secures him refuge in an inn, and pays the innkeeper to nurse him back to health.

In order to find people predisposed to the Samaritan view, Darley and Batson recruited students from the Princeton Theological Seminary and gave them basic personality tests including the Religious Life Inventory. Then, ostensibly for further assessment, they asked each student to give a short public talk. They assigned half the students a sermon on the Good Samaritan and the other half a more neutral topic, job prospects for clergy.

Once the students had prepared their talks, they were sent to present them before a waiting audience. The psychologists told a third of the students that they were late. A third were informed that they were right on time, but shouldn't tarry. The rest were told to head over, but that things were running behind schedule and they didn't need to hurry.

On the way, each student had to pass through an alley where a poorly dressed man slumped in a doorway, coughing and groaning as if having a medical emergency. If the student stopped, the distressed man said that he had a respiratory condition but he had taken medication that would soon kick in. Though obviously still distressed, he instructed the student to go on. If the student insisted on helping, the man asked to be taken into a nearby building.

This scenario, of course, was the real test, and the results surprised the researchers. They found no correlation between personality type and whether or not a student stopped, nor did it matter if the student had been primed to be thinking about the Good Samaritan. The only variable that proved statistically significant to the decision to stop was whether or not the student was in a hurry. Once a student offered help, the other variables correlated to his or her degree of persistence in providing it, but in general, only those students who thought they had time to spare reached out in the first place. "Ethics becomes a luxury," Darley and Batson concluded, "as the speed of our daily lives increases."

I read about this experiment in a book titled *The Sabbath World: Glimpses of a Different Order of Time*, by Judith Shulevitz, who notes:

> The psychologists weren't quick to judge these seminarians. Even though all the students who hadn't stopped admitted that they'd seen the man, Darley and Batson pointed out, several said that they hadn't realized that he needed help until after they'd passed him. Time pressure had narrowed their "cognitive map"; as they raced by they had seen without seeing.

Meanwhile, the students who had realized that the man required assistance but who had withheld it from him showed up for their talks looking "aroused and anxious." Darley and Batson speculated that their subjects felt torn between their duty to help the man and their desire to live up to the expectations of the psychologists whom they had committed to help. "This is often true of people in a hurry," Darley and Batson wrote. "They hurry because somebody depends on their being somewhere. Conflict, rather than callousness, can explain their failure to stop."

The sense of being starved for time is real and pervasive, and like caloric malnutrition, it clouds the mind. Finding a workable compromise among competing responsibilities is always a delicate calculus, and I suspect many of us recognize moments in our own lives when we have been so in thrall to an immediate responsibility that we have compromised our deepest values. In our push to be "on time," we can lose sight of where we are heading. We hunger for the time to be true to ourselves.

Time is money, Benjamin Franklin so famously said, but we know, too, that time is a gift. As MacArthur Fellow Lewis Hyde pointed out in his landmark book *The Gift: Creativity and the Artist in the Modern World,* we live within two economies, a market economy and a gift economy. Within the market economy, we earn money, we buy things, and if we stockpile them, we can build an estate. A gift, on the other hand, is something that is bestowed on us. It comes to us through no effort on our part but brings with it a reciprocal responsibility. It only has value if we give it away.

The Good Samaritan is a story from the gift economy. When we stop to help someone change a flat tire, we don't expect payment. In fact, we take offense if the person we aided presses payment upon us. The assumption, instead, is that he or she will help someone else down the road. In other words, we give the gift of time, and we expect that gift to keep moving.

"A decade ago," writes Judith Shulevitz in the introduction to *The Sabbath World,* "I began to take a passionate interest in the Sabbath, the ancient day of rest. . . . I was ravenous for something, though I didn't know what." She had grown up in a Jewish home where a great deal of tension attended the Sabbath—her mother observed it and her father did not—and she had left it behind as a relic of childhood. Now she realized that "at some point, we all look for a Sabbath, whether or not that's what we call it."

The Sabbath derives from the Fourth Commandment: "Remember the Sabbath day, to keep it holy. Six days shalt thou labour, and do all thy work: But the seventh day is the Sabbath of the Lord thy God: in it thou shalt not do any work, thou, nor thy son, nor thy daughter, thy manservant, nor thy maidservant, nor thy cattle, nor thy stranger that is within thy gates." The Sabbath, in other words, is the day we give back not only to God but also to others, a time to turn from things we buy and sell to things we give away.

Shulevitz finds meaning as she tries to abide by Jewish Orthodox observance, but she stresses that "organized religion need not be involved." To imagine what the Sabbath might mean to us, no matter what our religious views, she asks what it meant to God—why did he stop?—and draws on the eighteenth-century view of Rabbi Elijah of Vilna:

> God stopped to show us that what we create becomes meaningful only once we stop creating it and start remembering why it was worth creating in the first place. Or—if this is the thought to which our critical impulses lead us— why it wasn't worth creating, why it isn't up to snuff and should be created anew. After all, God, contemplating his first Creation, decided to destroy it in a flood.
>
> We could let the world wind us up and set us to working, like dolls that go until they fall over because they have no way of stopping. But that would make us less than human. We have to remember to stop because we have to stop to remember.

I did not grow up in a religious home; we did not keep the Sabbath on the ranch, and in fact we often took on extra work so that the hired men could have Sundays off. Nor, as an adult, do I set a day apart in either the religious or secular sense. Instead, like so many people I know, I habitually use the weekend to catch up, often finishing entities for this journal, no matter the fact that "Weekends Off" is in its title. I have responsibilities, after all, to this and so many other assignments. But like Judith Shulevitz, I am increasingly ravenous for the ritual or observance that provides space for larger concerns.

As the palliative care professional Bronnie Ware recently noted, two of the most common regrets of people on their deathbeds are that they worked too much and didn't give enough time to their families and friends. We often complain that we don't have enough time, but in fact we have all the time in the world, all the time that exists, and it only exists right now. We can bequeath the fruits of the market economy to our loved ones and leave them well-off financially, but from the moment we take our last breaths, we can't give them another minute of our time.

GRATITUDE

Thanksgiving: A Christmas Story

As we express our gratitude, we must never forget that the highest appreciation is not to utter words, but to live by them.
—JOHN F. KENNEDY

I would maintain that thanks are the highest form of thought; and that gratitude is happiness doubled by wonder.
—G. K. CHESTERTON

On December 17, 1933, a small ad appeared in the Canton, Ohio, newspaper offering hope in the middle of the Great Depression. A man who called himself B. Virdot wanted "to help from fifty to seventy-five families so they will be able to spend a merry and joyful Christmas." He asked those in trouble to write to him, care of general delivery, and describe their "true circumstances." He assured them that no one would ever know their identity and that they, in turn, would never know his.

It's hard to overstate the despair in Canton in 1933. Unemployment ran at nearly 50 percent, twice the national average, and both rich and poor had seen their life savings evaporate when the banks failed. Served one eviction notice after another, many families lacked even the seven cents it took to buy a loaf of bread. Children died of "inanition," the clinical term for starving to death; orphanages were filled to overflowing as desperate parents sought refuge for children they could no longer feed.

In the midst of this long, dark night, B. Virdot's offer came as a single point of light. He revealed almost nothing about himself except that he had $750 to spread around and that his offer grew out his own "remembrance of much darker days." The letters he invited came in such number and expressed such need that in the end he made 150 gifts of $5 apiece, equivalent to about $100 today. It wasn't enough to change anyone's circumstances permanently, but the mere fact that someone cared restored hope to not only the lucky recipients but to an entire community.

So begins the story of a generous act, born out of one man's sense of thanksgiving. Canton's secret Santa was not, as people had speculated, from one of the city's established families. Rather, he was Sam Stone, a men's clothier who had been born Sam Finkelstein, an Orthodox Jew, in Romania. He had spoken only Yiddish as a child and had walked across Europe in exile, one of the thousands of *Fusgeyers*, or "foot walkers," expelled from their homeland and rejected by one European country after another. He had been fifteen years old when his family arrived in America in 1902, and his Christmas gift twenty-nine years later gave him a way to say thank you to the only country that would take him in.

For nearly eight decades, B. Virdot's identity remained a mystery. Now it has been revealed in a book titled *A Secret Gift: How One Man's Kindness—and a Trove of Letters—Revealed the Hidden History of the Great Depression,* by Ted Gup. A best-selling author and investigative reporter whose previous books focused on the CIA and issues of national security, Gup did not expect, when his eighty-year-old mother gave him a suitcase filled with family papers, to be launched on an investigation that would take him sixteen months, require over five hundred interviews, and reveal the hidden history not only of the Great Depression but also of his family.

The suitcase contained a thick packet of letters and 150 canceled checks. Early on, Gup figured out that B. Virdot was his grandfather, who had chosen his pseudonym to honor his daughters, Barbara, Virginia (Gup's mother), and Dorothy. It took Gup longer to realize that the beloved patriarch he and everyone else knew as Sam Stone—"a good and loving father and husband, a veteran, a solid provider . . . a highly respected member of the community, a man of deep patriotic feeling"— had a secret past. No one but his wife knew he had not been born in the United States; Barbara could never remember the word *Romania* even being spoken in their home.

The people who responded to B. Virdot's offer came from all walks of life. Before the Great Depression, George Monnot's Ford dealership counted an inventory of one thousand cars and occupied a full city block; he owned a thirty-five-foot yacht and a lakeside summer home, and he contributed generously to his community. By the time he wrote B. Virdot, his family lived in an alley apartment, and he was penniless. "Have a family of six," he wrote, "and struggle is the word for me now. . . ." He used B. Virdot's gift to buy shoes for his girls and "other little necessities."

Thirty-nine-year-old Edith May had been born in Jamaica and had moved to the United States eight years earlier to marry James May, the grandson of former slaves, whom she had met through a pen-pal correspondence. "Four years ago we were getting 135 dollars for milk," she wrote. "Now Saturday we got 12. . . . Imagine 5 of us for a month." She wanted to buy shoes for her oldest son for school and clothes for the family. "I know what it is to be hungry & cold. We suffered so last winter & this one is worst." Her husband didn't know she was writing; it would have wounded his pride. She didn't even have a stamp, "but I am going to beg the mailman to post this for me."

Her daughter, Felice May, remembers the hardship of those years when the odor of the skunks her father trapped for their pelts was the "smell of money." But she also remembers an enchanted day just before Christmas in 1933. She was to turn four on December 23, a day, like Christmas, that usually passed without remark. But that day, her family went into town and took her to the five-and-dime. They showed Felice the shelves of toys and asked her to choose between a doll and a horse she could pull with a string. She chose the horse, and it not only became her most prized possession, it launched a lifelong passion. She grew up to raise Welsh ponies; today, at the age of eighty, she still has a herd of fifteen.

The letters reveal a landscape of hardship that we can hardly imagine now. People needed money for food, for coal, for medicine, to pay the undertaker for burying a child, to buy shoes so their children could go to school, or even to bring their children home from the orphanage for a week's visit at Christmas. As Gup writes, "Reading the letters put things in perspective. They reminded me of the difference between discomfort and misery, between the complaints of consumers forced to rein in their spending and the keening of parents whose children went hungry night after night."

Gup also came to understand the genius of the privacy his grandfather promised the letter writers. "If I thought this would be printed in the papers I would rather die of hunger first," wrote one applicant. "I haven't been a beggar all ways." Another thanked B. Virdot simply for the chance to share his circumstances:

> Whether the writer shares in your kind offer or not, you have made me feel good, and if more of the unfortunate Has Beens would write you & empty out their painful burdens to one that has taken such a unique plan of encouragement, the road would be easier to travel & this world a better place to live in.

Gup's research led him to the source of his grandfather's empathy. The Great Depression threw people into a harsh destitution from which there seemed no escape, and it was a world Sam Finkelstein had experienced firsthand, as described in the *Jewish Criterion* in 1900:

> The Romanian Jews possess, for the greater part, nothing but the few rags upon their bodies. The poorest among

them . . . drag themselves upon their wounded feet from one frontier to another. . . . They had to carry with them nothing else but the wanderer's staff and the unendurable burden of their memories and their fears . . . and when they ask in despair, "Where are we to go, what is to become of us?" the only reply they receive is a shrug of the shoulder and a turn of the hand, mercilessly pointing to the distance further on into the unknown, unto the blue away, far away.

Sam Stone kept the secret of his birth from even his own family, a dishonesty that disturbed Gup when he uncovered it. Finally, though, he came to understand that his grandfather reinvented himself as an act of both gratitude and self-affirmation. "'Mr. B. Virdot' was the gift he gave others, but it was also the gift he gave himself. It was the right to a second chance, to be reborn as someone else."

Today, as we remain mired in the harshest economic conditions since the Great Depression, the story of B. Virdot has especial resonance. Once again, Canton is suffering more than the rest of the country. Recently, with unemployment nearing 15 percent, over eight hundred people responded to the listing of a janitor's job. But generosity begets generosity, and the town woke up on Thanksgiving day to read in the Canton *Repository*, the newspaper in which B. Virdot made his initial offer, that three anonymous businessmen—inspired by B. Virdot's example so many years ago—had pledged to sweeten the holidays for 150 local families and individuals with gifts of $100 apiece.

Postscript (and notice of full disclosure): I have a personal connection to this story. My husband, Hal Cannon, plays in the musical group Red Rock Rondo. Almost two years ago, its leader, Phillip Bimstein, read Ted Gup's *New York Times* Op-Ed piece, "Hard Times, a Helping Hand," in which he described finding the letters.

The story so moved Bimstein that he immediately wrote Gup and asked if he could compose songs based upon the stories. A correspondence ensued, and Gup granted permission.

In October, Bimstein and Gup met for the first time when Gup came to the Utah Humanities Book Festival. Gup discussed *A Secret Gift* and read from the letters, his words interspersed with songs performed by Red Rock Rondo. The combination met with a prolonged standing ovation, and when the audience once again grew quiet, Gup mentioned that Red Rock Rondo would join him in Canton, Ohio, in a few days for the book launch in Canton's historic Palace Theater, where descendants of forty of the families would gather and several would read the original letters out loud.

A few days later, Phillip received a cashier's check, drawn on a Salt Lake City bank, to help with travel expenses for the group. The only clue to the source of the funds was a typewritten note: "Say hello to my grandson. (Signed) B. Virdot." Phillip thought the contribution had come from Ted Gup, but he learned it had not. Someone in the audience that day had taken on the cloak of anonymous generosity.

I went along with the group to Canton, and one of the highlights of the trip was the chance to meet Helen Palm, the only one of the original letter writers who lived long enough to learn the true identity of her benefactor. She had been fourteen years old when she wrote B. Virdot:

Dear Sir, I am writing this because I need clothing. And sometimes we run out of food. My father does not want to ask for charity. But us children would like to have some clothing for Christmas.

Seventy-seven years later, on the stage of the Palace Theater, Helen Palm heard her words sung back to her. It was a powerful moment in an evening that reminded all of us what we have to be thankful for, and how a single act of gratitude can reverberate for generations.

FORGIVENESS

The Heroic Choice

Forgiveness is the key to action and freedom.
—HANNAH ARENDT

It is easier to forgive an enemy than to forgive a friend.
—WILLIAM BLAKE

How does someone survive a childhood marked by cruelty and deprivation and go on to lead a confident, generous, and successful life? In the case of Mari Sandoz, the Nebraska author of twenty-six novels, biographies, and historical works on the American West, the answer lies in a combination of stubbornness, passion, and something that from a distance looks a lot like forgiveness, though she almost certainly would never have used that word to define her relationship with her abusive father.

Mari was the first of six children born to Jules Sandoz and his fourth wife, Mary Fehr. Old Jules, as everyone called him, had dropped out of medical school in Switzerland in the 1880s to try his fortune pioneering in Nebraska. He abandoned his first wife; his next two divorced him for abuse and neglect. They left because they could: they had no children, and at least one of them had independent means. Mari's mother, however, had handed over the funds she brought from Switzerland when she said her wedding vows. In the grinding poverty of the frontier, her first pregnancy sealed her fate. She stayed with her husband until he died in 1928.

"I learn her to obey me if I got to kill her!" he raged once after he beat her bloody with a wire whip. Her transgression? A bull that Jules had ordered her to hold had overpowered her.

He beat Mari, too, even before she could walk. In *Old Jules*, the biography of her father she published seven years after his death, Mari wrote about the experience, referring to herself in the third person as Marie:

> When the little Marie was three months old and ill with summer complaint, her cries awakened Jules. Towering dark and bearded in the lamplight, he whipped the child until she lay blue and trembling as a terrorized small animal. When Mary dared she snatched the baby from him and carried her into the night and did not return until the bright day.

Old Jules was a study in contradictions. A brilliant horticulturalist and visionary community builder, he worked passionately to tame the harsh Nebraska frontier through settlement and husbandry. He invited new settlers into his home for weeks, even months, while he helped them locate homesteads, taking little or no fee for his services. He opened his house for community gatherings and spent a rare inheritance on a phonograph and three hundred records, providing music and entertainment to a starved community. This, even though he was deeply in debt and his children needed shoes. He stood up for the settlers against the large cattlemen when no one else would. Yet he was quick to pick a fight and often feuded with the very neighbors he had previously helped to survive. People depended on him, and they also feared him. He was madman and genius, prophet, protector, and terror in one.

He traveled tirelessly around the Sandhills, but at home he was downright lazy. Once, when his wife asked for help, he threw her up against the wall: "You want me, an educated man, to work like a hired tramp!" That, however, was exactly what he expected of his family, and he demanded they build fence, take care of the stock, and tend his extensive crops and orchards. His wife returned to the fields within days of giving birth to their sixth child. When a blizzard scattered the cattle, Mari and her next younger brother set out alone to dig them out, a task that took them from sunrise to dark and left Mari snow-blind. She suffered terribly for a week and never regained the sight in her left eye.

Perhaps the cruelest deprivation for Mari, however, was intellectual. Old Jules refused to send his children to the "inferior" prairie schools, nor would he take time to educate them himself. Only when a truant officer turned up at the door did Old Jules relent. At that point, the children spoke no English. Jules spoke several languages fluently but used only Swiss German at home. Nine-year-old Mari had to struggle with a new language even as she began to read and write.

Still, she immediately recognized her life's passion. As her biographer Helen Winter Stauffer phrased it, "she never got over the thrill of discovering that those little black marks always meant the same thing and could unravel the mystery of words." Mari used every spare moment to pore over vocabulary, spelling, and grammar. She yearned not only to read books but also to write them. At the age of twelve, she saw her first story published in the Omaha *Evening News*. When the paper arrived at the homestead, Old Jules beat her and locked her in the cellar. Fiction, he told her, was appropriate only for hired girls and trash.

In glimpses we have of Mari during these years, she is shy and cringing, a child who "hid away, retreating into fancy." Yet she put up with her father when her younger siblings defied him or simply stayed out of his way, and he passed on to her much of his knowledge and love of the Sandhills. "He told me many fine stories when the others weren't around."

Within her quietness, though, burned a determination to escape. She passed her eighth-grade examination after only four and a half years of intermittent schooling, and soon after, without

Jules's consent, rode eighteen miles horseback to try for a rural teacher's license. She was sixteen years old, weighed seventy-five pounds, and had no more social skills than a weanling calf. In her faded gingham dress, she looked like a third grader.

[She] took the teacher's examination in such subjects as arithmetic and civil government, and the theory of teaching. It seemed impossible that she could pass. All the other candidates were well-dressed young ladies and she was a child, but she must get away—peacefully if she could, because of her mother, but get away.

When Jules heard what she had done he was violent. "I want no goddamn lazy schoolma'ams in my family. Balky, no good for nothing!" But after Marie got her certificate he bragged about it when she wasn't around. "That's what comes of living with an educated man!"

She taught school for several years, writing in the evening. Then in her midtwenties, she made her way to Lincoln, where she eventually talked her way into the University of Nebraska, even though she lacked a high school diploma. She supported herself filling pharmaceutical capsules for pennies an hour, scrimping on meals almost to the point of collapse so she could buy postage to submit her stories. Friends suspected that she often subsisted on little more than the free sugar, tea, and crackers available in the University dining hall.

Professors who recognized her promise mentored her in writing and history. She won an honorable mention in an intercollegiate short-story contest. Though she had entered under a pseudonym, somehow Old Jules learned of the award and wrote her a single line of acknowledgment: "You know I consider artists and writers the maggots of society." Publishers' responses were less brutal but, beyond a few small successes, not much more encouraging. As she neared her fortieth birthday, she estimated that she had received over one thousand rejections and "had made $250 from published writings, $75 in prizes, and had a novel and seventy-eight unpublished short stories on hand."

Then, in 1935, the manuscript for *Old Jules*—which, over a period of seven years, had been rejected fourteen times and repeatedly rewritten—won the Atlantic Press nonfiction prize. It came out to enthusiastic reviews and became a Book-of-the-Month Club selection. There had never been a book quite like it before, nor has there been one since. She had captured Old Jules, that "strong, coldly savagely selfish, intelligent, lazy, vain, interesting, magnetic, detestable father of hers" (as one reader described him), in fascinating and objective detail. "She writes with the detachment of an impartial observer," wrote a reviewer, "with no perceptible tug of prejudice at all." Another remarked that her book revealed "the yet untapped layers and layers of historical soil of our own American heritage." She had written a stunning biography not only of a man but also of a place and a period of time.

Perhaps even more remarkable was the fact that she had transformed herself through the process of writing. When she first came to Lincoln in 1923, she had been shy and socially backward. One friend described her as a stereotypical old maid. As Helen Winter Stauffer points out, Mari "carried with her the psychic scars of her youth; her childhood feelings of alienation from her family, community, and schoolmates made her at times self-pitying and frustrated. She still felt strongly the lack of parental love, of physical attractiveness, and of social status."

Sandoz already knew that she wanted to write about the Nebraska frontier, and she knew that her family and neighbors were her richest material. She based characters in her first novel, *Murky River*, and several short stories on Old Jules and herself, but her anger and sense of offense made their encounters seem one-dimensional and overly dramatic. As she struggled to make the narratives work, her understanding of the real-life Old Jules deepened as well. He became both more human and more universal. "It dawned on me that here was a character who embodied not only his own strengths and weaknesses but those of all humanity—and his struggles were universal struggles and his defeats at the hands of his environment and his own insufficiencies were those of mankind. . . ."

Murky River never found a publisher, a fact Sandoz later acknowledged with relief, and even the long struggle with *Old Jules* worked in her favor. Chosen as a finalist in the 1932 Atlantic nonfiction contest, it ultimately lost out. This setback so demoralized her that she burnt seventy short stories in a washtub and swore off writing completely. But within a month she tackled *Old Jules* anew, and the version that *The Atlantic* chose in 1935 had been completely redrawn. Though the early drafts do not survive, those who read them remarked on the degree to which she cleansed the final version of her earlier accusatory tone.

As Mari's writing evolved, so did she. She never sugarcoated her father, but she no longer reviled him. As she researched his life, diving into the four thousand letters he left behind as well as reams of newspaper articles, first-person accounts, and other historical documents, she came to see him as a product of his time and place. "The maladjusted," she wrote, "the misfits—economic, social or emotional, men and women—normally drifted to the frontier. Many of these were further unsettled by the hardship and isolation, to end in a mental or penal institution or a suicide's grave." However painful the violence of her childhood, Old Jules had pulled his family through, and she came to feel a genuine gratitude that she had been privileged to "look upon the lightning."

The Pulitzer Prize–winning historian Bernard De Voto recognized that part of Sandoz's literary power lay in her ability to write from both pain and gratitude. In his words, "The scars of terror and adoration were plainly visible." Mari appreciated this insight and wrote De Voto, "Every time an Oh-you-poor-dear-how-you-must-have-suffered letter about *Old Jules* comes in I am tempted to write you a note of thanks for seeing that the Running Water of my childhood was a paradise, a paradise beyond anything the horrified can conceive, let alone attain in even the best of their conventionalized, dehumanized, civilized society."

As she let go of anger and blame, she let go, too, of those traits that could have handicapped her for life. She kept her father's will and feistiness—her battles with editors to retain the regional vocabulary and cadences that gave her writing authenticity were legendary—but she was free of his bitterness, anger, and suspicion. She always kept a part of herself private, and she could have an edge, but she was also playful and funny. She rarely held a grudge, and she enjoyed many deep and lifelong friendships. In contrast to Old Jules's narcissism, she mentored young writers so generously that even those who never met her felt the warmth of her support. As historian and novelist Dorothee Kocks wrote in *Dream a Little: Land and Social Justice in Modern America,* "I glimpsed a kindness in her books toward the learner in me."

The pleasure and success Mari Sandoz enjoyed later in life seem almost miraculous in light of her formative years. Her tenacity in the face of continued rejection is rare, but not enough, on its own, to earn her the wholehearted admiration that most people feel when they learn her story. Old Jules was a bulldog of tenacity, but however fascinating we find him, we don't want him as our neighbor, let alone our father. Mari, on the other hand, was well-rounded and engaging, her passion generously creative instead of something cruel and mad.

Her gift was the ability to let go of resentment, and the process that she stumbled upon through years of dedicated writing lies at the core of what is often called forgiveness studies within the emerging field of positive psychology. Pioneered by such scholars as Dr. Frederic Luskin from Stanford, Dr. Robert Enright from the University of Wisconsin, and Dr. Michael McCullough from the University of Miami, the therapeutic concept of forgiveness does not condone wrongdoing. Nor does it require reconciliation; in fact, the injured person can choose never to see the transgressor again. Enright defines forgiveness as an "emotional, intellectual, and moral response to unfair treatment from others," and its purpose is to free someone who has suffered at the hands of another from posttraumatic distress.

In the book *Forgive for Good*, often used as a textbook in courses on forgiveness, Luskin outlines a process in four steps that he summarizes under the acronym HEAL, standing for Hope, Educate, Affirm, and Live.

"Hope" stands for the acknowledgement of what one hoped for, something that begins with an unflinching assessment of wrongdoing. In Mari's case, her hopes for kindness, nurture, and tutoring were met with blows, humiliation, and neglect.

"Educate" refers to educating oneself in the larger context of human behavior in order to take the wrong one has suffered less personally. We all hope for loving parents, but objectively we recognize that many parents neglect and abuse their children. Through her research, Mari came to understand that her father's cruelty and self-absorption were not unique, and the hardships of pioneer life pushed many people past the breaking point.

"Affirm" stands for a positive intention the wronged person chooses to embrace, and it often grows directly out of earlier deprivation. Treated unfairly as a child, Mari Sandoz knew exactly what she wanted to do as an adult. "The underprivileged child," she told an interviewer in 1959, "if he becomes a writer, becomes a writer who is interested in social justice, and destruction of discrimination between economic levels, between nationalist levels, between color levels and so on." The theme of social justice underlies many of Sandoz's books, and she was one of the first scholars to write Indian history from an indigenous point of view. *The Battle of the Little Bighorn* and *Crazy Horse: The Strange Man of the Oglalas* are seminal works. In addition, Sandoz helped young writers, driven by her own childhood longing for education and creative support.

"Live" asks for a long-term commitment to live true to one's positive intentions, something Sandoz did through her more than

two-dozen books, hundreds of stories and articles, and her men-
toring activities.

Luskin stresses that the ability to heal is a process, a journey
that begins with a heroic choice. "This choice exists whether or
not someone asks for forgiveness," writes Luskin, and is something we can decide to embrace whether or not the transgressor
deserves it. It is an act of courage born out of enlightened self-
interest, acceptance of reality, compassion, understanding, and a
desire to be free. In Luskin's words, "When we choose forgiveness, we release our past to heal our present."

I suspect that Sandoz would be amused and even annoyed by
my attempt to condense her life's struggle into a quick formula.
Certainly, she would take issue with the concept of forgiveness
itself, scoffing that she had nothing to excuse. "There is no reason
for bitterness at all," she replied to one of the hundreds of letters she
received after *Old Jules* was published. "No family of my acquain-
tance has been better equipped against the vicissitudes of life as it
must be lived than his six children. Don't forget that we got our
ability to dream dreams far above our surroundings from him."

Nonetheless, the field of positive psychology might well have
intrigued her with its attempt to understand the processes of repair
and growth. She was an advocate of creative writing courses and
believed that instruction could have saved her years of effort as
she struggled to figure things out on her own. She wanted to write
well, and she wanted to live fully; at some level she knew that her
ability to do both was due, at least in part, to her willingness to
release her resentments. Her own heroic journey was long and
arduous. She might have appreciated some help along the way.

CONTROL (AND FAITH)

The Green Bean Testament

There are two ways to live your life. One is as though nothing
is a miracle. The other is as though everything is a miracle.
—ALBERT EINSTEIN

Let the mystery be.
—IRIS DEMENT, from her *Infamous Angel* album

On the night before my father's funeral, longtime friends in
Cheyenne invited my husband, Hal; my brother, Blade; and
me, along with other family members, for dinner. Our family ties
went back a long way. Beth and I had known each other since
childhood. Her father had been my father's best friend, and when
Beth had been Miss Frontier for Cheyenne Frontier Days, I served
as her Lady-in-Waiting. Her husband, Bill, had partnered with
my father on several occasions.

We all hung out in the kitchen while Beth prepared dinner—
steak, crab legs, Caesar salad, and baked potatoes. I was
particularly delighted to see a big pan of fresh green beans ready
to put on the stove. "Green beans!" I said. "I love green beans! I
grew up green bean deprived. Dad never let us have green beans
when we were kids."

"That can't be true!" Beth said.

"No, really," I replied, and I explained that Dad had eaten
so many green beans in the army that he banned them from our

home. We could only have them if he was away, which wasn't
often.

"I just can't believe that," Beth said. "Everybody eats green
beans. Blade," she said, turning to my brother, "you really didn't
eat green beans?"

"I don't know," Blade answered. "I don't really remember, but
then I don't care much about green beans one way or the other."
The conversation moved on to other topics, and soon Bill ushered
us into the dining room while Beth finished a few last things.

We were seated when Beth called Bill back to the kitchen. We
could hear them rustling around in there, and then they brought
the pan of green beans into the dining room. The lid was stuck.
They passed the pan around, but none of us could remove the lid,
so we all ended up in the kitchen again, offering suggestions. We
pegged the problem as a vapor lock, and we ran cold water on
the pan and then put it back on the stove. No luck. We took the
pan outside and stuck it in a snowdrift. The lid held fast. Bill got
a screwdriver to pry it off but couldn't get a wedge under the lid
without ruining the pan. Finally, we gave up and enjoyed the rest
of the dinner while I said a little thank-you under my breath to
Dad for backing me up.

My father liked to be in control. He had written out instruc-
tions for his funeral at least a dozen years in advance and made
occasional revisions to the form he kept on file at the mortuary.
He requested three poems be read "by someone who knows how
to read poetry": "If," by Rudyard Kipling; "High Chin Bob," by
Badger Clark; and all four verses to "The Star-Spangled Banner,"
recited, not sung. For music, he wanted "Life is Like a Mountain
Railroad," the hymn that the hired gun Tom Horn had requested
for his own funeral. Finally, he stipulated that no minister should
preside. A lifelong agnostic, he considered it hypocritical to try to
gain favor on his way out. "If there is a God and he is just," he
liked to say, "I trust Him to treat me fairly."

As Blade, Hal, and I sat down to plan the service, we added a few
embellishments. We chose three of Dad's friends to read the poems

and asked them to add personal remembrances. I had a story of my own I wanted to tell, and I decided to recite the twenty-third psalm, a text that is dear to my heart. I figured Dad wouldn't be too mad. Since it was my idea instead of his, he couldn't be blamed for trying to tip the scale on the way out. Besides, he had always loved the language of the King James Bible, and I hoped that the twenty-third psalm, the only text many of the early cowboys knew by heart, might appeal to Dad's sense of tradition.

The service was warm and genuine, short enough that we thought Dad would approve. At the end of it, we adjourned to his favorite restaurant and bar to fulfill his final request and buy everyone a drink.

Blade and Hal and I arrived last at the reception, but we had arranged in advance for a selection of photos and mementos to be set out on a table. When we came in, we saw that Beth had added the pan of green beans to the display. The lid still held tight, and as Beth told the story to people gathered around, everyone took turns trying to remove it, like King Arthur's knights lining up to pull the sword out of the stone.

Leonard, the foreman of our ranch for many years, met me at the door, and after he gave me a hug, he told me that he'd like to buy my dad a drink for old time's sake. I thought that was a fine idea, and we went to the bar and ordered a double shot of Old Forester bourbon. (Dad had been a Jack Daniel's man until the company lowered its proof from 90 to 80. From that point on, he boycotted the brand. "A gentleman," he said, "doesn't water his whiskey.")

Leonard carried the glass over to the table and placed it in front of my father's picture. The moment he set it down, everyone behind us started to laugh. We turned around to see one of the guests standing with the open pan of green beans in one hand and the lid in the other. "What's so hard about that?" she said.

What's so hard, indeed? It had been a long day, but it looked like Dad had finally relaxed, relieved that we hadn't messed things up too badly. "Gee, Dad," I said under my breath. "You could have had a little faith."

BALANCE

On the High Wire

If I see three oranges, I have to juggle. And if I see two
towers, I have to walk.
—Philippe Petit

What I dream of is an art of balance.
—Henri Matisse

One of the earliest stories my family tells about me comes
from a time I was too young to remember. As soon as I
learned to crawl, they say, I loved to climb. One day, one of the
men on the ranch set his extension ladder against the wall of our
two-story house so he could repair our roof. He was working
on the peak when he heard me gurgling behind him, voicing the
toddler equivalent of "whatcha doin' up here?"

I have always loved high places, but I am not agile. With
unsteady balance and poor proprioception, I have little sense of
where my body is in space. Strong and with good endurance—in
midlife I took up marathoning—I am a creature of the earth, not
the air. However much I aspire to the ether, I do best when my
feet are firmly placed upon the ground.

Perhaps that explains why, from the moment I first saw the
newscast of Philippe Petit's walk on a high wire strung between
the Twin Towers of the World Trade Center in New York City
in 1974, I have been obsessed with the French aerialist. Over the

years, I have learned everything I can about him, including this: on the sole of his right foot, he has a small tattoo. It represents a wire strung between two planets, an impossible link. For this, I love him. He has dedicated his life to the impossible, forging links that defy mortal imagination.

In 1971, at the age of twenty-one, Petit strung a wire between the towers of Notre-Dame Cathedral in France, 226 feet above the ground. He spent three hours on the cable, though he had never been on a wire higher than twenty feet before.

Three years later, in the middle of the night, he and his accomplices stretched a 450-pound cable between the Twin Towers. Manhattan woke to find him walking, unannounced and without fanfare, on a filament a quarter mile above its streets.

For nearly an hour he passed back and forth between the towers—strolling, striding, running, dancing, kneeling on one knee and offering a salute—while beneath him traffic came to a complete halt and the sidewalks filled with pedestrians gazing skyward. Sometimes he lay down on the wire, relaxed and almost dozing, mesmerized by the clouds above, only to pop up after a few moments and resume his passage. Each time he approached one tower or the other, an "octopus" of angry police officers surged forward, reaching out to snatch him, and he would pirouette on the wire and skip out of their reach until finally, after his sixth crossing—or maybe it was his eighth; even the police were so entranced they lost count—he leapt into their arms and let them drag him away, having successfully completed not only the most audacious art crime of the twentieth century but arguably its most ascendant moment of grace.

He has completed many walks since, including a performance on an inclined wire connecting the Jewish and Arab quarters of Jerusalem. In 1987, when he came to Oregon to help open the new Portland Center for the Performing Arts, I had the chance to interview him. "Perhaps life is to link things," he told me. "The notion of linking two points that were doomed to be separated, it is a very important miracle. So I am happy to be a carrier of that task of linking. It lasts an instant. Those things that last an instant, they are worth, sometimes, a lifetime of work."

Lately I have found myself thinking a great deal about Philippe Petit, perhaps for obvious reasons. In a time when our nation seems hopelessly out of balance and divided against itself, I find solace in turning off the news and spending time, if only in my mind, with someone who has devoted his life to bridging impossible chasms, maintaining balance against all odds.

Petit's historic Twin Towers walk took place on August 7, 1974. Home for summer vacation after my freshman year of college, I found the image I saw on the news that night of his lithe figure, clad in black all alone in graceful motion 110 stories above the ground, both the most beautiful and the most miraculous thing I could imagine. A few years later, I came across his book, *On the High Wire*. Ostensibly a guide to tightrope walking, its chapters on such topics as walking, running, practice, falling, and fear provide a manual for living a passionate and masterful life, topics that engaged me as much then as now. When I heard he was coming to Portland, where I lived at the time, I had to find a way to meet him. Although I had not written for the newspaper before, I talked *The Oregonian* into giving me an assignment for their arts weekly.

I called Petit's publicist to request an interview. Petit was too busy with rehearsal and rigging, she told me, for a formal interview, but he had to eat. He liked sushi. If I took him to dinner, we could talk. Nine at night would be good, she said, and she suggested a date three days away.

I made a reservation at a Japanese restaurant a block from the Center for the Performing Arts and requested a tatami room, one of the small, private dining cubicles where we could sit on mats to eat and talk with minimal interruption. We met after what had been a long day of work for Petit. Although the restaurant had a good reputation, that night the service was terrible. Our food took over an hour and a half to arrive. That gave me undistracted time with Petit, but he was exhausted and needed food. At one point he yawned. "I'm tired," he said, "no point in hiding it." I apologized for the wait and thanked him for his time. "I know what it costs you," I said.

"But I always find it interesting, an interview," he replied. "Very honestly. There are bad interviews and good interviews, and I am being asked very much, sometimes, the same questions, but I don't have quick answers. At the press conference, yes, I can do a dance. But actually, I always take a question and try to really, on the moment, express what I think, so it's an interesting exercise for me, and I love that." At that point, Petit had been interviewed literally thousands of times, in dozens of countries. And yet I could tell that he spoke honestly and attended to our conversation with freshness and care. It's one reason I will never forget that evening. Here are some of the things we discussed:

ABOUT CONFIDENCE AND HUMILITY:

"You have to work so hard," I said, "and yet you can't force it." I had just quoted lines from *On the High Wire*—"The tendency is to want to calm [the wire] by force. In fact you must move with grace and suppleness to avoid disturbing the song of the cable."

"That's the beauty of it," he said. "It's a live adversary, an opponent."

"An adversary?" I asked, "or a friend?"

"At times, it turns," he answered. "It goes from being an opponent to a friendly accomplice. You can't impose [yourself] on the wire. You have to place [yourself] humbly. If you impose even a foot on the wire, the wire will vibrate and throw you off. You have to glide it in and hold your breath. That's an imposition, but if you do it well, then the wire will receive it with no doubt. You need a total confidence, very, very, very fierce confidence, but you need as much—I was going to say humility, but that's not the term. It's humbleness. You need a lot of respect for this stage that you have chosen."

ABOUT MASTERY:

Petit is master of a dozen talents. A sublime magician, juggler, toreador, visual artist, writer, pickpocket, and lock picker (something that has been particularly useful on some of his clandestine walks), he even delivered his own daughter, not only tying off her umbilical cord but also sewing a tear in her mother's birth canal. He has an artist's soul and an engineer's mind; he does all his own rigging, and his success on the high wire would be impossible without his grasp of architecture and physics.

"You have to have an inside fire," Petit said. "Technique is not really what makes it. You can be juggling for twenty years, practicing, throwing things in the air, and catching them, but you might not be a good juggler. To be a good juggler is to have this madness that makes you keep on doing it eight hours a day furiously. This is how I do what I do.

"I never learned anything [in schools or from teachers]." (In fact, Petit had been expelled from five schools by the time he was eighteen.) "I didn't learn how to write [from other people]. I didn't learn how to juggle and to do magic and to walk on the wire. I learned by myself. I do it by intuition and by *gourmandise.*"

Gourmandise. The word intrigued me. "It's like a sweet tooth," he said, "but more than that. It has a hungry, hungry sense. A romantic sense."

"Passion," I suggested, an insatiable hunger for beauty and excellence.

"Yes, yes, yes," he said. "That's all. It's passion. Early on, I caught an incurable disease, the excess of passion."

ON SOLITUDE:

I told him that the loneliness of his art touched me. "It's one of those paradoxes," I said, "that when you perform, a huge crowd gathers. But in your art, the solitude is extraordinary."

"It is not extraordinary," he said, "because any performance should be an act of solitude. To me, the best performance in the world is somebody chained and nailed and locked into his own world. 'I'm going to open the box and see something and close the box.' There is nothing more powerful than to witness somebody chained to his own passion. There are some exceptions. A stand-up comic has to play with his audience. But there is a beautiful distance. If you lose that distance, if you are just trying to get the audience to react, then the performance becomes a fantasy, a fake, an apparition."

"It strikes me," I said, "that no performance is as far away from the audience as for instance your walk between the Twin Towers, yet nothing involves the audience as much as that."

"Yes," he agreed. "It is beautiful to be disconnected and united at the same time. Which makes the beauty, I think, of the wire."

There were other topics we touched upon but skirted around, primarily faith and fear. Petit had said in other interviews that when he was on the wire, he was too busy to be afraid, and that he took no risks because he planned each walk for years. "My safety net is my preparation."

In *On the High Wire,* he wrote that anything that could be done on the ground could be done on the wire, and theoretically I understood how a person, with obsession and practice, could develop grace and confidence. But how to maintain that ease 1,400 feet above the ground? "Tell me," I implored clumsily, "about faith, that moment of faith when you step onto the wire. How do you describe your spirituality? What is God to you?"

Petit replied without hesitation. "God to me doesn't exit. I don't believe in any religion. But I of course believe in many things, many, many things. I believe in people who believe in themselves. I believe in myself. I hold in my hands my entire destiny, my life, my way of thinking. So that's one thing. And I believe in minutes in life, because perhaps life is to link things. I believe in beauty because it is useless and it is ephemeral. It lasts an instant."

Those answers didn't satisfy me, but I was too shy to probe further. I don't think they satisfied Petit, either, and as I have followed his career these many years, I have watched his articulation deepen. Since 1980, he has been artist-in-residence at the Cathedral of St. John the Divine in New York City, the seat of the Episcopal diocese of New York and the largest Gothic cathedral in the world.

"I am not a man of belief, but I really belong in this cathedral," Petit told Calvin Tomkins, who profiled him for *The New Yorker*. "When you think about it, wire walking is very close to what religion is. 'Religion' is from the Latin *religare*, which means to link something, people or places. And to know, before you take your first step on a wire, that you are going to do the last one—this is a kind of faith."

In 2008, Petit published *Man on Wire*, a reminiscence of his World Trade Center walk that was the basis for the Oscar-winning documentary of the same title. In a chapter titled "Meeting the Gods," he remembers his sense of gratitude during his walk. He gave thanks to:

> the gods in me,
> the gods in the balancing pole,
> the gods in my feet,
> the gods in the wire-rope,
> the gods of the void,
> the gods in my friends who are watching from the street,
> the gods of the towers, the gods in my friends who are standing
> on the rooftops,
> the gods of all dimensions, the gods of arrival
>
> and you,
> gods of a billion constellations,
> gods in the crowd,
> gods in the air below, gods in the air above,
> gods of the wind . . .

Why is it, this morning, the first time you gather?
Why don't you congregate more often?
Will there be a next time?

To receive an answer, I lean back and lie down again, I stare
straight into the sky.

The Very Reverend James Parks Morton, Dean Emeritus of St. John the Divine Cathedral and the man who invited Petit to be artist-in-residence there, told Calvin Tomkins that Petit is one of the most religious people he has ever known. "Sometimes very unusual people turn out to be the most religious. I think of this as God's joke."

"Philippe does not believe in God," Dean Morton said another time, "but God believes in Philippe."

Before 9/11, Petit always referred to the Twin Towers as his towers. After the tragedy, he always called them "our towers." At the end of *Man on Wire*, he offered to walk again after the Towers were rebuilt. "Together," he wrote in the book's closing lines, "we will rejoice in an aerial song of victory. I will carry my life across the wire, as your life, as all our lives past, present, and future—the lives lost, the lives welcomed since."

MANNERS

The Good Hand

The test of good manners is to be patient with bad ones.
—Solomon ibn Gabirol

Manners should be a technique of inclusion, a way of ensuring that in our company no one will ever be made to feel he is an outcast.   —Quentin Crisp, *Manners from Heaven*

When my brother and I were small, we had, like most ranch kids, reasonably good manners. We said please and thank you, asked to be excused from the table when we were through eating, and—once telephone service came to our isolated ranch community—identified ourselves whenever we made a call. Though it sometimes took some prodding from our mother, we wrote thank-you notes whenever we received gifts. (Always loquacious, I tended to be flowery, but my brother cut to the chase. One Christmas, acknowledging the soap-on-a-rope he received from our cousins, he wrote simply: "Thanks for the soap. I needed it.")

Being kids, we sometimes came up short, but we never forgot our manners in the barn. To this day, I say "whoa" to announce myself whenever I enter one. A startled horse may strike out in fear; if I was rude or alarming or simply self-absorbed, I could get kicked in the head. It was an object lesson in the purpose of manners: to make another feel safe and at ease.

Although manners and etiquette are related, they are not the same thing. Etiquette has to do with the rules, such as which fork to use for salad or how to address the Queen. The word derives from Old French *estiquette*, meaning "label" or "ticket," and refers to the small cards or "little signs" once used at court to codify proper behavior.

The word *manners* derives from the Latin word for *hand, manus,* and refers to the "method of handling," how we handle ourselves and others. As Emily Post put it, "Manners are a sensitive awareness of the feelings of others. If you have that awareness, you have good manners, no matter what fork you use."

A good horseman is called a "good hand," and I began to make the connection between horsemanship and manners as I watched *Buck*, the just-released documentary about legendary horse trainer Buck Brannaman. Brannaman inspired Robert Redford's character in *The Horse Whisperer* and is one of the leading practitioners of what has come to be known as natural horsemanship, a quiet revolution that started in the cowboy West in the 1960s and is gradually changing the way people work with horses all over the world. Documentary films seldom do well in the box office, but *Buck* enjoyed great reviews and ranked among the top twenty-five box-office draws for several months after its release, a surprising success when you consider that fewer than 2 percent of American households own a horse. But *Buck* is as much about how we treat each other as it is about how we treat horses.

However courteous my brother and I were when we stepped into a barn, we did not inhabit a world where horsebreaking would be called considerate. Rather, we inherited the tradition Will James described in his famous novel *Smoky the Cowhorse*. Clint, the hero of the tale, gathers Smoky off the range, ropes and "busts" him (tripping him so he falls hard enough to knock out his breath), and then ties his four feet together to keep him down. After Clint puts a hackamore on the horse, he lets it get up and fight him:

The cowboy played his rope and held his horse; he'd held many like him before and most all had fought the same as Smoky was now fighting. That pony's eyes was afire as he seen there was no chance for any get away even when he was on his feet. He couldn't at all shake that two legged hunk of terror, and as he snorted and fought the rope that still held fast around his head and neck, he begin to tire some; and came a time when as the cowboy stood still a few yards away he stood still too, and legs wide apart, sweat a dripping from his slick hide, he took in a breathing spell.

After this initial session, Clint ties Smoky to a log so he will learn that pulling back on a rope is useless; later he "sacks" him with a saddle blanket to get him used to noise and touch, and then he slaps a saddle on him, swings on, and bucks him out. In each stage, the terrified horse only settles down after he learns he can't escape. Once he quiets, Clint offers comfort, and over time he earns the horse's trust. He had broken hundreds of horses this way and "had never made an outlaw." He is the good guy in the novel, compassionate in comparison to the horse thief who abuses Smoky to try to break his spirit. Under the best of conditions, the traditional method of horse breaking roughed up the horse, something captured by the fact that the art was known variously as bronc breaking, busting, twisting, or fighting. A man who tried to gentle a horse before he threw on the saddle was seen as something of a sissy.

The new horse trainers talk about "making" a horse rather than breaking it and describe themselves as horse gentlers rather than bronc busters. One of their central insights is to make a young or troubled horse feel secure rather than working to exhaust its terror. Another tenet is to arrange things so a horse will choose to cooperate because it is more comfortable rather than because it is less painful, something Brannaman described in his book *The Faraway Horses* as "making the wrong thing difficult, and the right thing easy, as opposed to making the wrong thing impossible through intimidation."

This is not new; four centuries before Christ, Xenophon advised the Greek cavalry to handle colts so that they were "gentle, tractable, and fond of man," and there have always been those who preferred to give a horse no reason to buck rather than taking pride in their ability to ride it out. But leaders in the natural horsemanship movement have been able to articulate their understanding of the horse in ways that have shown people how to relate better not only to their horses, but also to each other.

Buck Brannaman and his brother Smokie were terribly abused by their alcoholic father. After their mother's death, their father's violence spiraled out of control, and several times he beat the boys almost to death. Finally, a teacher helped remove them to a foster home. "When something is scared for its life," Brannaman says, "I understand that." This empathy gives him a special understanding of troubled horses, but he knows, too, that someone who has been abused needs more than just sympathy. He started learning this the first day he met his foster parents, Forrest and Betsy Shirley, and Forrest gave him a pair of gloves and took him out to fix fence.

"If the Shirleys had dwelled on [our] troubles," Buck wrote in his book *The Faraway Horses,*

> instead of providing us with discipline and a sense of direction, we would eventually have become spoiled . . . because we'd have realized that Forrest and Betsy were willing to make exceptions for us because of our situation. Thank goodness they didn't do that.

> That time in my life . . . made me understand the needs of horses that have been treated poorly and are scared

or troubled. You can't just fix things by showing them love. . . . You have to give them some direction, a purpose, a job. They need . . . a vision of the future so that the past eventually becomes irrelevant. A mistreated horse has more needs than a horse that has had a nice upbringing. You need to be understanding, and you need to have empathy, but you also need to know that an excess of empathy can get you into trouble. You need to provide discipline without forcing it.

If good manners—making a horse feel safe and secure—comprise one half of natural horsemanship, discipline makes up the other. Having good manners need not mean getting run over, and knowing the difference between discipline and punishment is key. As Buck puts it, "Whether riding a horse or working with a kid, there's no crime in saying no. But always saying no will take away all the horse's desire to try, and pretty soon the horse or the youngster will believe there's nothing he can do right."

Buck teaches the art of redirection, of heading off inappropriate behavior by providing an alternative, a job to do, and rewarding the slightest try. "Whether you're dealing with a kid or an adult or a horse," he says, "treat them the way you'd like them to be, not the way they are now."

It is one thing to talk about such concepts and another to incorporate them into your own life. The ability that the best of the natural horsemen and women possess to work with even deeply troubled horses, transforming fear and aggression into eager confidence, can seem nothing short of miraculous. It comes from a respectful way of handling not only one's horse but also oneself—manners, if you will—that is deeply imbedded in the mind but speaks through the heart and the body. I suspect that one reason natural horsemanship has begun to fascinate people far beyond the horse world is that it suggests that if such growth is possible when we treat horses differently, it can happen if we change the way we treat each other.

"Horses don't care what color you are," says Buck Brannaman, "how tall or short or how small or large you are, or whether you're rich or poor, attractive or unattractive. None of that means anything to the horse. A horse takes you at face value for how you make him feel at that moment. It seems to me this would be a good way for all of us people to behave with each other, too. Lord knows, in this day and age, the whole world could stand a bit more of that."

MODERATION

All I Want for Christmas . . .
Is a Truce in the War on Christmas

Avoid extremes; forbear resenting injuries so much as you
think they deserve. —Benjamin Franklin

While you are proclaiming peace with your lips, be careful to
have it even more fully in your heart. —St. Francis of Assisi

Though I'm shy to admit this to some of my more cynical
friends, I still retain an almost-childlike enchantment with
the whole spectacle of Christmas. The season runs far too long,
of course, and I pretty much ignore it until at least the middle of
December, but I love the sparkling lights, the traditional music,
the Salvation Army Santas with their musical bells, and the
general sense of generosity that calls out to our better natures.
When I open a Christmas card and run my fingers across the
raised letters, "Peace on Earth, Goodwill Toward Men," I feel a
palpable warmth, a genuine sense of hope. I'm not naive enough
to think world peace is nigh, but this time of year it seems possible to relax our animosities, if only for a moment. I think of the
story of the Christmas Truce, the scattered and unofficial cease-
fires that broke out along the Western Front in 1914 when British
and German soldiers shared Christmas carols across the trenches.
So I'm both disappointed and fatigued to see this year's replay

of the hyped-up "War on Christmas." The Catholic League and American Atheists spar with dueling billboards in the Lincoln Tunnel; Gretchen Carlson on Fox expresses outrage that Tulsa's Christmas Parade is now called the Holiday Parade; and Jon Stewart on *The Daily Show* is outraged by Carlson's outrage. As Stewart puts it, "the season wouldn't be the same without people going out of their way to be offended by nothing," and he turned his own sense of affront into a lengthy segment for his show. Like the folks at Fox, he knows that indignation keeps us tuned in, and that, in turn, keeps the sponsors happy. Ire is a commodity, and like so many other guilty pleasures, it is addictive. As Mike Fisher, founder of the British Association of Anger Management, has pointed out, outrage and its attendant adrenaline rush can give life "shape, form, texture, and meaning. . . . It is like extreme sport."

Outside of the 24/7 news cycle, however, most of us feel simple gratitude when someone wishes us joy in the season, no matter how they phrase it. And I'm always encouraged to witness the respect and openness with which people of different traditions respond to each other when they have the chance.

Early in our marriage, Hal and I lived for several years in Starr Valley, Nevada, a ranching community in the northeast corner of the state. Our first December there, we searched the papers and local bulletin boards for Christmas programs and other festivities, and one event in particular caught our eye. A group of Tibetan monks was scheduled to perform a concert of sacred music in Wells, our nearest town, population 1,250, fifteen miles away. We decided to go. We both knew how hard it is to attract an audience for an event under any circumstances, and Buddhist monks in Wells, ten days before Christmas—we figured they needed all the warm bodies they could muster.

The night of the concert, we stopped first at a potluck dinner in the Fellowship Hall of the Presbyterian church. Beneath paper snowflakes and foil garlands hung from the ceiling, a dozen monks joined us to eat braised ribs, green beans, scalloped potatoes, and blackberry pie, and then we moved to the Mormon church for the performance. On the way over, Hal and I admitted to each other our concern: the Mormon church has the biggest hall in town, and we dreaded walking into a sea of empty seats. With the exception of the truck stop/casinos, the church also has the largest parking lot, and we were surprised when we pulled in and had trouble finding a place.

Snowpack made the parking lot treacherous, and we helped an older woman cross from her car to the sidewalk. She had a slight accent, and she told us that she came originally from Germany; she'd settled in Wells nearly forty years before. We mentioned that the turnout surprised us and asked what had attracted her. "These things don't happen very often around here," she told us. "When they do, I like to take advantage."

We could hardly find seats in the basketball court that doubled as an auditorium. Almost immediately, the lights dimmed, and the monks came on stage. They wore long burgundy robes, brilliant saffron shawls, and high, fringed hats like bright-yellow cockscombs. They carried long horns that reached clear to the floor and curved back up again, drums, cymbals, and a variety of other instruments.

A hush came over the room. When the hall had grown completely silent, the monks with the long horns stepped forward. They blew several deep notes, making sounds that were almost animal, like elephants trumpeting before a charge. Short horns joined in, running up and down atonal scales like hyenas, and the cymbals, bells, and drums broke into a wild cacophony. In time, the monks began to chant. Each one produced a three-note tone from deep in his throat. The tones started low and gradually climbed, creating a sound like a convoy of heavily loaded trucks ascending a steep grade.

Please understand: I mean no disrespect with these descriptions. I want only to capture how foreign this music seemed to us, ranchers and miners and teachers and truck drivers whose own traditions of sacred music were so different. We grew restive, squirming in our chairs, coughing, clearing our throats. I feared a mass exodus at intermission. But in time, our ears grew accustomed to the strangeness of the sounds. We began to hear it as music, to understand its nuances. When the break came, no one left. Instead, long lines formed at the table where the monks sold CDs and prayer scarves to support their monastery. During the second half, we sat quietly, transported by the ancient power of sacred traditions we didn't need to fully understand in order to respect. When the performance ended, the applause went on and on.

When the hall once again quieted, a spokesman for the group stepped forward and told us a bit about their lives. They belonged to a monastery in exile in India. They had suffered dearly under the Chinese occupation of Tibet that had sacked their monasteries and killed so many of their brethren. They traveled around the United States to present what is sacred to them. As we learned that night about the great injustice that had been served upon them, many of us sat in awe to hear no enmity in the spokesman's voice. The monks simply wanted us to know who they were. They trusted that once we did, we would insist on the most basic of all rights, which is the right to exist.

We emerged from the church hall into a night shimmering with diamonds. The temperature had dropped and frozen the moisture in the air so that it glittered like the star-strewn sky above us, and a light skim of ice glassed the sidewalks and the parking lot. We saw our German friend looking askance at the slippery walk, and we each took one of her arms. When we asked what she thought of the concert, she chuckled. "Boy," she said, "that was weird."

And then she added, quite simply, "I'm glad I came."

AFTERWORD

God has no Religion.
—Mahatma Gandhi

If the word God means a being that exists outside time, I'm
not sure I believe in Him. But if it means something in us that
is on the side of justice, then yes, I do believe that, in spite of
all the crimes, there is a moral purpose to the world.
—Jorge Luis Borges

Most discussions of virtue and vice suggest a certain hierarchy. When Pope Gregory the Great codified the seven
deadly sins in the sixth century, he deemed pride the mother of
corruption, as it led man to put himself not only before other men
but also before God. On the other side of the ledger, in the 1800s,
Benjamin Franklin placed temperance at the head of his list of
thirteen virtues as the trait that would best facilitate the others.

In the zeitgeist of our day, greed often ranks as the king of vice.
The Great Recession officially ended five years ago, but much of
the nation still reels, even as those at the top of the food chain
grow fatter than ever. Eighty-five people own as much as the
combined wealth of the bottom half of the world's population,
and voices as various as *Forbes Magazine*, Pope Francis, and
the 2013 economics Nobel Laureate Robert Shiller have singled
out increasing economic inequality as the most destabilizing and
urgent problem we face today.

When we are victims of greed, it can feel as if the flesh is being
ripped off our bones. The financiers and institutions that figured
most prominently in the worldwide economic meltdown are

often likened to carrion birds, and in fact the mutual funds that profit from toxic debt, the rubble of that implosion, are called Vulture Funds.

Real vultures are not greedy; they are just hungry. They feed on the dead, on bodies that no longer serve their owners. Efficient recyclers, they make our world cleaner and healthier. Vultures will gorge themselves: they never know when they will happen upon their next meal. But they will also disgorge. If they feel threatened, they regurgitate to lighten their load and survive. We humans have a hard time with this; no matter the threat from world economic collapse, climate change, diminishing resources, or the suffering of other people, many of us never seem to have enough.

If it is important to make the distinction between greed and hunger as we look at carrion birds, the same is true when we look at our own behavior. Greed carries with it a degree of intention. Hunger is more thoughtless, by which I don't mean careless, though it often is, but rather without thought, an instinct rather than a conscious decision. A hungry vulture eats what it can find, and so do we. In the end, I find myself less interested in greed than in our mindless, insatiable hunger.

The Zen teacher Thich Nhat Hanh has introduced Buddhist practice to the West in a way that is useful to followers of any faith. In the Buddhist tradition, Mara attempted to thwart the Buddha's search for enlightenment by tempting him with beautiful women and other earthly delights. Nhat Hanh describes Mara as roughly equivalent to Satan and suggests that these days, Buddha manifests in mindfulness and Mara in forgetfulness. The Buddha lives in each of us, or can. Mara lives in each one of us as well. Whenever we give in to temptation or simply fail to act from our deepest beliefs, we forget what matters to us most. We forget that we can choose where to place our attention. We even forget that we *have* chosen. If we don't remember we have eaten, we are hungry all the time.

Forgetfulness, which in our over-scheduled and gadget-laden lives often plays out in distraction, comes at the cost of our better natures. I think of the Good Samaritan Experiment, in which 90 percent of the seminary students who thought they were late to an obligation rushed by a man in obvious distress. In their haste, some didn't notice him even as they literally stepped over him. In contrast, the majority of the seminarians who believed they had plenty of time stopped and offered aid. The results were so consistent that the researchers concluded, "Ethics becomes a luxury as the speed of our daily lives increases."

It may seem a stretch to connect the momentary lapses of divinity students with the obscene risks taken by the lords of commerce. I believe in evil, and some of the players were evil or at least psychopathic. A psychopath is defined as someone completely lacking in empathy and moral reasoning, and one study suggests that as many as 4 percent of our top CEO's would qualify when measured by the standard inventory used in law enforcement, the Hare Psychopath test. But even if we take that figure at face value, it leaves the majority with at least some degree of fairness intact.

Most Americans believe that talent and effort should be rewarded, but they question the degree to which relative compensation has skewed over time. In the 1950s, the average CEO took home twenty times as much as the typical worker. Now, according to the Economic Policy Institute, the ratio is over 230 to 1, and that is just on average. In 2011, the ratio for Walmart CEO Michael Duke was almost 800 to 1, leaving many of his employees reliant on food stamps in order to feed their families. On the other end of the scale, the ratio at Costco that year was less than 50 to 1. Costco's employees consistently rank it among the best American companies to work for, and this fairness has not impaired its financial viability. The company stands as the third-largest retailer in the country and places twenty-fourth among the Fortune 500.

I suspect that many if not most leaders of business and finance have functioning moral centers, but I doubt that many of them find time to listen to the still, small voice within that might question whether their compensation and corporate decisions are in accord with what they know, deep down, serves not only their employees and the world at large but also their own sense of moral congruence.

As the Rabbi Abraham Joshua Heschel reminds us, "Some are guilty, but all are responsible." If I can't affect the behavior in the towers of power, I can at least affect my own. The theme that emerged most consistently throughout my year of weekly reflections was the need to create space in which that still, small voice can make itself heard. Benjamin Franklin, speaking through Poor Richard, advised that "the idle man is the devil's hireling," but compulsive busyness itself has become a curse, something Buddhist master Sogyal Rinpoche calls active laziness and poet David Whyte suggests causes us to betray our marriage with time. Neuroscience supports the observations of ethicists, spiritual leaders, and poets, for stress impairs the production of oxytocin, a hormone and neurotransmitter deemed the "moral molecule" for the role it plays in evoking trustworthy behavior. Psychopaths don't respond to oxytocin; stress reduces its effectiveness in us all. To say that distraction distorts our sense of decency is not to speak in metaphor but rather in scientific fact.

Thich Nhat Hanh addresses the forgetfulness and hunger at the core of distraction by reminding us that we already have enough conditions to be happy. On its surface, this can sound facile; in practice, it is transformative. Hostage Terry Waite found moments of peace and transcendence chained to the floor of a filthy cell in Lebanon; quadriplegic Brooke Hopkins experienced moments of bliss struggling for breath on a respirator. During the last phase of his long battle with MS, our friend Rich McClure could move only his eyes, but he remained engaged and communicative, using assistive software to blink out profound if cryptic messages to friends. "u no id" he emailed my husband, "wt otsd wndo e da" which we eventually translated as "you have no idea what's outside your window each day."

Waite, Hopkins, and McClure made conscious choices to draw sustenance from what was immediately at hand. Thich Nhat Hanh suggests that we don't need to experience the pain of imprisonment or severe physical impairment to do the same. We choose where we place our attention. When we take time to fully taste a strawberry or focus on what goes on outside our window, even if only for a moment, our unspoken hunger begins to subside.

As I searched for stories with which to understand the various aspects of virtue and vice, I repeatedly encountered the importance of stillness in creating a meaningful life. On retreat at a Trappist monastery, I began to realize how the monks' practice of silence prepared them to speak "at the right time and in the right way." As I studied confrontations in Iraq during my research for the chapter on defense, I learned how an American officer's ability to hear the deeper meaning of a shrieking mob averted a disaster that might have otherwise turned into a massacre. When I looked into humility, both through the eyes of a young boy encountering a new culture and a businessman teaching leadership at Harvard, I came to understand that its grace comes not in hiding the self but rather in respecting others by listening, deeply listening, not only with the ears but also with the body, the mind, and the heart.

In the beginning I said that I didn't expect the year to change me. Certainly I wanted to protect myself from any expectation that I was or could become a paragon of virtue, and I can safely say that I am no more virtuous now than I have ever been. But the year *did* change me. After writing about the poet William Stafford's habit of clearing his desk each day so he could meet a new poem fresh each morning, I somehow abandoned a lifetime habit of clutter to find myself tidying my workspace each evening before I left my desk. After exploring the new frugality, my husband and I decided to downsize. Other bad habits

remain. No matter how insightfully I considered wrath and procrastination, I ended the year still quick to temper and slow to
get things done.

We can know something without *knowing* it. We can even know
something for a while and then forget it. I was aware of the value
of mindfulness before I undertook *The Year of Living Virtuously*.
I had practiced meditation sporadically since I first encountered
Transcendental Meditation in college. Two of my previous books,
one on the Grand Canyon and another on Yosemite, came from
sojourns into the wilderness. A retreat with Byron Katie after my
father's death helped me understand and heal from our troubled
relationship. But in retrospect, my spiritual practice had a certain
inoculatory rhythm: anxiety or a life crisis would lead me to a
"shot" of enlightenment, I would practice for a while, and then
the busyness of life would distract me until I stepped on the meta-
phorical nail that would send me back for a booster.

I emerged from *The Year of Living Virtuously* with a desire
for more consistency. I had read about Thich Nhat Hanh when
I learned how Captain Cheri Maples integrated mindfulness
training into her police work. I liked the idea of practice as a part
of daily activity, and when I learned that Nhat Hanh was visiting
the United States, I told Hal I hoped to attend one of his retreats.
To my surprise, Hal wanted to go, too.

We registered for a five-day retreat at the Magnolia Grove
Monastery in Mississippi. It is a small monastery, and we
expected the retreat would serve eighty or a hundred people. We
arrived to find ourselves among nearly eight hundred. I couldn't
imagine how so many could interact without an element of chaos,
and I found myself nervously assessing the limited toilet facilities.

Much of the retreat was held in silence. We dressed in silence,
had morning tea in silence, made our way to the meditation hall
in silence, ate in silence. Waiting quietly in line for meals turned
into a restful pleasure. Food itself had never tasted so good. We

had all been assigned chores when we first arrived—cooking or cleaning or helping keep up the grounds—and we found our places and settled into our work with surprising ease when we weren't distracted by our own questions. In this environment of quiet and respect, even waiting in line for the toilet seemed restorative. In between designated periods without conversation, we could speak if we wanted to, but we often felt no need.

In the afternoon, we broke into small groups with the monks to share questions and experiences. People had come to the retreat from all over the world and for many reasons: some to strengthen an already well-established practice, others to begin one or to address a crisis in their lives. Over the course of the five days, we each spoke about what mattered to us. Although sometimes the monk commented, the rest of us did not; we simply listened wholeheartedly, and there was something in the quality of attentiveness that brought clarity and healing.

I dropped into a deep peace, a receptive quiet that I had never touched before. The blog had turned into a practice of concentrated listening on an intellectual level; the retreat helped me integrate organically what I had learned. When Hal and I left, we were committed to downsizing and incorporating mindfulness into our daily fabric.

We returned home and listed our house. Although we didn't intend to move until Hal retired a few months later, we thought our home would take a long time to sell in the depressed economy. In the interim, I would turn the blog into a book, and we would sort through a lifetime of accumulation to prepare for a simpler life.

To our amazement, the house sold in a day. The buyers needed it immediately, and by the time we knew the deal would go through, we had only a few days to pack. We threw things into boxes, swept up in a tsunami of moving and resettlement that would take months to sort out. We had not fully recovered by the time Hal retired and we left for a two-month performing tour of Australia and New Zealand . . . life, in other words, resumed its customary busyness, and in its wake, old habits took hold. Mindfulness was swept out to sea.

A few months ago, I had the chance to present a book award to a writer whose work I admire. Although I felt honored by the request, I had agreed reluctantly. Even though the move was more than a year behind us, it had deeply unsettled me. I had only just reestablished a rhythm with my work, and the idea of leaving home filled me with anxiety. I arrived at the event feeling attenuated and off balance, fighting an impulse to flee rather than interact with those seated at the head table.

The writer proved to be down-to-earth and engaging, generous in his discussion of his own work and interested in turn in what the rest of us had on our plates. Everyone took part in the conversation, but in time, I found myself talking more than I had intended, in part because I often try to mask nervousness with exuberance but also because the writer was working on a book about a subject I had researched in depth. By the time the conversation turned to *The Year of Living Virtuously*, I knew that I was talking more than anyone else. Someone asked what virtue I had found most engaging. I wanted to answer "listening," but I was doing such a poor job of it that I launched instead into a long exposition about one of the chapters, veering into a know-it-all stance that I very much dislike about myself.

My experience at the awards luncheon haunted me throughout the day. I found it hard to sleep that night. My transgression had not been so great, but if *The Year of Living Virtuously* had alerted me to anything, it was that balance, deep listening, and generous calm are available if we pay attention. At the very moment I might have shared this insight, I was not living by what I knew. More than the day's careless talking kept me awake that night. As I tossed and turned, I confronted the fact I had been anxious for some time, short tempered at home and impatient with colleagues and friends. I knew how to live with more balance, but I had forgotten. Inattention is in itself a choice. By default, I was choosing to live in a way that was damaging my personal relationships.

When people don't practice their native language, they forget it. Values are the language of the soul. I knew I had to return to practice. And I knew something else: I would need to remind myself to do so time and again.

Mindfulness can take many forms. William Stafford wrote each day before dawn. Trappist monks pray and chant the hours. Cheri Maples brings sitting meditation and mindful action to police work. I don't know what habits of mind underlay Lieutenant Colonel Chris Hughes's ability to quiet a seething mob, except that his gesture came from a deep-seated sense of fairness and respect. Examples like his may be the reason the U.S. Marines recently began integrating meditation practice into training as a way to enhance resilience under fire. All of us can use more resilience under fire. In the spaciousness of attention, each one of us has more choices than we otherwise might know.

In 2010, Warren Buffett and Bill Gates began something called The Giving Pledge, asking the world's wealthiest people to join them in divesting themselves of at least half of their wealth. To date, over 120 individuals, couples, and families have taken the pledge. The participants choose how to direct their gifts; there are infinite ways to make the world a better place. The impact these decisions can make on the future boggles the mind. Bill and Melinda Gates's focus on world health has saved an estimated 3.3 million lives from malaria since 2000.

Those who sign the Giving Pledge are able to give away half their worldly possessions without negatively impacting their own lives. Few of us can do the same, but we don't need to be billionaires to make a difference, and we also don't need to become monks or ascetics. We just need to ask if the ways in which we use our time and our money are nourishing us or mindlessly feeding an infinite but unnecessary hunger.

———◄○►———

When I first conceived of *The Year of Living Virtuously*, I added "(*Weekends Off*)" to the title as something of a joke, to suggest a vacation from the arduous pursuit of decency. I agreed with Benjamin Franklin's assessment at the end of his life that "extream nicety" could be "a foppery in morals" that verged on the ridiculous. Now I realize that weekends off are a more serious concern, for without periodic time for renewal, we forget what we care about. We may even lose the ability to care at all, as stress shuts down the parts of our brain that connect us to others. As Judith Shulevitz wrote in *The Sabbath World*, "We have to remember to stop because we have to stop to remember."

Aristotle saw happiness not so much as a state of mind as an activity, and in the end, practice interests me more than perfection. The *Oxford English Dictionary*'s first definition of *practice* is eloquently simple: "to pursue or be engaged in." This project started as a way to practice writing. It continues to engage me, long after my self-assignment of weekly reflections has expired, as a way to practice life.

ACKNOWLEDGMENTS

My great thanks to:

The online readers whose generous conversation helped shape this book;

Andrea Carlisle, whose friendship and wise critique have enriched me for more than a quarter of a century;

Public artist Larry Kirkland, whose use of "conversation benches" (as well as our own conversations) inspired the dialogue that introduces each chapter;

World Interbeing Sangha, a long-distance community of practice in the Plum Village tradition. Especial thanks to Lynne Dagostino and Kevin Hutchinson, whose kind and steadfast facilitation (and the miracle of Google hangouts) makes it possible for us to meet face-to-face twice a week across five continents;

Phillip Bimstein and Charlotte Bell, Ralph Beer, Melissa Bond, Betsy Burton, Anne Collier, Hal Cannon, Anneliese Cannon, Jean Cheney, Greer Cheser, Brenda Cowley, John Daniel, Candra Day, Greta deJong, Kathryn Dixon, John Dofflemyer, Deb Durban and Steve Masefield, Fae Ellsworth, Judith Freeman, Scott Hansen and Peggy Norton, Brooke Hopkins and Peggy Battin, the Iron Mountain Community, Linda Hussa, Carolyn Jenkins, Carlie Jimenez and Roly Pearson, Dorothee Kocks, Blade Jordan, David Kranes, Mary Lindblom and Patrick Zwick, Gretchen and Paul

Reynolds, Sean Sexton, Kim Stafford and Perrin Kerns, Gail Steiger and Amy Auker, Amy and Peter Stempel, Bonnie and Dennis Timmerman, Steve Trimble, Andy Wilkinson, Russell and Lori Wrankel, and Paul Zarzyski;

And to Jack Shoemaker and the dedicated community at Counterpoint who still believe in books and midwife them beautifully into the world.

SOURCES

INTRODUCTION

Franklin, Benjamin. 2005. *Benjamin Franklin: Autobiography, Poor Richard, and Later Writings.* Ed. J. A. L. Lemay. New York: Library of America.

RESOLUTION: ON THE EVE OF A NEW YEAR

Plimpton, George, and Frank H. Crowther. 1969. E. B. White, The Art of the Essay No. 1. *Paris Review* 48.

Shenker, Israel. 1969. E. B. White: Notes and Comment by Author. *New York Times*, July 11.

White, E. B. 1977. Coon Tree. In *Essays of E. B. White.* New York: Harper and Row.

———. 1944. Memorandum. In *One Man's Meat.* New York: Harper & Brothers.

CLEANLINESS: CLEANLINESS AND ITS CAVEATS

Ashenburg, Katherine. 2008. *The Dirt on Clean: An Unsanitized History.* New York: North Point Press.

Brown, Kathleen M. 2009. *Foul Bodies: Cleanliness in Early America.* New Haven, CT: Yale University Press.

Bryson, Bill. 2010. *At Home: A Short History of Private Life.* New York: Doubleday.

Heise, Jennifer A. 2007. *A Short History of Bathing Before 1601.* http://www.gallowglass.org/jadwiga/herbs/baths.html.

ScienceDaily.com. 2010. Is Cleanliness to Blame for Increasing Allergies? April 14.

Moseman, Andrew. 2009. Let Kids Eat Dirt: Over-Cleanliness Linked to Heart Disease. *DiscoverMagazine.com,* December 11.

Stuller, Jay. 1991. Cleanliness has only Recently Become a Virtue. *Smithsonian Magazine,* February.

U.S. Department of Labor and U.S. Bureau of Labor Statistics. eds. 2010. Consumer Expenditures in 2008. Washington, DC: Bureau of Labor Statistics.

Zaccone, P., Z. Fehervari, J. M. Phillips, D. W. Dunne, and A. Cooke. 2006. Parasitic worms and inflammatory diseases. *Parasite Immunology* 28 (10): 515–523.

SILENCE: MAKING SPACE FOR CONVERSATION

Franklin, Benjamin. 1730. On Conversation. *Pennsylvania Gazette,* October 15.

Isaacson, Walter. 2003. *Benjamin Franklin: An American Life.* Kindle ed. New York: Simon and Schuster.

O'Donnell, Terence. 1980. *Garden of the Brave in War.* New York: Ticknor and Fields.

COURAGE: THE TRUTH OF THE LAND

Braucher, Scott, and Bette Ramsey, eds. 2005. *Buck Ramsey's Grass: With Essays on His Life and Work.* Lubbok, TX: Texas Tech University Press.

Cannon, Hal, ed. 1990. *Cowboy Poetry: A Gathering.* Salt Lake City, UT: Gibbs Smith.

———, ed. 1975. *New Cowboy Poetry: A Contemporary Gathering.* Salt Lake City, UT: Gibbs Smith.

Jordan, Teresa, ed. 1994. *Graining the Mare: The Poetry of Ranch Women.* Salt Lake City, UT: Gibbs Smith.

Lawson, Henry. [1896?] Past Carin'. Available from http://
www.poemhunter.com/best-poems/henry-lawson/past-carin/.
Norris, Kathleen. 1992. A Crowded Writer on the Lonely
Prairie. *New York Times*, December 27.

PRIDE: THE PRIDE OF WORK, THE WORK OF PRIDE

Baumeister, Roy. 2005. The Lowdown on High Self Esteem.
Los Angeles Times, January 2005.
Christensen, Clayton M. 2010. How Will You Measure Your
Life? *Harvard Business Review*, July–August.
Collins, Jim. 2005. Level 5 Leadership: The Triumph of Humility
and Fierce Resolve. *Harvard Business Review*, July–August.
Keisling, Phil. [1981?] Personal conversation about interview with
Studs Terkel for article in *Willamette Week*. Portland, OR.
Schechter, Jennifer. 1995. The Packwood Diaries. *Washington
Monthly*, November: 5.
Terkel, Studs. 1974. *Working: People Talk About What They
Do All Day and How They Feel About What They Do*. New
York: Pantheon / Random House.

SLOTH: EVERYTHING I NEED TO KNOW ABOUT SLOTH
I LEARNED FROM CRITTERS

Norris, Kathleen. 2008. *Acedia & Me: A Marriage, Monks, and
a Writer's Life*. New York: Riverhead Books.
Wasserstein, Wendy. 2005. *Sloth: The Seven Deadly Sins*. New
York: Oxford University Press.

INDUSTRY: THE HARD WORK OF STAYING STILL

Abbey of Our Lady of the Holy Trinity. 2013. History. http://
www.holytrinityabbey.org/history.html.
Rinpoche, Sogyal. 2010. *The Tibetan Book of Living and
Dying*. New York: Harper.

Whyte, David. 2001. *Crossing the Unknown Sea: Work as a Pilgrimage of Identity*. New York: Riverhead Books.

LISTENING: LISTENING TO THE DEVIL'S TRILL

Hicks, Scott, director. 2007. Glass: A Portrait of Philip in Twelve Parts.
Weingarten, Gene. 2007. Pearls Before Breakfast. *Washington Post*, April 8.

ORDER: A POMEGRANATE OF IMPOSSIBLE TASKS

Stafford, Kim. 2002. *Early Morning: Remembering My Father*, William Stafford. St. Paul, MN: Graywolf Press.

HABIT: SOME THOUGHTS ON IN-HABITATION

Jordan, Teresa. 1992. *Riding the White Horse Home*. New York: Pantheon.

FRUGALITY: STEPPING OFF THE HEDONIC TREADMILL

Jordan, Teresa. 1982. *Cowgirls: Women of the American West*. Garden City, New York: Anchor Press / Doubleday.
Revkin, Andrew C. 2009. Are You on a "Hedonic Treadmill"? *New York Times*, August 31.
Rosenbloom, Stephanie. 2010. But Will It Make You Happy? *New York Times*, August 7.

HOMECOMING: RETHINKING NOSTALGIA

Carpenter, Novella. 2010. *Farm City: The Education of an Urban Farmer*. New York: Penguin.
Gruchow, Paul. 1995. *Grass Roots: The Universe of Home*. Minneapolis, MN: Milkweed Editions.

Jackson, Wes. 1996. *Becoming Native to this Place.* Berkeley, CA: Counterpoint.

GOVERNANCE: WHAT GEORGE MIGHT SAY

Americans for Tax Reform. 2011. Available from atr.org.
Faler, Brian. 2011. Reagan's Tax Increases Have Democrats Recalling Republican Hero. *Bloomberg.com*, July 21.
Needleman, Jacob. 2003. *The American Soul: Rediscovering the Wisdom of the Founders.* New York: Tarcher.
Tippett, Krista. 2011. The Inward Work of Democracy: Interview with Jacob Needleman. In *On Being*, ed. Krista Tippett. Collegeville, MN: American Public Media.
Washington, George. 1796. Farewell Address. Yale Law School, 2008. http://avalon.law.yale.edu/18th_century/washing.asp.

SINCERITY: GIVING VOICE TO UNTOLD STORIES

Cuch, Forrest S., ed. 2000. *A History of Utah's American Indians.* Salt Lake City: Utah State University Press.
Hebner, William Logan, and Michael L. Pyler. 2010. *Southern Paiute: A Portrait.* Salt Lake City: Utah State University Press.
Tippett, Krista. 2010. Desmond Tutu's God of Surprises. In *Speaking of Faith*, ed. Krista Tippett. Collegeville, MN: American Public Media.

GREED: IS IT GREED OR IS IT GRAVITY?

Craig, Susanne. 2010. Wall Street Gets Its Groove Back. *New York Times*, November 3.
Frank, Robert H. 2009. Post-Consumer Prosperity: Finding new opportunities amid the economic wreckage. *American Prospect*, March 24.
———. 2000. Why Living in a Rich Society Makes Us Feel Poor. *New York Times Magazine*, October 15.

Meyers, Robin R. 2004. *The Virtue in the Vice: Finding Seven Lively Virtues in the Seven Deadly Sins*. Deerfield Beach, FL: Health Communications, Inc.

Yardley, Jim. 2010. Soaring Above India's Poverty, a 27-Story Home. *New York Times*, October 28.

JUSTICE: FOR THE HORSES

Pinker, Steven. 2011. *The Better Angels of Our Nature: Why Violence Has Declined*. New York: Viking Adult.

Wister, Owen. 1894. Balaam and Pedro. *Harper's Magazine*, January.

————. 1885–1900. Journals. American Heritage Center, University of Wyoming, Laramie.

————. 1902. *The Virginian*. New York: Macmillan.

WRATH: COMING BACK TO OURSELVES

Gordon, Mary. 1993. Anger. In *Deadly Sins*. New York: Quill / William Morrow.

GLUTTONY: A RE-ENCHANTMENT WITH FOOD

Miller, Lisa. 2010. Divided We Eat. *Newsweek*, November 29.

Prose, Francine. 2003. *Gluttony, The Seven Deadly Sins*. New York: Oxford University Press.

Shipley, Orby. 1875. *A Theory About Sin in Relation to Some Facts of Daily Life*. London: Macmillan and Co.

CHASTITY AND LUST: A PSYCHOLOGY OF SEX

Branden, Nathaniel. 2009. The Psychology of Sex. In *The Vision of Ayn Rand: The Basic Principles of Objectivism*. New York: Laissez Faire Books.

Coburn, Marietta M. 2010. Rachel L. Wagley: Explaining the right way in a world that turns left. *TheCrimson.com*, December 10.

Fields, Marguerite. 2008. Want to Be My Boyfriend? Please Define. *New York Times*, May 4.

Godbeer, Richard. 2004. *Sexual Revolution in Early America*. Baltimore: John Hopkins University Press.

Hobbs, Roger. 2008. Instant Message, Instant Girlfriend. *New York Times*, May 25.

Jaime-Becerra, Michael. 2010. *This Time Tomorrow: A Novel*. New York: Thomas Dunne Books.

Reimold, Daniel. 2010. *Sex and the University: Celebrity, Controversy, and a Student Journalism Revolution*. New Brunswick, NJ: Rutgers University Press.

Walkowski, Joel. 2008. Let's Not Get to Know Each Other Better. *New York Times*, June 8.

CREATIVITY: WHY WE NEED ART
(AND WHY WE MAKE IT OR WE DON'T)

Auden, W. H. 1940. September 1, 1939. In *Another Time*. New York: Random House.

Briggs, John. 1988. *Fire in the Crucible: The Alchemy of Creative Genius*. New York: St. Martin's Press.

Brodsky, Joseph. 1988. Some Tips: A Commencement Address. University of Michigan, Ann Arbor.

Hyde, Lewis. 2009. *The Gift: Creativity and the Artist in the Modern World*. New York: Vintage Books.

Yeats, W. B. 1919. The Second Coming. Available from http://www.poets.org/viewmedia.php/prmMID/15527.

ENVY: ENVY AND ITS DISCONTENTS

Epstein, Joseph. 2003. *Envy*. New York: Oxford University Press.

Schimmel, Solomon. 1992. *The Seven Deadly Sins: Jewish, Christian, and Classical Reflections on Human Nature.* New York: The Free Press.

HUMILITY: THE LISTENER

Chaplin, Jeremiah. 1876. *The Life of Benjamin Franklin.* Boston: D. Lothrop & Company.

Franklin, Benjamin. 2005. *Benjamin Franklin: Autobiography, Poor Richard, and Later Writings.* Ed. J. A. L. Lemay. New York: Library of America.

Isaacson, Walter. 2003. *Benjamin Franklin: An American Life.* Kindle ed. New York: Simon and Schuster.

JEALOUSY (AND OTHER TRIALS OF LOVE): CUPID: THE SOAP OPERA

Apuleius, Lucius. 1566. *The Golden Asse.* Trans. William Adlington. Available from http://www.gutenberg.org/ebooks/1666.

Bulfinch, Thomas. 2006. *Bulfinch's Mythology.* New York: Barnes & Noble Classics.

TRANQUILITY: THE LONG ROAD: TERRY WAITE'S STORY

Frankl, Victor. 1975. *Man's Search for Meaning.* New York: Pocket Books.

Waite, Terry. 1997. *Footfalls in Memory: Reflections from Solitude* New York: Doubleday.

———. 1993. *Taken on Trust.* New York: Harcourt Brace.

TRANQUILITY: THE LONG ROAD: BROOKE HOPKINS'S STORY

Hogsten, Leah. 2010. Learning to Live Again: A Photo Essay.

Salt Lake Tribune. Available from http://extras.sltrib.com/
multimedia/2010/LearningToLiveAgain/index.html.
———. 2010. Metamorphosis: A Photo Essay. *Salt
Lake Tribune.* Available from http://extras.sltrib.com/
multimedia/2010/TragicMetamorphosis/index.html.
Hopkins, Brooke, and Peggy Battin. 2008–2011. Various blog
entries. In *Brooke Hopkins & Peggy Battin.* Salt Lake City,
UT. Available from http://brookeandpeggy.blogspot.com/.
Stack, Peggy Fletcher. 2009. *Learning to Live Again: Brooke
Hopkins Struggles Through Rehab After Bicycle Accident.*
Salt Lake Tribune, September 4. Available from http://www.
sltrib.com/News/ci_13270592.
———. 2009. *Tragic Metamorphosis: Ethical Debates Turn
Personal for U. Professor.* Salt Lake Tribune, June 2.
Available from http://www.sltrib.com/news/ci_12480371.

SELF-RELIANCE: BENJAMIN FRANKLIN, AYN RAND, AND THE AMERICAN SPIRIT

Branden, Barbara. 1986. *The Passion of Ayn Rand: A
Biography.* New York: Doubleday & Co.
Branden, Nathaniel. 1984. The Benefits and Hazards of the
Philosophy of Ayn Rand: A Personal Statement. *Journal of
Humanistic Psychology* 24 (4): 39–64.
———. 1989. *Judgment Day: My Years with Ayn Rand.* New
York: Houghton Mifflin.
Burns, Jennifer. 2009. *Ayn Rand and the American Right.*
Kindle ed. New York: Oxford University Press.
Doren, Carl Van. 1973. *Benjamin Franklin.* New York:
Bramhall House.
Franklin, Benjamin. 2005. *Benjamin Franklin: Autobiography,
Poor Richard, and Later Writings.* Ed. J. A. L. Lemay. New
York: Library of America.
Hauptman, Don. 2004. The "Lost" Parts of Ayn Rand's
Playboy Interview. *Atlassociety.org*, March.

Heller, Anne C. 2009. *Ayn Rand and the World She Made.* Kindle ed. New York: Anchor.

Isaacson, Walter. 2003. *Benjamin Franklin: An American Life.* Kindle ed. New York: Simon and Schuster.

McConnell, Scott. 2010. *100 Voices: An Oral History of Ayn Rand.* New York: New American Library.

Modern Library. 2013. 100 Best Novels: The Readers' List. Available from http://www.modernlibrary.com/top-100/ 100-best-novels/.

Morgan, Edmund S. 2003. *Benjamin Franklin (Yale Nota Bene).* New Haven: Yale University Press.

Rand, Ayn. 2005. *Atlas Shrugged.* Kindle ed. New York: Plume / Penguin.

———. 1984. Faith and Force: The Destroyers of the Modern World. In *Philosophy: Who Needs It.* New York: Signet.

———. 2005. *The Fountainhead.* New York: Plume / Penguin.

———. 1959. Interview by Mike Wallace. CBS.

———. 1964. The Objectivist Ethics. In *The Virtue of Selfishness.* New York: Signet.

Rand, Ayn, and Peter Schwartz. 1998. *The Ayn Rand Column: Written for the Los Angeles Times.* New Milford, CT: Second Renaissance Books.

Toffler, Alvin. 1964. Playboy interview with Ayn Rand. *Playboy,* March 1964.

Wood, Gordon S. 2005. *The Americanization of Benjamin Franklin.* Kindle ed. New York: Penguin.

CURIOSITY: GROWING PAINS

Doren, Carl Van. 1973. *Benjamin Franklin.* New York: Bramhall House.

Kashdan, Todd. 2009. *Curious?: Discover the Missing Ingredient to a Fulfilling Life* New York: William Morrow.

Yoffe, Emily. 2009. Seeking: How the brain hard-wires us to love Google, Twitter, and texting. And why that's dangerous. *Slate,* August 12.

PROCRASTINATION: DO IT . . . NEXT

Andreou, Chrisoula, and Mark D. White, eds. 2012. *The Thief of Time: Philosophical Essays on Procrastination*. New York: Oxford University Press.

Perry, John. 2011. Structured Procrastination. Available from http://www.structuredprocrastination.com/index.php.

Slate.com. 2008. Just Don't Do It: A special issue on procrastination. May 15.

Surowiecki, James. 2010. Later: What does procrastination tell us about ourselves? *New Yorker*, October 11.

GRUMPINESS: THE GROUCH SETTLES IN

Abumrad, Jad. 2009. Seeking Patterns. *Radiolab*. New York: WNYC.

Bloom, Paul. 2008. First Person Plural. *The Atlantic*, November.

STUBBORNESS: HOLDING ON FOR DEAR LIFE

Goleman, Daniel. 2006. *Emotional Intelligence: 10th Anniversary Edition; Why It Can Matter More Than IQ*. New York: Bantam.

Heller, Anne C. 2009. *Ayn Rand and the World She Made*. Kindle ed. New York: Anchor.

Rand, Ayn. 2005. *Atlas Shrugged*. Kindle ed. New York: Plume / Penguin.

———. 2005. *The Fountainhead*. New York: Plume / Penguin.

———. 1959. Interview by Mike Wallace. CBS.

Whyte, David. 2001. *Crossing the Unknown Sea: Work as a Pilgrimage of Identity*. New York: Riverhead Books.

TRUST: WILL ROGERS, WHERE ARE YOU NOW?

Carter, Joseph H. 1991. *Never Met a Man I Didn't Like: The Life and Writings of Will Rogers*. New York: Avon Books, Inc.

————. 2005. *The Quotable Will Rogers*. Layton, Utah: Gibbs Smith.

Meacham, Jon. 1994. What Will Rogers Could Teach the Age of Limbaugh. *Washington Monthly*, January–February, 7.

Ono, Keiko. 2005. Electoral Origins of Partisan Polarization in Congress: Debunking the Myth. *Extensions* (Fall).

Poole, Keith T. 2005. The Decline and Rise of Party Polarization in Congress During the Twentieth Century. *Extensions* (Fall).

White, Richard D., Jr. 2011. *Will Rogers: A Political Biography*. Lubbock: Texas Tech University Press.

Yagoda, Ben. 1993. *Will Rogers: A Biography*. New York: Alfred A. Knopf.

DEFENSIVENESS AND FAITH: CHOOSING OUR BATTLES

Baum, Dan. 2005. Battle Lessons. *New Yorker*, January 17.

Beauvois, Xavier, director. 2010. *Of Gods and Men*. France.

Phillips, Jan. 2011. When Doctrine Isn't Enough: A Former Nun Awakens to the Responsibility of Her Own Spirituality. Blog post. Available from http://www.onbeing.org/ blog/when-doctrine-isnt-enough-former-nun-awakens- responsibility-her-own-spirituality/2635.

Tippett, Krista. 2009. Brother Thay: A Radio Pilgrimage with Thich Nhat Hanh. In *Speaking of Faith*, ed. Krista Tippett. Collegeville, MN: American Public Media.

GLADNESS: THE MYSERIOUS LIGHTNESS OF BEING

Gilbert, Jack. 2005. A Brief for the Defense. In *Refusing Heaven: Poems*. New York: Knopf.

Harrington, Anne, and Arthur Zajonc. 2006. *The Dalai Lama at MIT*. Boston: Harvard University Press.

Salzberg, Sharon. 2002. *Lovingkindness: The Revolutionary Art of Happiness*. Boston: Shambhala Classics.

PUNCTUALITY: THE GIFT OF TIME

Hyde, Lewis. 2009. *The Gift: Creativity and the Artist in the Modern World*. New York: Vintage.

Gleick, James. 1999. *Faster: The Acceleration of Just About Everything*. New York: Random House.

Shulevitz, Judith. 2010. *The Sabbath World: Glimpses of a Different Order of Time*. New York: Random House.

Ware, Bonnie. 2009. Regrets of the Dying. In Inspiration and Chai, November 19. http://bronnieware.com/regrets-of-the-dying/.

GRATITUDE: THANKSGIVING: A CHRISTMAS STORY

Bimstein, Phillip. 2012. *Live at the Symphony: A Secret Gift*. Conducted by Robert Baldwin. Red Rock Rondo, 884501778114 (compact disc).

Gup, Ted. 2008. Hard Times, a Helping Hand. *New York Times*, December 22.

———. 2010. *A Secret Gift: How One Man's Kindness—and a Trove of Letters—Revealed the Hidden History of the Great Depression*. New York: Penguin.

FORGIVENESS: THE HEROIC CHOICE

Enright, Robert D. 2011. *Forgiveness is a Choice*. Washington, D.C.: American Psychological Association.

———. 2012. *The Forgiving Life: A Pathway to Overcoming Resentment and Creating a Legacy of Love*. Washington, D.C.: American Psychological Association.

Kocks, Dorothee. 2000. *Dream a Little: Land and Social Justice in Modern America*. Berkeley: University of California Press.

Luskin, Frederic. 2003. *Forgive for Good*. New York: HarperOne.

Nicoll, Bruce H. 1965. Mari Sandoz: Nebraska Loner. *The American West* 2 (2): 32–26.

Sandoz, Mari. 1935. *Old Jules*. Boston: Little, Brown, and Company.

Stauffer, Helen Winter. 1992. *Letters of Mari Sandoz Edited and with an Introduction by Helen Winter Stauffer*. Lincoln: University of Nebraska Press.

———. 1982. *Mari Sandoz: Story Catcher of the Plains, Western Writers Series*. Lincoln: University of Nebraska Press.

BALANCE: ON THE HIGH WIRE

Higginbotham, Adam. 2003. Touching the Void. *Observer*, January 19.

Jordan, Teresa. 1987. Between Two Worlds. *Orgonian*, August 23.

Kinkead, Gwen. 1987. Alone and in Control. *New Yorker*, June 15.

Petit, Philippe. 2008. *Man on Wire*. New York: Skyhorse Publishing.

———. 1985. *On the High Wire*. New York: Random House.

———. 2002. *To Reach the Clouds: My High Wire Walk Between the Twin Towers*. New York: North Point Press.

Tomkins, Calvin. 1999. The Man Who Walks on Air. *New Yorker*, April 5.

MANNERS: THE GOOD HAND

Brannaman, Buck. 2001. *The Faraway Horses: The Adventures and Wisdom of One of America's Most Renowned Horsemen*. Guilford, CT: The Lyons Press.

Brannaman, Buck, and William Reynolds. 2004. *Believe: A Horseman's Journey*. Guilford, CT: The Lyons Press.

Desmond, Leslie, and Bill Dorrance. 2007. *True Horsemanship Through Feel.* Guilford, CT: Lyons Press.

Dorrance, Tom, and Milly Hunt Porter, ed. 2009. *True Unity: Willing Communication Between Horse and Human.* Bruneau, ID: Give-It-A-Go Enterprises.

James, Will. 1929. *Smoky the Cow Horse.* New York City: Scribner.

Meehl, Cindy, director. 2011. *Buck.*

MODERATION: ALL I WANT FOR CHRISTMAS . . . IS A TRUCE IN THE WAR ON CHRISTMAS

Fisher, Mike. 2008. Anger Management: Control. Available from http://www.videojug.com/interview/anger-management-control.

Stewart, Jon. 2010. The Gretch Who Saved the War on Christmas. In *The Daily Show with Jon Stewart*, ed. Jon Stewart.

AFTERWORD

Bercovici, Jeff. 2011. Why (Some) Psychopaths Make Great CEOs. *Forbes Magazine*, June 14.

Christoffersen, John. 2013. Robert Shiller: Income Inequality Is "Most Important Problem." The Huffington Post. October 15.

CNN Money. 2012. "Fortune 50 CEO pay vs. our salaries." Available from money.cnn.com/magazines/fortune/fortune500/2012/ceo-pay-ratios/.

Egan, Timothy. 2014. Billionaires and Boasts. *New York Times*, January 23.

Franklin, Benjamin. 2005. *Benjamin Franklin: Autobiography, Poor Richard, and Later Writings.* Ed. J. A. L. Lemay. New York, Library of America.

Fuentes-Nieva, Ricardo, and Nick Galasso. 2014. Working for the Few. Oxford: Oxfam International.

The Giving Pledge. 2014. The Giving Pledge. Available from http://givingpledge.org/index.html.

Hurley, Dan. 2014. Eureka: Breathing In vs. Spacing Out. *New York Times*, January 14.

Thompson, Mark. 2014. World's 85 richest own as much as poorest 50%. *CNN Money*, January 21.

ACKNOWLEDGMENTS AND PERMISSIONS

ACKNOWLEDGMENTS

A portion of "All I Want for Christmas ... is a Truce in the War on Christmas" was first published as "The Truth of the Land" in *The Native Home of Hope*, Wallace Stegner Center for Land, Resources, and the Environment (Salt Lake City: University of Utah, 1996).

A portion of "The Pride of Work, the Work of Pride" was first published in "The Conceit of Girls" in *Jo's Girls: Tomboy Tales of High Adventure, True Grit, and Real Life*, ed. Christian McEwan (Boston: Beacon Press, 1997).

The poem "Looking Back" was first published in *Riding the White Horse Home* by Teresa Jordan (New York: Pantheon, 1982).

PERMISSIONS

Party Polarization 1879-2013," ©2014 Kieth T. Poole and Howard Rosenthal, voteview.com. Used by permission.

"Old Vogal," from Write *'em Cowboy*, by Peggy Godfrey (Lake City, Colorado: Peter Carlyle Elliott Pub, 1993. Used by permission.

"When Cowboys Cry," ©1994 Judy Blunt, first appeared in *Graining the Mare: The Poetry of Ranch Women*, ed. Teresa Jordan (Layton, Utah: Gibbs Smith Publisher, 1994. Used by permission.

INDEX

Printed in the United States
by Baker & Taylor Publisher Services